Wood, Silver and Gold

a flutist's life

John Wion

Copyright © John Wion 2007

John Wion
180 Riverside Drive
NY, NY 10024

http://johnwion.com

johnwion@aol.com

ISBN 978-1-4303-2039-5

For Russell and Anthony
&
Charlie and Annie

and
dedicated to my companion through most of this journey

Victoria Simon

Foreword

These memoirs began when I started reminiscing to Helen Spielman, a new friend from the internet FLUTE LIST, about my early time in New York. She enjoyed the stories and encouraged me to write them down. Not long after, Larry Krantz, of the same list, similarly asked me to record my stories.

Encouraged, I began at the beginning and emailed them my recollections of my early years. Their enthusiastic responses led to a second chapter and a third. Other friends joined my list of recipients and I kept writing whenever time permitted.

After creating my internet site I added some pictures and uploaded the chapters already completed. Spurred on by many kind responses, I kept adding to my story.

After deciding to publish this print version so I could leave something tangible for my grandchildren, I received invaluable support from friends and family in turning my colloquial narrative into written prose. The people who wrought this magic were primarily Jennifer Gardner, Helen Spielman, Marjorie Pawling, and Betty Caroli. When it came time to layout my book I found another friend in Robert Bigio, who guided me through the intricacies of InDesign and corrected my amateurish efforts. In addition to this invaluable advice, he made many corrections to my prose and astute observations about my stories. Nancy Toff and Nathan Zalman generously advised me about proofreading and publishing. Leonard Spira, an early and enthusiastic supporter, undertook to design the cover. His wife Gail provided the photo for the back cover. I learned much from all of these friends and cannot thank them enough for their time, support, and patience.

I have been blessed in so many ways throughout my life, but I have made my mistakes, and things have not always gone as I wished. As John Lennon said, "Life is what happens to you while you're busy making other plans." I hope my life will be as interesting to read about as it has been to live.

Contents

Foreword	5
My Early Years	9
My high school years	14
My university years	21
Settling in to New York	39
A new life	49
New York City Opera	71
Expanding horizons	91
Crisis looms	120
Crisis	135
Reassessment	142
NFA years	152
My fifties	169
My sixties	197
Afterword	217

My Early Years

I was born in Rio de Janeiro, Brazil, January 22, 1937, to a Pennsylvania Dutch father and an Australian mother. My father, an electrical engineer who became an expert in railroad signals, was born in Bellefonte, Pennsylvania in 1886. The family name is an anglicized phonetic version of the German name Weyandt. These German Protestants came to Pennsylvania at the invitation of William Penn in the early eighteenth century. After a generation or two their names became whatever the local census taker or other civil servant heard. Weyandt became Wyant, then Wyan or Wian, and in our branch, Wion. John and Catherine Wyan moved to central Pennsylvania from further east around 1800. While some of their large family of thirteen participated in the expansion of the colonies to the West, my own branch stayed farming in Mifflin and Centre Counties for the rest of the century.

My father, George Henry, or Harry as he was then called, was the first Wion to go to college, graduating from Penn State in 1908. He married a local girl and began working for the Pennsylvania Railroad. In 1914 they went to Melbourne, Australia, where my father assisted with the electrification of the railroads. In 1925, his wife, not enjoying life in Australia, left him and returned with their two daughters, Jocelyn and Kathryn, to the States. My father chose to stay. Now calling himself George, he met and married my mother.

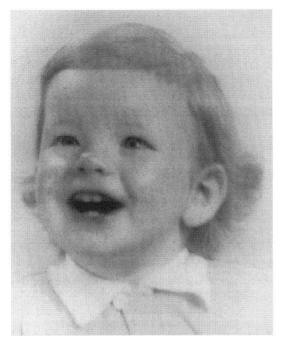

My hand-tinted baby photo.

Marianne Turner, although Australian born, was herself half German, descended from the same kind of farmers as her new husband. Her maternal ancestors, the Bretags, had migrated from the eastern part of Germany to Australia in the mid-nineteenth century. Her Turner ancestors were from Glasgow, Scotland. She was an only child and an accomplished pianist. My father, too, was musical – I have a photo of him as a cornet player in the Bellefonte town band.

Very soon after their marriage in Melbourne in 1930, the couple moved to Chicago when Dad was offered a position with General Railways Signal Company of Rochester, New York. My oldest brother, Frank, was born there in 1931. After two years, they moved back to Australia, where their second son, David, was born in 1934. In 1935, they packed up once more and sailed to Brazil, where my story begins.

The electrification of the Central Brazil Railway System took until 1938 when we gave up the tropical warmth of Rio for the freezing cold of

George and Marianne Wion at New Year's Eve party.

The Wion family in Rio de Janeiro, 1937.

Rochester. I do not remember Brazil, but the sepia toned family photographs show nannies, and beaches, and sun-bleached siblings (apparently Portuguese speaking). Nor do I have memories of Rochester and the birth of my younger brother, Richard, nor the trip via London and Capetown to Melbourne, where my father, unwilling to tolerate the East Coast winters any more, decided we would all grow up. My mother told me that a fortune-teller on the ship predicted a musical life for me.

My earliest recollection is sitting in a high chair refusing parsnips. We moved soon after (probably not for this reason) to the house where I grew up. Mabel Street in the suburb of Camberwell was then on the fringe of the city. It was a beautiful street with "nature strips" of deciduous plane trees alternating with evergreen shrubs. Our house was a big, two-story, white stuccoed brick rectangle set in the middle of the lot. In the Australian fashion, the lot was fenced all around, tall wood paling providing privacy around the back half, shorter fences on the front sides and a white brick fence matching the house on the street front.

The front yard was grass, planted with numerous trees and shrubs. A sprinkler system kept the lawn reasonably green and provided immense diversion for growing boys. Tall cypresses flanked the front door and along the house front were hydrangeas bursting with blue and violet clusters. We had fruit trees – almond, plum, lemon, orange, grapefruit, and fig; decorative trees – crab apple and jacaranda. Rose bushes ran the length of the front fence. The back lawn grew smaller each year with the expansion of the vegetable garden, but room was still found for apricot, peach, plum, quince, guava, lemon, fig, and apple trees, not to mention the passionfruit

The Wion family in Melbourne, 1940.

vines that draped the fence. As we children grew, further space in the backyard had to be found for the chicken coop and the pigeon aviary. All of this had to be cared for, of course, and one of my early memories is of lying in my upstairs bedroom taking a required afternoon nap and being delighted to find that some light trick was throwing onto my ceiling the picture of my parents working in the garden below.

The double brick walls of the house kept it cool in the hot Australian summers. The right half of the house consisted of one large room downstairs, a rarely used, carpeted "lounge," and the master bedroom upstairs. The left side contained the living area downstairs (dining/living room, kitchen, "breakfast room," laundry), with two more bedrooms and a family bathroom upstairs. A central staircase, at the foot of which was the family telephone, connected the two floors. Along the rear of the house was a tiled, covered verandah, which was eventually closed in to provide another sleeping space. At first, my oldest brother slept there. After he went to boarding school my younger brother moved in, leaving David and me upstairs in one bedroom and my maternal grandmother in the other.

Dad watering at Mabel Street.

Starched hair and foreign snowsuit.

When I was three I started going to a kindergarten in a nearby church hall. Apart from a general memory of being there, my only specific recollection from this year is of being frightened by a dog outside our house.

Just after my fourth birthday I started at the local Canterbury State School — motto *semper paratus* (always prepared). My early memories are very few — the classroom, the desks, the alphabet, my school bag, the cupboards with wire fronts where we placed our lunch on arrival. However, sometime during that first year I was led across the internal hall to the first grade classroom diagonally opposite. In this way I advanced a year for my age. My new teacher, Miss Greenwood, forced me to write with my right hand, against my body's natural design but in accord with then current theory. I learned about perspective that year. The drawing assignment, in chalk on brown paper, was to copy a picture of "the old woman who lived in a shoe" which hung on the classroom wall. When my rendition was deemed to have no perspective I was kept after school.

The next year's teacher, Miss Stewart, was altogether more kind and friendly. However, my only real memory is of the discussion at year's end as to whether I should spend another year in her class to "mature." I decided to press ahead.

Grade 3. I am top center.

The final year of co-ed classes was with Miss LeCoutier. Again my recollections are vague, with only the embarrassment of having to go home during school one day for clean underwear remaining vivid. I also recall drawing class where I would move the chalk to my right hand as the teacher moved past my desk, then back to the left to continue work.

In the fourth grade we boys were supervised by a severe little man. I wonder which student made up "Mr. Besant, the wonderful ant, went to church on Sunday, and prayed to God to give him strength to belt the kids on Monday." Schoolwork was easy for me, and I always got a gold honor certificate at the end of each year, but I was often bored and stared out the window. My report cards for these next years show "ten" for most quantifiable things like math, spelling, and grammar. Not surprisingly, my handwriting was less well received, as low as seven one semester. I topped the class once and generally placed third. The principal's final report commended my "fine work and keen interest throughout." My father wrote on it, "We are very pleased with John's progress." I never got a ten for music, but that year I joined the school fife and drum band — I believe only because my older brothers were already fifing members.

That was the year the wars ended. The one in Europe didn't mean too much emotionally. The Australian men who had gone to support the Empire were either dead or fighting the Japanese in New Guinea. It was the end of *this* war that meant so much to us. I roller-skated home to announce the news to my mother. Ironically, my father, who would surely have played an important part in the U.S. military had he been in the States, was not called for service in Australia. He was finally flown to Darwin, in the north, as part of a civilian program, but was suddenly sent home for the removal of a growth on his leg.

During this time I remember more about my home life, particularly Sunday summer visits to the beach. First the garden chores had to be done while the picnic lunch was being prepared. Then it was into the black '38 Buick for the trip to Rickett's Point on Port Philip Bay. We would play on the sand and

The school band, 1945 – I am in the second row, fourth from the right. My brother David is next to Mr. Stevens, standing on right.

walk over the sandstone rocks at low tide, investigating all the rock pools and checking that our names carved in the stone had not been too much erased by the water. I would fight my mother who tried to protect my fair skin from the fierce Australian sun. After lunch we would hide beside the tea-tree-lined path on the cliff face to surprise our father as he came strolling by, leaning on his cane. When summer passed, Sunday returned to being more of a church day. We didn't care for church, and certainly were not encouraged by our dad's own lack of interest. We soon developed the habit of taking our "collection" money to the miniature golf course.

We started taking a beach house a bit further down the bay at Macray. The only place to visit was the general store down the road run by a "Chinaman" whom we ethnically abused on at least one occasion. We were left very much to our own resources for amusement, but the four of us seem to have managed. We had the beach, of course, and I particularly remember walking up the hill behind the house through native blue flowers to the top known as Arthur's Seat. Otherwise, images are of the sound of the sea at night in bed and the hot sun on the verandah.

In Mr. DeReske's fifth grade, apart from being strapped for the first time over a faulty geometric design, my recollections are of the band. I was made captain that year and our enthusiastic leader, Mr. Stevens, arranged uniforms for us and took us to the inter-school competition. This had always been won by the brilliantly uniformed and well-drilled Sandringham school, but in this and the following year Canterbury was the stunning upset winner – what tension, what excitement!

In sixth grade Mr. Stevens also became my classroom teacher. I will always thank him for his math exercises. He had a board in front of the class with numbers on it. With his pointer moving to different numbers he would say "add, add," or "from a hundred subtract, subtract."

The band was again a big part of my life. I was playing the piccolo rather than the fife, and provided the solo line for Offenbach's *Barcarole*. I recall being insulted at being criticized for a loud squawk, which I knew was not from my sweet piccolo at all but the uncouth fife next to me! We read no music – the system taught was one of numbers – one was B, two was A. Big sheets were put up in front of the band with the charts on them. I suppose the rhythm and tempo came from Mr. Stevens's pointer.

This was the year I began the flute. Our band had a weekly visiting coach, Stanley Baines, a well-known professional flutist. One week he drew out a real wooden flute, which he announced was for sale. I couldn't wait to get home after school. "Quick, phone!," I said to my mother, imagining all my schoolmates acting with the same urgency. Like a good mother of the time she said to wait until Dad got home from work. He went on his next lunch break to the music store in the city to inquire about flutes and teachers. One Friday afternoon soon after, I was taken from sports period to the Melbourne Conservatorium to play *The Whistler and His Dog* on my tin piccolo for Leslie Barklamb. He was apparently sufficiently impressed that he arranged a flute for me (a high-pitched wooden Rudall Carte) and study with his former student, Dorothy Jelbart. My first public appearance was during that same year, when I performed Saint-Saens's *The Swan* over the school public address system. That was also the first time my memory failed, though I managed to bring the work to some kind of cadence.

It was a full year for me. I was a leader in the Cub Scouts and suddenly developed an overriding passion for sports. I don't know where this came from – certainly not from my American dad who only played softball with us on the front lawn. Cricket, football, and later tennis now meant everything to me and were the driving passions in my life until music surpassed them several years later. I started a paper route, using the income to buy a cricket bat, and eventually I had all the equipment necessary.

I was studying the banjo-mandolin at a Saturday morning class, so much against my will that I would pretend to be asleep when my mother came to get me ready. More interesting was the ukulele, which my brother David was studying at the same school. I would watch his lessons and picked up enough to provide great enjoyment over many years of camp and party evenings.

Suddenly it was time to make plans for high school and my father had me sit for a scholarship exam at one of the church-run private schools, termed public schools. As I was unsuccessful, I enrolled at the local Camberwell High School.

My High School Years

1948

My interests were becoming ever more divergent. Academic work in high school was no problem, and I topped my class for the year. I was still near perfect at mathematics and caught onto Latin, my first foreign language, easily. Typically, music was not a subject, though art and sheet metal work were. Practicing the flute was a tiresome chore that my mother kept me at. I played my first annual exam at the conservatorium and received a glowing report from Mr. Barklamb. I played a few public appearances and the praise for my talent was, not surprisingly, good for my ego. Yet I was a reluctant performer. One incident the year before I recall with sadness and regret. My father had taken me to play in an afternoon concert at the local church. As we approached I said something like, "You know you'll be the only man there." Either hurt or embarrassed, he stayed outside. I waited inside the door for a while, then came out saying I was through. My parents must surely have learned that I didn't play, but they never said a word to me.

Seventh grade athlete.

Sports and scouting were the most important activities for me. At school we played "hand tennis" at every available opportunity. Small courts were painted onto the asphalt yard. The ball was a dirty old tennis ball; the racquet the palm of one's hand – I got to be very good. At real tennis I was also becoming quite proficient. I also started to get the hang of "footy" – Australian Rules Football – though I was disappointed at not making the junior team at school. I was fast on my feet and represented my school, unsuccessfully, as a sprinter. The team photo shows a skinny kid with freckles and protruding ears.

A highlight of the year was going to my first football Grand Final at the Melbourne Cricket Ground. My team, Melbourne, seemed on the way to defeat by its rival Essendon, so I began to squeeze my way through the jammed arena to an exit. With each minute of progress my team closed the gap. Absolutely riveted I watched it pull even, but in the last agonizing moments even my heroes, the veterans Jack Mueller and Norm Smith, couldn't turn a goal area scramble into that one extra point. The following week, in an unprecedented play-off, Melbourne won.

I had graduated to the scouts and was doing the camping and other requirements to qualify for the forthcoming Pan-Pacific Jamboree. This event, over the Christmas break, was my first exposure to non-Australians. I was impressed by the native dress of the Fijians and the red silk scarves of the Filipinos. I enjoyed a concert which included *The Dance of the Hours* played by the Victorian Symphony Orchestra, of which Mr. Barklamb was a member. But I was too young to fully appreciate and participate in the broader opportunities of the jamboree and spent too much time hanging around our campsite playing cards.

In real terms, the most important events of the year were the scholarship exams. My father was determined I was to get a public school education somehow. First were the tests for Melbourne Grammar. These took place over two days – a compulsory first day of English and Mathematics, followed by an optional second day of languages. I found the first day really tough, and prevailed on my parents not to send me back. I was in the middle of my first year of Latin, so didn't think I would do well.

Dad had me hard at work preparing to retake the exam for Scotch College when the phone rang to say I had won an entrance scholarship to Melbourne Grammar. I was glad to have won the scholarship, but much more delighted that I could stop studying and run off to my scout meeting. So I did not follow my older brothers into Wesley College, the Methodist school, or join the Presbyterians at Scotch College but headed with great trepidation toward the ivied, blue-stone buildings that were the home of Melbourne's Anglican aristocracy.

1949

The class in which I was entered had an odd assortment of students, either new like myself or too old to be in the corresponding class in the two junior schools. This was the last year of the authoritarian regime of headmaster Joseph Sutcliffe and things were scary. The prefects were grown men who stayed an extra year in school to strengthen the sports teams, and who used the cane to keep discipline. Lists of misdemeanors were published, and at every break a line of quaking boys would form outside the prefects' study waiting for their inquisitions to begin. We had to "turn-out" for sports twice a week after school. Not to do so would surely lead to a caning. Showers after sports were cold water so one had to be pretty dirty to suffer them.

I eventually settled down to the new life and began to enjoy myself. Classes were a riot of misbehavior. The teachers were characters. The school was divided into "houses," which competed with each other. In my house, Witherby, was an older boy who was outrageous in his flaunting of all the rules. His name was Barry Humphries, and he went on to an international career on the stage, most famously as Dame Edna.

Inter-house and inter-school sporting events were major activities to be attended. I got my first and only taste of boxing, which I found most unpleasant. Fortunately I was eliminated after receiving a few hits to the head in the try-outs. The boy who inflicted this on me was chosen to represent us in the inter-house competition and was knocked out in the first round of his fight. This same boy put an end to my sprinting career with a decisive victory, and I moved my interests towards hurdling. The coaching and facilities for all the sports were excellent, and my spare time was devoted to cricket or football, depending on the season.

In general I was an insignificant figure in the school this first year and largely just tried to keep out of trouble. I topped my year and took prizes in mathematics and "general subjects."

I was just adjusting to all these routines when my father died on April 11 at the age of 62. He was lying on the living room floor with some blood on his face as I was getting ready to leave for school. I had been promised money for some treat by my mother and apparently didn't feel that whatever my father's problem was should alter the situation. Her "How can you ask when your father may never work again?" was a bit above me, and I left for school miffed.

I became involved in the school day and remembered my father's situation only when, walking home down our street, a neighbor asked if everything was all right. "Dad's not too well," I said. I walked in the door to find my sobbing mother being comforted by friends. "Daddy's gone," she said. "To the hospital?," I asked. She lost control, and one of the friends made the situation clear to me. I went upstairs to my room, not feeling anything much, not crying, and generally wondering how I was supposed to react.

The funeral was held in our lounge. I stayed upstairs reading, periodically checking out a window that the people hadn't come in yet. I didn't understand that these were people who were not invited to the service, and suddenly I was summoned to join the ceremony. Walking through the assembled friends and family in the darkened room was the worst part. I hadn't gone to see the body the previous night and certainly didn't want to go to the crematorium after the service. It was decided I should go to the home of a friend's mother instead – good, I thought, now I can play. It's all very strange in hindsight, and I spent many guilty hours as I grew up wondering about my behavior.

George Wion, 1921.

I think the truth is that, while I liked my father, he was a somewhat remote figure in my life. I had always been my mother's child. She had wanted a daughter, and at some level I became that for her. She kept my hair long when I was a baby and dressed me in dresses, probably not too unusual for the times. But I always related to her rather than Dad. I would crawl into their bed when I couldn't sleep or was delirious, and he would go to my bed. I did things like knitting and cooking without feeling particularly abnormal. I think that Dad moved away from me because of my closeness to my mother. Certainly my older brothers enjoyed and missed him much more than I did.

What actually bothered me more over the next few years were the consequences of his death. I had always felt different from other kids – my parents were older and my father "foreign;" on cold days, when I was young, I was sent to school dressed in a fleece-lined snowsuit from Rochester; our hair was always kept firmly in place with a homemade starch paste. Now I felt embarrassed at school, for example, when a teacher would say, "Ask your father," and I would have to say, "He's dead."

My mother changed dramatically as the entire focus of her life turned to providing for us. One way or another we never went without necessities, but little was left for extras. Friction among us all was on-going, and no one maintained any sense of order or control. Although we appreciated the sacrifices our mother was making, it became very difficult to be continually reminded of them. The atmosphere at home became tense and hostile. Generally speaking, Frank was the only one to express his anger openly, which he did with nasty sarcasm. He was working now and felt that his supporting role gave him more rights. The rest of us kept to ourselves and quietly suffered, each in our own way. Frank's savage tongue was directed at all his younger brothers. If I called him a rat in a moment of frustration at some meanness, he would smile pleasantly and remind me that I was his brother. Richard and I, being so close together in age, were always fighting. He was bigger and stronger; I was smarter. Everyone loved David, but even he became silent and was often best left alone. As each of us grew older and began to assert our individuality, the general level of tension increased still further. If we borrowed the family car for a date we had to be prepared to suffer through a lecture. Then Mom would stay awake till we came home and make us clearly aware of how thoughtless we were to be so late. Of course our girlfriends were never good enough for us anyway.

One of our jobs during this time was to assemble indoor clothes-drying racks that our father had designed. On one of my "shifts" we received a visit from the husband of my half sister, Jocelyn. Herbie Wiere was an absolutely charming vaudevillian. He and his two brothers, Harry and Sylvester, were touring Australia with their clever violin playing act, and the three of them did many kind things for us during their stay. I was to meet up with them again in California several years later when I went to their ranch to meet Jo.

My flute teacher had gone to live on a farm, and I had started studying with Leslie Barklamb at his house. When Dad died we had no money for lessons, but Mr. Barklamb insisted on teaching me for free. This he did until I entered university on a scholarship several years later. He was a very generous man and a wonderfully enthusiastic teacher and person. He was always lending flutes and music to people, and I know that he lost a lot of both. Now that I was traveling by tram into the city to go to school, I started taking my lessons at the conservatorium each week. I was in awe of him, and the highlight of each lesson was playing a duet with him. He played in the old English/German style without vibrato, drawing a very strong, rich sound from his wooden flute. His own teacher had been the world-renowned John Amadio, but Barklamb himself had never traveled out of Australia. His experiences were limited to visiting performers and conductors whom he worked with, first in touring companies, and then in his position as second flute with the Victorian Symphony, Melbourne's professional orchestra at that time. Because of his enthusiasm he became the major teacher in the area, despite the fact that his colleague in the orchestra, Dick Chugg, had studied in Europe and played in a most elegant French style. We were not encouraged to appreciate his playing, and it was not until I had the opportunity to sit next to Dick in the orchestra and get to know him that I fully appreciated what a loss this was for us all.

My holidays at this time consisted of chaperoning my mother, though I did not understand this at the time. She was being wooed by an old friend, who invited her on two different trips. The second took us to Sydney and into an airplane for my first time. I recall being particularly impressed by the sun setting on fleecy clouds seen from the window of the DC3.

Around the same time, I was also invited to stay on the new farm of my former teacher, Dorothy Jelbart. She and her husband, Lloyd, introduced my brother David and me to a new life. After a breakfast of peppered lard spread on toast, we went to the milking sheds. We trapped, killed, and skinned rabbits, the major pest in this environment. We learned to ride on an old white horse called Bonnie, and helped out in the intense heat of summer, clearing dry bracken and erecting an electric fence around the bull paddock.

1950

With an influx from two junior schools, my class the next year at Melbourne Grammar was divided into six divisions. Without my understanding its importance, this was also the year when a choice among courses was first offered. With no guidance from home and no advice at school, my future was decided in most haphazard fashion. Our entire class was assembled in the quadrangle at the start of the school year. The school's acting principal began giving instructions. Those taking this subject were to go to this room; those taking that.... The ranks began thinning. I had no idea what the choices represented and was too shy to ask. Finally he told those taking geography to go to this room. It seemed the easiest thing to do, so I went. As a result I missed taking science courses that were prerequisites for certain physics and chemistry courses. As my friends went on to become doctors and engineers, I was steered by default towards liberal arts, with Latin, French, history, and, as mentioned, geography.

The geography teacher was "Tickle" Turner, a First World War veteran. Classes consisted primarily of his reading works of fact or fiction to us. Any misbehavior resulted in being straddled face down across his lap and paddled on the seat of the pants.

Again sports were the most important school activity to me, and scouting the most important non-school activity. I particularly enjoyed camping and hiking – especially the social aspects, including the campfires where I was starting to become quite a performer, singing and playing the ukulele and telling stories.

1950 football player.

1951

School became more serious with the arrival of the new headmaster, Brian Hone. Although he spent his first year sizing up the situation before instituting changes, his dynamic presence was felt immediately. He was my football coach that year and paid particular attention to me for my remaining time at school, becoming a major influence on my development. Nobody at school knew that I played the flute – it was something that might be held against you. However, over the next few years, things began to change. A music teacher was hired from England. Musical events were introduced, and we closet musicians were encouraged to emerge and participate. I eventually became the first "Captain of Music" in the school's history.

We all joined the school's Cadet Corps and began playing at being soldiers with great seriousness. This interest began to replace scouting, and at the end of the year I went to a camp for training to become a non-commissioned officer. Eventually I would become an officer, an elite member of the school.

1952

School changed for me this year as teachers started asking us to think about things as opposed to knowing facts. History, for example, was no longer about the date of an event but its cause or effect. I was generally too immature to make this adjustment and my grades suffered accordingly. I became involved in school plays, though I was still thrilled principally by sports, both playing and watching. I was always in my age group's football team, and played in the second cricket team and hurdled for my House. As a corporal in the cadets I became enthusiastic about the ritual of the changing of the guard at the annual camp. I was actually considering a career in the army but wisely decided that becoming a school teacher was a better idea. I passed my annual flute exam at the conservatorium with honors and my life took a major turn when Mr. Barklamb recommended that I attend a music camp over the summer holiday.

Music was not yet an important part of my life. I had not grown up with music at home. We had no phonograph and had bought a piano only a year before Dad died. I remember that my first experience with recorded music was while baby-sitting for the family next door. They had a cylinder-playing machine and I heard my first Caruso. The closest I came to fun with music was when Dad used to sit with me at the new piano and play oom-pah chords, until Mom would complain at the poor example he was setting for me. Most of my musical experience was what I heard over the little radio on our living room mantelpiece – short excerpts such as arias or overtures, or the theme music for the different programs we listened to, like *The Search for the Golden Boomerang*. My mother took me to visiting opera companies, and occasionally my class would attend an orchestral concert for schoolchildren. But these were all events to which I was dragged, resentful that my brothers didn't have to go, or that I was missing some other more important activity. I was certainly not looking forward to two weeks of music!

The camp was held at Geelong Grammar School, the other Anglican school, fifty miles from Melbourne. The opening night concert by the Victorian Symphony Orchestra, many of whose members were the camp coaches, consisted of all unfamiliar music – including the Ibert Concerto, played by our leading camper, David Cubbin. In the auditions I placed in the first of three orchestras, fifth flute in a section of six. The first rehearsal began with Vaughan-Williams's *Folk Song Suite*. I was nervous, never having played in an orchestra before. With my fingers set for the first note, I waited for the downbeat from the white-maned conductor, John Bishop. Suddenly life opened for me – this beautiful sound, divided in its textures and components around me, and centered and united in me. I sat stunned, and it was some time before I was able to join in. It is hard to define this being in an orchestra – all-encompassing, vibrating. No other experience in my life is like it.

We also performed the Bruch violin concerto, the Liadov *Eight Fairy Tales*, and the second symphony of a composer unknown to me, Jean Sibelius. At first sight it looked quite uninteresting. But by the time the concert arrived, nothing was as important as this work, as I blew away unheard on low notes in the grandeur of the final moments. How well I later appreciated critic Bernard Shore's comment about how, in Sibelius, one never tires of the endless "unimportant" chords and ostinatos – it is enough just to be participating.

An incredible two weeks of excitement and tension, hot summer days, the breeze from the sea at night, new friends, love, riotous fun at meals was suddenly finished. The first week at home in my room I lay in stunned loneliness playing a newly acquired 78 recording of Bruch over and over. I slowly returned to normal, but for the whole next year I counted off the days till camp.

1953

I was less mature than most of my classmates in this my "senior" year, yet full of enthusiasm, and for the first time I really worked hard. Apart from scouts and sports I had a small part in the school play and was very involved with the cadets. I was an officer now and in charge of a platoon of recruits. At the annual camp during the winter break this year, I enjoyed the privilege of a private room, the officers' mess, and the freedom from discipline. I was popular with my platoon and we had a good time.

I made the school's second football team and won my "colors" for representing the house in football, cricket, and track. I also made my only century at cricket, scoring a hundred runs in a church game, something of which I was enormously proud.

I decided that my life would be in music and not teaching and accepted the advice of the headmaster to return to school for another year before going to the university. I was just old enough to matriculate, but benefitted greatly from this extra year.

The long awaited music camp time finally arrived, and I was able to approach it with more experience and maturity than before. I placed first in the orchestra this year, but only because the four ahead of me the previous year were not present. I enjoyed myself socially, catching up with last year's friends and making new ones, but my inexperience at leading a flute section showed.

1954

I had already passed the exams necessary to enter university, sitting with hundreds of others in the vast space of the Exhibition Hall the previous spring, and waiting for the results to be published, by number, in the daily paper. For this reason my classes in this final year were no longer important to me. I took flute and theory, dropped Latin and English Literature, and stayed with French, English Expression, and a calculus course I had enjoyed. I was now one of the leaders in the school, being appointed a "probationer," a rank below prefect. My musical interests and abilities were in the open, and a new environment of cultural acceptance permeated the school. I became the aide to the recently appointed music teacher from England, Donald Britton, in organizing a competition and presenting a concert. I participated in the school play again, and helped run a new cafeteria. In the cadets I took over the medical platoon; there was a visit by the Queen, and a parade for the Governor-General. The annual cadet camp was highlighted by my running the camp concert – rough, clever, and a huge success, marred only by one pretty rude skit on which a "teacher-officer" had the curtain lowered.

Officer in the cadet corps.

I had been taking serious tennis lessons from a friend of the family whose own career had been cut short by an eye injury, so I played tennis instead of cricket in the first term. I suffered a nasty sprain early in the football season when I was hit on the right side while kicking the ball with my left foot. My right ankle and knee caved in and the initial pain was followed by the realization that I was unable to walk. In my final term I became a rower. My competitive career consisted of about two strokes, after which our lead rower's seat came off its runner. By the time he fixed it the race was over and we rowed leisurely to the finish line.

A member of the school tennis team.

The annual exams went well except for music theory, particularly counterpoint, which was new for me. It was the last exam, and I was already working at my summer job in a tobacconist's and participating in all the end-of-year parties and dances. I had gone to bed late, and to work early, then to the exam where I promptly dozed off. Aroused by the starting bell I somehow squeaked the pass necessary for entrance to the university's music degree program.

My best friend at school at this time was Jeremy Barrett, who later became an artist. We were partners in the school tennis team and spent a lot of time together, including a camping trip to nearby rugged Wilson's Promontory. He began speaking to me about joining him as a residential student at the university, something that had never occurred to me, and something that was nowhere near as common in Australia as it is in the US. Most high school and university students were commuters. I sat for the entrance exam to Trinity College, the Anglican residential college, and due more to Mr. Hone's recommendation than my scholarship I suspect, won a minor residency. I had already been awarded a Commonwealth Scholarship to cover my tuition. No sooner had I committed to Trinity than I learned that Jeremy was to go to school in Adelaide, some five hundred miles away, and into a family business there.

Once again it was music camp time, my last. I placed third in the orchestra, the first being a wonderfully mature player from Perth, Dierdre Hall. Still, I played the Mozart D Major Concerto with the orchestra, and many chamber music concerts. My life was now completely devoted to music and I was thoroughly engrossed in practice and performance.

My University Years

1955

From the pinnacle of high school I plunged with trepidation into the unknown of university, a new residence away from home, and the degrading status of freshman. From the tedium of a summer job putting sticks into popsicles I moved to the cloisters, ivy, academic gowns, and sherry of Trinity College. Several of my school friends were also becoming Trinity gentlemen, and we were joined by a similar number from the rival Geelong Grammar. The rest of our class was made up of students from country towns.

Among my close friends were Russell Meares, son of psychiatrist Ainsley Meares, who later became distinguished in the same field, and Tony Casson, grandson of two British acting greats, Sir Lewis Casson and Dame Sybil Thorndyke. Russell had been an admired scholar, leader and sports-companion at Grammar, and had gone so far as to invite me to dinner at his family's home in aristocratic Toorak. As an outsider to the social set of my school friends, I found such formal occasions to be something of a trial. Tony Casson's family, though very British, lived in more modest circumstances, and I felt more comfortable there. My other friends of the time were Jim Grimwade, another Toorak aristocrat whose home I had visited when he formed a "Dixieland" band in which he played piano and I played ukulele, and John "Baron" Bryson, son of a wealthy businessman who served as Australia's Jaguar dealer. The Brysons lived in a mansion on the waterfront at Brighton, where John invited me for billiards and excursions on the family yacht. John went into law, car racing, and eventually writing, having a considerable success with his book on the Lindy Chamberlain case, which became the movie, *Cry In the Dark* with Meryl Streep.

Bryson was only a day boy at Trinity, but the others joined me in residence. A friend from Grammar, Ian Langford, a jock heading into law, was assigned as my roommate ("wife" in Trinity terminology). Our room, called The Barn, a vast space in the oldest building, had at one time served as the chapel, at another the library. The arched roof receded into shadow as light faded, and became the floor for scurrying rats and possums throughout the night. A large fireplace, despite consuming great quantities of wood laboriously lugged from the distant woodpile, did not begin to take the chill off the room. Two beds seemed dwarfed in one corner; our desks by the window looked out over the center court of the college and its large oak tree. To see that beds were made and rooms kept in order, inspections were scheduled at irregular intervals. But their imminence was always leaked, and only on those rare occasions did the room look presentable. The rest of the time it was a sordid, carefree shambles. Because of its size it quickly became the rendezvous for the fifty or so freshmen. Most of them lived in "the wooden wing," a temporary addition that never managed to get demolished, and whose small rooms were not ideal for partying. We had an "instant-coffee" party every hour for unexpected visitors, and I began to broaden my intellectual horizons through new acquaintances and deepening friendships.

A much admired Grammar boarder, now a Trinity boarder, was John Michie, a seemingly uncouth country boy whose brilliant intellect and sharp humor became ever more obvious as he developed from a beer-drinking oarsman, sailor and womanizer, to the head of Penguin Books in Australia. He would turn it into a world-class house before succumbing tragically to Alzheimer's disease. I can hear him, wild eyed, roaring drunk, "Bring me me brass-bound buggerin' box – these boys split too easy!" And I can see him many years later in my New York living room, bathed in afternoon sunlight, discussing the possibility of a Robert Kennedy presidency.

Altogether we led a carefree life at Trinity, with social balls, parties, common room dances, movies, arguments, joke sessions, beer drinking, and sherry parties. Formal occasions, which included chapel each morning and dinner each night, required the wearing of an academic gown.

The end-of-term dinner was a truly formal event, at least at the beginning. By the end it had degenerated into a drunken shambles. Brilliant speeches were made, and after-dinner stories told, and people wondered which "fresher" would make an inebriated display. On one occasion it was one of my close friends, probably better left nameless. With our table's attention turned toward the speechmaker, he managed to consume the major portion of a bottle of port on top of the already consumed beer, sherry, and wine. Out in the fresh air, he took a flying tackle at some poor soul, badly mistimed, and lay gurgling in the grass. We all went off to see the corniest movie possible, where we made complete fools of ourselves by disrupting the show with our loud comments and laughs. My friend disappeared, was found prone on the bathroom floor, and was manhandled back to college where he spent a fitful twenty-four hours, more on the floor than in bed, dry retching and vowing never to drink again.

The inter-college boat race was a big event. The senior student, dressed in a green checked suit, with a bowler hat, red socks and umbrella, was responsible for stopping traffic by the river so we could pass. Between races we congregated at the Riverside Inn for refreshment and afterwards re-ran the day's events at the Mayfair, a pub near the university.

We traditionally met for a pre-dinner drink at Norton's, a pub just across the road from college. At that time in Australia the bars closed at six o'clock – the thought being that this would limit inebriation and prevent workers from avoiding family responsibilities. More often you saw a number of glasses of beer ordered at "last call" lined up before each patron.

One week before third term the gentlemen convened for "swot vac." This vacation from hard work was a week of sporting activities, the highlight of which was Jutoddie, a handicap race for brick-toting freshmen in academic dress, over the obstacle course around the chapel's field. All the gentry appeared in period dress and placed their bets with the "bookies." A suitable presentation was made to the winner, and the chaplain graced the proceedings with a speech.

The saying "first term freshmen work, second term no one works, third term everyone works" was largely true. The traditional time to hit the books was the first leafing of the college oak. This took most people by surprise and led to sudden penitence, abstinence, and complete seclusion.

In addition to participating in all of the college social activities, I was also a student, enrolled in a double major of music and art (which amounted only to a French course this first year). I quickly discovered the boredom and restriction of lectures, which ones I could miss, and how best to while away the time during the rest. Lectures were just that at the University of Melbourne. Whether you came or not, whether you took good notes, was your own responsibility. All you had to do was pass the final.

Serious study for me began two weeks before exams. Because my history notes failed me, I read Paul Henry Lang's *Music in Western Civilization* twice, around the clock, with the help of black coffee and a currently available phenobarbital tonic, in the hope that enough would sink in to get me through. I got undeserved passes all round.

As a performer I began breaking into small-time circles. Chamber music and solo engagements for local groups and a radio act with a coloratura soprano kept me busy most nights. Then in mid-year, with activity at its highest, and in preparation for a performance of the Chaminade Concertino with the conservatorium orchestra, I injured my right pinkie playing in an inter-college football match. Such an activity was against everyone's advice and can only be explained in retrospect as the bravado of youth.

"Rover Wion was winning around the packs for Trinity."

The doctor said I had a tiny crack in a bone. I should keep the finger strapped to its neighbor till it reset itself. But I had engagements, so, despite the pain, I played on – and played more football too! I allowed myself to be manipulated by physiotherapists to no avail, and finally Mr. Barklamb marched me in to see Sir Bernard Heinze, Director of the Conservatorium. He immediately arranged for me to see Tom King, the leading orthopedic surgeon. Mr. King advised me that the first joint was dislocated and that a bone chip had now grafted itself back in a place that would prevent the joint being relocated. He would operate. For the first and, I hope, last time I was placed under full anesthesia and awoke to find my mother by my bed and an enormous cast up to my elbow. A month later, this cast, along with stitches and a steel pin, was removed. Before beginning the required physical therapy, of course, I had a concert to play. So, padded with cotton and tape, I went off to Canberra for a performance of the Milhaud *Sonatine*. How I played the low Cs I can't imagine. Two months of therapy made no difference to the finger's mobility and I accepted the fact that this would have to do. Although the finger was stiff, I had no pain. The joint had been set at an angle so my pinkie was curved, and this meant it was quite serviceable for playing. I met the doctor's assistant a couple of years later on the college squash court. He was not surprised that I had no movement, and hinted that that was why the joint had been set bent.

Immediately after final exams we got our opportunity to serve Australia. Compulsory national service meant that eighteen-year-olds were enlisted for a three-year period made up of basic training, followed by reserve service entailing weekend drills and annual camps. The elite university students got special treatment to fit their military service around the academic year and did their basic training all together for three months over the summer vacation. Following this, they served in the University Regiment until discharged.

First came physicals. I think they must have had some kind of quota system for each session, with the necessary adjustments up or down being made toward the end of the day. How else to explain the strange aberrations? One friend, a star runner, was exempted with flat feet; another, opening bat for the college cricket team, with poor eyesight. Yet they accepted a third, who, bespectacled, had trouble recognizing a face at fifty yards.

We medically fit ones reported early in the morning for entrainment to Puckapunyal Army Camp, fifty miles north of the city, where we were issued all the necessary equipment. The farcical nature of the exercise became apparent when two days later we were sent to Watsonia, a small camp just twelve miles from Melbourne. After a week or so of hard drilling in the hot sun we were sent home for Christmas. We spent most of the remaining time following our return preparing to form an honor guard for a visiting dignitary. We drilled a lot, but most importantly we cleaned our equipment. We shined the brass, even down to the little stud that kept up one side of the Australian slouch hat. We "blancoed" the canvas webbing of the belts and gaiters with the green paste that heightened the color. We spit-and-polished our boots to a mirror surface – this was serious stuff! The photos show Australia's finest lined up beneath the eucalyptus trees, presenting arms, then standing ramrod to attention as the Governor-General makes the inspection. Before and after, we proudly marched to the regiment's brass band.

In an interesting life lesson I discovered the power of preconception and prejudice. I had decided that I would not admit to having been an officer in the cadet corps; I thought my ability would surely show itself. Not so, and I was passed by for the promotion that all my friends got. In similar style I had at an earlier training camp decided not to seem eager to answer questions. By waiting to be called on, I would surprise the instructor with my correct response. Yet my

The university regiment being inspected by the Governor-General, Watsonia camp, January 1956.

knowing the answer never seemed to make up for my apparent lack of enthusiasm!

The drill sergeant was a regular army veteran who regaled us with stories of the Korean War and got drunk on crème de menthe. By far the worst part of our training was a week's bivouac on the exact site of my earlier scout jamboree. We had to "dig in" to the rocky, clay hill and suffer the heat, sweat, dirt, and incessant flies (until sundown when mosquitoes replaced them). Cold food was covered with flies. We had to deal with surprise raids and sleepless nights. Relief consisted of rolling down one's sleeves, putting hands in pockets and a wet towel over the head, and trying to get some shade from one of the scraggy little bushes. After this, the marquees, hard bunks, regular army food, and hot showers were pure luxury.

All in all, the army was a great experience. I met a lot of people and had never been so healthy. I was fit, and I filled out to an ideal weight of one-fifty-four. We had lots of laughs, and I became a good rifle shot. Unfortunately, I also started smoking – that seemed the thing to do to accompany the hot sugared tea that arrived in urns at mid-morning breaks in training. I managed to stop when camp ended, but it would become a nasty habit over the next years.

1956

While I did scrape by in my first year, my piano studies had been a problem. I had had no keyboard training before university, and although my teacher, June McClain, was patient and warm, I found it difficult to deal with playing at such a beginning level and making so little progress. I actually failed and was told to take a make-up exam before the start of the second year. As the army camp had no piano for me to use, I obtained permission to go home each afternoon after training. I passed the make-up exam, but decided to change my second instrument to percussion, largely as a result of some encouragement at music camps from one of the VSO's percussionists, Ernie Leighton, who now became my teacher.

As school started for the second year, new pairings were made for roommates. Not having arranged anything, I was stuck with another random single and began "wifing" with Mick Long. We scarcely knew each other. He was a medical student, a nice person who rarely stopped studying long enough to be sociable, whereas I was just the opposite. Things were a bit strained at first. He knew absolutely nothing about music, and I even less about medicine. We soon got to talking, however, and by year's end he was coming out of his shell, and I was starting to settle down and get more serious.

Our study was in the same building as the previous year, across the hall from The Barn, and we each had a separate bedroom. Toilets and communal showers were at the other end of the building with its dark corridors always ringing with the shouts of students and the clomping of feet. The only phone was downstairs near the common room. That would become a big problem as I began freelancing more. A student was always supposed to be on telephone duty to page people getting calls, but I would learn that many times the phone went unanswered. On the other hand, if you were trying to avoid a former girlfriend it was an ideal situation.

Mick was the son of a wealthy self-made man, already deceased, whom Mick had really hated. I later got to know his mother, a wonderful person who lived in a flat in Toorak, and his brother and sister. The family still owned a sheep farm, though they no longer lived there. Mick had been sent off to board at Geelong Grammar and now wanted just two things: to become a surgeon and to learn to fly. He would achieve both. Along the way he managed to become an ardent lover of classical music too, and with great generosity began paying the balance of my Trinity board.

Early in the year I was hired to join a state tour of Gilbert and Sullivan's *The Gondoliers* for its final week. This turned out to be an absolute riot. Every day was a new town: drive in, drink, play matinee, drink, play evening show, drink till two or three; next morning, hung over, move on. The final night, an exaggeration of the others, ended with a 4 A.M. train back to the city. Full of a cold, I hoped to rest before facing a concert that evening. My bed, however, had been taken in my absence, and the study couch didn't help much. I got up, uniformed, and went off to a required army drill, with only black coffee to keep me going. After going home to change, I ran off for a quick run-through of my contribution of Handel and Chaminade, changed again, and went off to the concert. My voice now gone, I somehow got through, and felt glad that it was not a very important engagement. I was, therefore, horrified to learn that the concert had been attended by a critic and reviewed in one of the papers. Remarkably, I had been the hit of the evening. The time had definitely come to settle down to some hard work and clean living.

On Mr. Barklamb's advice, I entered the Australian Broadcasting Commission's annual Concerto and Vocal Competition – the competition that David Helfgott failed to win in *Shine*, the movie about his life. The ABC, a government organization, was the primary presenter of classical music in Australia. Many years earlier, a decision had been made that land lines were an unsatisfactory option for disseminating music in this large but sparsely occupied country, so the commission created orchestras in each of the six state capitals. Then it began a program of importing conductors and soloists and presenting series of orchestral concerts and recitals. Everything was broadcast live. By the time I was growing up, tape was available, and studio concerts were also recorded for later broadcast.

Our choice for the competition was the *Konzertstück*, opus 98 by the late-nineteenth-century Berlin composer, Heinrich Hofmann. Hofmann had been a successful composer in his lifetime, and this piece was sufficiently popular that the great John Amadio had recorded the dazzling finale along with the Chaminade Concertino. Although I was not yet aware of this recording, Mr. Barklamb did tell me that his teacher had had great success with the Hofmann. To everyone's amazement, including my own, I was chosen as a state finalist to appear with the VSO under conductor Henry Kripps on the stage of the Melbourne Town Hall. What an incredible thrill, though a sober analysis had to include the possibility that I was needed to balance the other finalists who were pianists and singers.

Now life started getting complicated. John Amadio was ending his career by playing principal flute of the Tasmanian ABC orchestra, based in that island's capital, Hobart. He was taken ill and scheduled for surgery in Melbourne, and a replacement was needed. With no one at hand locally, I was asked to play second flute and piccolo (the current second would move over). I obtained permission from the conservatorium to miss classes, had my first publicity photo taken for the competition program, and flew off to this latest adventure. The trip from the airport was through bush, until suddenly the Derwent River appeared, with its sweeping bridge across to the quaint city of Hobart. I discovered it was really a country town, with none of the nightlife, espresso bars, continental food, fashions or art of Melbourne. Mount Wellington hovered over the town with its narrow streets, little trams, trolley buses, and air of general leisure. Only the Melbourne *Herald* arriving each day, weather permitting, prevented a sense of total isolation. The chill air and the dim five o'clock gray of winter were new experiences.

Accommodation had been arranged at Amadio's rooming house, indeed in his lovely room overlooking the harbor. Mrs. Lucas ran this house for single men, all of whom were good fun and addicted to multiple solitaire. They had great stories of Amadio, whom I had still not met, though Mr. Barklamb had snuck me into the hall some years before to hear him play the Mozart D Major.

In his room I investigated an old unlocked steamer trunk and found it filled with music. A born snoop, I started going through it – an amazing collection, mostly of old editions of nineteenth century show pieces. Each was heavily blue-penciled, teaching me an important lesson. He never played an entire piece — just the bits that showed off his astonishing technique. Apart from his need to accommodate pieces to record size, he was an active vaudevillian, playing these solos at more than one theater a night, opening one program, then jumping into a cab to appear somewhere else just before intermission, and then again, last on another program. He had false teeth, and I was told that he wore out the plates with his tonguing practice. He was also a great ladies' man. In a later visit, when he was back but not yet playing, I heard him charming someone on the telephone.

Publicity photo, 1956.

After getting over my usual shyness and anxiety, I began to settle into the job. The "band" had a very relaxed attitude to the job. They worked a twenty-one-hour week, largely recording light "dinner music" for later broadcast. We played table tennis right up to rehearsal time, and no one would dream of warming up or practicing or even taking his instrument home. The studio was a church hall with great acoustics. The players had to be arranged strategically, however, to avoid drips from the leaky roof. At this time of year the weather was cold and damp. The conductor was a nice, but somewhat limited Englishman.

I was apprehensive about my first program, particularly William Walton's *Facade Suite* with its tricky piccolo part. "Don't worry," said the first flutist, Don Davidson, "and don't practice it." I did, of course, though without great success. However, after listening to the broadcast of the session later, everything became clear. That scrawny thirty-piece ensemble, where the trombones put bowler hats over their bells to play the third and fourth horn parts, became a hundred piece orchestra of world class. I couldn't hear the piccolo, much less its errors — just one big, beautiful sound.

I became fond of Don and his wife Marilyn, and spent many evenings at their home listening to recordings of the great English players. We also laughed our way through Winthrop Sargeant's hysterical *Geniuses Goddesses and People*, particularly his stories of life in the New York Symphony. Another close friend was the orchestra's pianist, David Fox, who took me to his isolated home for sessions of Sibelius.

So time passed pleasantly and I learned an enormous amount of new orchestral repertoire. For the first time in my life I was practicing extremely hard. I was concerned about the brilliant sixteenth note passage that ends the Hofmann, worried that the conductor might press me beyond my single-tongue ability. The time had come to learn to double-tongue.

The orchestra had one of its not so frequent concerts, this one in the north coast town of Launceston (playing among other things the *Emperor Concerto* with Paul Badura-Skoda), so I could not be excused for the competition's first rehearsal. I went straight to bed after the concert but at midnight was still awake with nervous tension. After an early breakfast and a bumpy flight, I arrived in Melbourne feeling somewhat nauseous. My mother drove me to the hall as the final rehearsal was ending. I played twice straight through and went home to rest.

A scratchy acetate disc made of my performance that night records a dreadfully slow tempo for the first movement and a slight falling out with the orchestra during the second. The conductor had me play the opening just before going on stage, but he still didn't get the tempo right, and I was not experienced enough to know how to handle it. After the post-concert deliberations, the judging panel, which included the orchestra's director, Kurt Woess, came on stage to announce the winners to go on to the commonwealth final in Sydney. To my absolute shock I won the instrumental division. All of a sudden life took on new meaning. Backstage, a beaming Mr. Barklamb introduced me to an elegantly dressed John Amadio, who had been in the audience. I received congratulations all round, new admiration from friends, and, later, telegrams, letters, and supportive reviews. Great my performance wasn't, but it was a start. I was on my way.

Mr. Amadio congratulates me as Mr. Barklamb looks on.

Russell Meares had a party afterwards, and the next morning I flew back to Hobart for two more weeks. Now I had two habits – cigarettes (elegant, Black Russian Sobranies with their gold tip when the occasion demanded), and Vincent's – a dreadfully bitter powder that I swallowed dry for my frequent throbbing headaches.

Following Hobart, I had two more weeks back at school before flying to the competition finals in Sydney's lovely town hall. The conductor this time was our director, Sir Bernard, which was comforting. I played better as a result of my earlier experience and another month of preparation, and was pleased to receive an honorable mention from the judge, the newly arrived English composer, William Lovelock. The review said I "played expressively with excellent tone, clean tonguing and nimble fingering," and noted "his fine musicianly instinct for shaping a phrase and the technique and breath control to achieve his object."

Back in Melbourne I was starting to play percussion with the VSO and over the next couple of years became a regular performer in this capacity. I began with bass drum and cymbals, and progressed, following my lessons, to snare drums and even some mallet work. Apart from having a wonderful opportunity to participate in great music with a good orchestra, I learned how to count bars of rest and play rhythm.

One of my Amateur Hour radio appearances.

I had my moments. In the Tchaikovsky *Fourth* I stood up to play the triangle solo thinking everyone must be looking at me. But between watching the conductor and following the music, I missed the triangle with my quavering beater. Another time I was trying to place an enormous bass drum beat in the middle of a giant seven bar in the "Great Gate of Kiev" section of *Pictures at an Exhibition*, when the bar was beat as a colossal two-arm circle without subdivision.

The funniest moment (in retrospect only) was my xylophone solo in the Shostakovitch *First* – the conductor my very own Henry Kripps. I had been fooling around with the instrument during the first rehearsal break when my teacher came up and asked if I wanted to play it in the slow movement – what confidence in this first year student! I spent the rest of the break memorizing the solo and after counting my hundred or so bars made a perfect entry, but played it twice too fast. Maestro stopped the orchestra and said, "Mr. Wion, you are an excellent flautist, but a terrible percussionist!"

I was still playing flute whenever and wherever I could and played my first Stravinsky when someone got sick in Adelaide. David Cubbin, who played first flute there, kindly took me through the piccolo part of *The Firebird* beforehand. The concert, which also included the Bruckner *Seventh*, was a challenging but exciting experience.

AUSTRALIAN BROADCASTING COMMISSION

presents

CONCERTO AND VOCAL COMPETITIONS
COMMONWEALTH FINAL CONCERT

SYDNEY SYMPHONY ORCHESTRA

Guest Conductor

SIR BERNARD HEINZE

Commonwealth Finalists

MARY WARNECKE (pianist) S.A.
JANETTE HAMILTON (pianist) N.S.W.
RUSSELL COOPER (bass-baritone) N.S.W.
JOHN WION (flautist) Vic.
BARBARA RIDGWAY (soprano) Qld.
JOSEPHINE McKIMMIE (pianist) W.A.
CORNELIA BRAIN (pianist) N.S.W.
BRIAN HANSFORD (bass-baritone) Vic.
MAX MACKAY (pianist) Vic.

Adjudicator: Dr. WILLIAM LOVELOCK

TOWN HALL, SYDNEY

Saturday, 14th July, 1956, at 8 p.m.

When I came back to school from Hobart, I heard about this tough professor, Keith Humble, who had just returned to Australia and was conducting the conservatorium orchestra. I immediately went to introduce myself and found myself staring down at a curly headed little man with an impish grin. He said he had been hearing about me too; so began a friendship that lasted until his death in 1995.

Keith was ten years older than I, and a brilliant pianist. After working his way through school by playing for silent movies, he had gone to England to study. He then went to Paris to study composition with Schönberg's disciple, René Leibowitz. Unable to work legally, he began copying parts for tuition and playing on some recordings, notably the *Guerrelieder*. His wife, Jill, also a pianist, supported them by typing for Unesco.

A fiercely national Australian, Keith had returned after five years to make his country more aware of twentieth century atonal music. He became my mentor, my drinking buddy, and my friend. I would arrive unannounced at the Humble flat at all hours, and he would sit me down with scores of Mahler (just beginning to be played in Melbourne) and Schönberg and play the recordings. I was introduced to such exotic food as pancakes with maple syrup and sausage. Then, truly looped, we would tackle some sonata like Hindemith. He taught me about twelve-tone theory and the excitement of life in Paris. We talked about "dead" music (like Beethoven) and "living" music (like his own), and he gave me books and texts to read. He conducted the *Meistersinger* overture like a piece of chamber music, a reading still unmatched in my career. Then suddenly, at year's end, he announced he was going back to Paris. I was terribly angry, knowing what he still had to offer, thinking him selfish. It was only several years later when we met again in Paris that I was able to understand that Australia's total refusal to accept his philosophy and music was destroying him; he felt unable to withstand the combination of resentment and apathy. This wise, tough little man, leaving his country for the second time, was all of twenty-nine years old.

Keith Humble

The next year I was to meet another Australian composer, Percy Grainger, of an earlier generation. He also felt unable to live in Australia but had built a museum for his artifacts and scores on the university grounds, to which he regularly sent material. He was there on a visit to unpack and arrange his shipments when a couple of us knocked on the museum door to seek his support for the music camp. A small man, gray haired, with the most piercing pale blue eyes, opened the door. He could not possibly support such a project he told us, seeing that he did not believe there was a future in live music. Ouch!

As the school year approached its end, Olympic fever was growing. Melbourne was preparing to host the summer games, and television became a part of life – at least for the wealthy. We music students participated in chamber music concerts at the quarters erected to house the visiting athletes, and we Trinity gentlemen went to the Melbourne Cricket Ground to cheer for our Australian athletes, particularly the great miler John Landy.

In this festive way my second year at the university ended. I had given up French due to missing so many lectures, and I had failed theory, mostly due to my inability to make the very pretty chord progressions that my teacher liked. When I presented a progression I had discovered in Sibelius, he would criticize it as weak. Besides, I was much more interested in twelve-tone music at this point.

At home for the holidays I found life strained. My mother was quite opposed to my current girlfriend. I was so poor I couldn't afford carfare to get away and couldn't ask her to provide it. I was saved by the annual three-week army camp where I had been assigned to the regimental band. This was a brass band, so I was made the bass-drummer. After breakfast each morning the band would march out of camp playing until it was out of earshot. Then we would be dismissed, to lie around in the bush until it was time to march back. After morning tea the real band would rehearse, and the outcasts like myself would sit in our tent and play cards. The afternoon was a repeat of the morning. At night we would buy illicit beer from the regular army mess and drink it in darkness behind locked doors. Occasionally we would pile into someone's car hidden off-site and drive to Melbourne, returning for reveille. Playing soldiers was great fun!

My good trumpet-playing friend, Brian Coogan, was one of the hardworking bandsmen. Brian's claim to fame at our music camps was that he was such a heavy sleeper that his whole bed was carried one day into the shower room and doused before he awoke. Our friendship continued in New York, and he still teases me about these camps.

1957

My third year at Trinity was ever more turbulent and stimulating. Mick and I were now confirmed "wives." Our new study, quite attractive but progressively disorganized as the year passed, was still the hangout for our friends. We had regular times, such as Sunday nights when the BBC's *Goon Show* with Spike Milligan and Peter Sellers had us rolling in hysterics, and impromptu ones, when friends drifted in for a quick cup of coffee and stayed for an hour or two, never quite relaxed because they knew they should be studying. Russell Meares would stop by with his latest beautiful poem, and I was becoming fascinated by another medico, Bill Grant, a brilliant iconoclast, scion of a Tasmanian brewer. Arguments with him were fierce. He had me reading Jung and Nietzsche and made me aware and critical of politics and organized religion. Very religious in an emotional, personal way, I became thoroughly disillusioned when chastised by the warden for wearing slippers to chapel one morning. I stopped participating thereafter and became progressively atheistic in my thinking.

I was painting in oils, including a portrait of Sibelius from a photograph, and listening to recordings of Mahler. I was also composing, particularly a symphonic poem, *Gertrude*, about André Gide's heroine in *La Symphonie Pastorale*. This reworking of an earlier quartet attempted to portray her mind from its nebulous beginning to catastrophic end, where I was now able to rework the final thematic material into a twelve-tone row.

In March I went to Sydney as principal flute of the first Australian Youth Orchestra, borrowing the necessary money for the trip. I was a heavy smoker of sixty "racehorses" (self-rolled cigarettes) a day, and my flute playing lips were consequently a mess. My girlfriend came along, although we were both so unstable that the relationship was rapidly falling apart. I stayed with my cousin Buzzy and her husband, but we were always out late. My behavior led to some embarrassing playing in the concerts. I was quite ashamed.

Emotionally I was a mess during the whole first half of the year. In addition to my stormy relationship with my mother and my religious anger, I had a final separation from the girl who had been a tumultuous focus of my life for the last three years. For two weeks I sat in total lethargy, erupting at the slightest interruption, sleeping twelve hours a night, smoking incessantly. Mick was a huge support throughout this depression.

At school the orchestra read through my *Gertrude*, and I was quite pleased. I didn't have any creative talent in this area, however, and eventually stopped composing. I kept up with my painting a bit longer, creating a self-portrait in

My 1957 portrait of Sibelius.

oil as a gift for my closest musical friends, Pam Webster and Len Spira. They became romantically attached at music camp and went on to become architects. They were first-class performers, clarinet and horn, and for several years we played wind quintets and any other combination of chamber music we could put together for a Sunday afternoon session. The painting was a wedding present for them, and I regretted that it disappeared when they later went their separate ways.

Pam and I decided to play the Bloch *Concertino* with the orchestra at the school's August concert this year and, unable to get the parts from Schirmer in the States, I drew them out of the piano reduction, and Len copied them. We gave a good performance. I later tried to get the parts from the librarian only to be told that she had destroyed them, part of her agreement with the publisher.

In the ABC concerto competition I played the Ibert without rehearsing with the pianist, and made it only to the semifinals. I played quite poorly, spending most of my energies trying to stay with the erratic accompaniment.

I played in most of the VSO concerts either on percussion or on flute whenever they needed an extra player, as in Strauss's *Sinfonia Domestica*, which Efrem Kurtz conducted. Kurtz was married to flutist Elaine Shaffer, though I didn't think to arrange to play for her. David Cubbin in Adelaide did however, and was invited by them to go to The Curtis Institute of Music in Philadelphia to study with Shaffer's teacher, William Kincaid. To my shock, David turned this down.

I was starting to have my own visions of studying in America. My friend Nicki Snekker had played for me a recording of Julius Baker playing the Bach sonatas, which someone had bought overseas. Solo flute recordings were virtually unknown at the time, so this was a thrilling experience for me. I listened to this pure, spinning, liquid gold sound, and tried to copy it. I taped myself and listened and tried again. Totally frustrated, I decided I had to go and study with him. Travel grants were not available in Australia at that time, so I went to the U.S. Consulate and got a list of foundations, writing to as many as seemed warranted. One by one the negative replies came back, and I eventually gave up. Instead I went in August for another six weeks to Hobart, a stay that included the orchestra's tour of the entire island. If nothing else I was surely gaining experience.

In Melbourne I was also expanding my expertise. Mr. Barklamb had been having hand problems for many years, and after two operations he was contemplating relinquishing his place in the orchestra and focusing entirely on teaching. I became acting second flute in the orchestra, sitting between Dick Chugg and the piccolist, Audrey Walklate. The orchestra's principal winds were all superb players – the exquisite Jiri Tancibudek on oboe, Tim White on clarinet, Tom Wightman on bassoon, and Roy White on horn – and it was an exciting time. I began to appreciate Chugg's beautiful sound and revel in his stories. He was a great raconteur. One story he told was of meeting Arthur Gleghorn, the great English flutist, at the Rudall Carte premises in London, and watching him, challenged, pick up a flute and some virtuoso piece from the store and read it brilliantly at

Richard Chugg, principal flute, VSO.

sight. On another occasion he got misty-eyed describing a broadcast he picked up on short wave radio from America of Kent Kennan's *Night Soliloquy*. Wryly he told how he had gone to Europe to develop his tonal skills and on his return had that tone praised for its trombone-like quality. He was very relaxed in his demeanor at rehearsals, usually having an art book or something similar on his stand. If a Straussian high D presented itself he would just turn to Audrey and ask her to play it on piccolo. His early life, before he taught himself the flute, had been spent at sea, and he never lost his love of sailing.

Toward the end of the year I heard indirectly that the J. C. Williamson company, which produced most of the theater in Australia, had me in mind for second flute for an upcoming visit of the New York City Ballet. I had started subbing in their orchestras when someone had been unable to play for a ballet matinee of Schumann's *Carnaval* and Tchaikovsky's *Nutcracker Suite*. The first flute was an elderly Italian, Americo Galliardi. I was struggling to keep up with the Schumann and thinking what a long overture it was, when I suddenly realized that we were well into the ballet. The silence of dance was a new experience for me.

> As Wednesday fades once more from sight
> I feel the urge to state my plight,
> So boldly here it is – to whit,
> I'm jack of all this elephants....!
>
> For three long years I've come to eat
> At Sid's, for lunch, in search of meat;
> Yet, once a week, nought of the species
> But sliced up hunks of elephants......!
>
> I hope and pray that day will come
> When no more speaks that mighty ...
> So brethren all just sign my sighin'
>
> SH   Yours sincerely Jack H. ....

My plea for better food in the 1957 Trinity College suggestion book.

The New York City Ballet, like most things American, was totally unknown in Australia. I was angling for the permanent second flute position in the VSO and had my graduating year ahead of me, so I declined to investigate further. Instead, after a year of minimal study and honors in every subject, I took off in my newly acquired car for Adelaide, where the music camp was to be held.

The car question had been a problem since I turned eighteen and obtained a license. We had a family car, a small Renault which my father had bought just before he died. I learned to drive in this and the old Stutz that my brother Frank had bought. When I moved to Trinity I became dependent on the generosity of my more affluent friends, Russell Meares and Jim Grimwade, to lend me their cars for special dates. Now my mother had sold me the aging Renault and I was a free man.

I sold my tape recorder to buy a car radio and set off on New Year's Day, 1958 – the start of my last year in Australia, though I didn't know it. I was no longer an official camper, so I lived in a tent and visited during the daytime, playing quintets and generally hanging out with my friends, the newly married Len and Pam Spira. I found it a strange week; when it was over I drove back for my annual army camp, overtired, underfed, and generally run down.

The army was more fun, seeing my old buddies, the laughing and swearing picking up just where it had left off the year before; tears ran down my face throughout the day. The routine was much the same as previously except that now I was one of the lucky car people. I went down to Melbourne at the first opportunity to bring it back and hide it in the scrub. Now we could go to movies or to the city for a night – a good holiday all in all. Back home a letter from J. C. Williamson was waiting.

1958

After much deliberation I decided to accept the second flute position for the New York City Ballet tour, primarily because the company would be bringing their principal flute with them. I thought that would be a good experience, with the possibility of both taking lessons and making contacts. Then came a second letter saying that the American flutist was not coming after all, and I was to play first. This was not to my taste, but after more thought and some haggling over pay, I accepted.

Right after Easter I took the train to Sydney for the start of this four-month engagement, booking into the Railway Hotel near the theater. The rehearsals went smoothly under the principal conductor, Hugo Fiorato; I enjoyed his open, American assurance and professional skill. I moved twice before settling down to the eight-week Sydney season. Most of my salary went home to pay for my car, and my spare time went into preparing assignments and sending them to the conservatorium. The orchestra was not terribly good, with some weaknesses in brass and percussion. Most of the repertoire was new to me – Hershey Kay's *Western Symphony* and *Stars and Stripes*, Debussy's *Afternoon of a Faun*, Tchaikovsky's *Swan Lake* second act and *Third Piano Concerto (Allegro Brillante)*, Barber's *Souvenirs*, Banfield's *The Duel*, Turner's *Pastorale*, Britten's *A Young Person's Guide to the Orchestra (Fanfare)*, Glinka's *Pas de Trois* and *Valse-Fantaisie*, Stravinsky's *Firebird*, Glazounov's *Pas de Dix (from Raymonda)*, Mendelssohn's *Scotch Symphony*, Gould's *American Concertette (Interplay)*, Rossini overtures (*Con Amore*), Bizet and Gounod symphonies, Chabrier's *Bourée Fantasque*, Minkus's *Pas de Trois*. Most of these were ballets of George Balanchine and Jerome Robbins.

As I felt more secure with my performances I began to be able to look at the stage while counting rests and started assessing the young ballerinas, one in particular. This was fantasy time, as I had no social contact with the company. Apart from the three conductors, the only Americans with whom we associated were the two players who came from New York, concertmaster Henry Siegl and clarinetist Eddie Wall (soloist in the Copland Concerto).

One night I was approached by one of the male soloists, Roy Tobias, with an old wooden flute he had bought and wanted to know how to blow. We became good friends, and he started inviting me to participate in some of the social events that had been arranged for the company on its days off, including a lovely sail on Sydney Harbour. Sunday was the free day in this very Victorian, Christian country, and the dancers, many of them Jewish, looked forward to their single day of leisure. To the question, "What is open on Sundays?" the answer was, "The churches."

I started soliciting information from Roy about one dancer I had my eye on, and he finally decided it must be Vicky Simon. So I had a name to my fantasy, until the day I took him by ferry to the zoo. As we arrived, some of the girls were just leaving. "That's Vicky," he said. "No," I said, "not her, *her*." "Oh, that's Joysanne Sidimus." So, a new name for my fantasy.

I flew to Melbourne to try once more to win the concerto competition, this time with the Nielsen. However, I didn't even make it to the semifinal and was now quite convinced that my success two years earlier had been a fluke. The thrilling eight-week Sydney season ended – an ecstatic moment as the curtain closed and the audience, which had been building weekly through word of mouth and reviews, went wild. Then I sadly went home, alone in a drizzle.

I couldn't wait to get back to Melbourne to show Roy my life. I took him to the university, to Trinity, to my mother's new house, and to the hills out of the city, and introduced him to my family and friends.

My return to Trinity following Sydney NYCB season.

As well as playing the next eight weeks of the ballet's Melbourne season, I had to get back into my schoolwork and my social life at Trinity – it was football season after all! Mick and I were in a new building, opened at the beginning of the year, and immediately named Jeopardy. The warden was always telling his unruly charges that if their behavior did not change for the better their place at Trinity would be in jeopardy. I was busy preparing my final year paper (on Sibelius's orchestration) and plotting how I could meet Joysanne.

I talked Mick into offering his mother's flat for a Sunday night party, and then Roy into asking Joysanne and her friends to come. Five of them had taken a house in the suburbs and we went to pick them up. Despite my efforts to appear casually sophisticated, I felt sure my subterfuge must have been transparent as I missed the introductions and my eyes went straight to Joysanne – the most quiet and most reticent of them.

The rest of the season disappeared in a flash as our romance bloomed. Mick had another party, this time at his farm, where we barbecued fresh-killed lamb. I started meeting Joysanne after performances, going to Bim's, one of the few places open late, or Troika, where I actually took out my flute one night and played Debussy's *Syrinx* for those present. I was getting to know more of the company members and to participate vicariously in their life. Melissa Hayden at the coffee bar would flash her eyes and say that the Australians couldn't appreciate her. The dazzling, kooky Allegra Kent could bewilder a tea party with her zany humor. I became a regular at 31 Ercildoune Street and watched the line of empty bottles grow down the driveway. Inside we lay on the floor listening to Ginette Neveu play Sibelius and Chausson, and I was introduced to *matzoh brei* and other Jewish and American traditions. Four of the girls, Joysanne, Joy, Judy and Vicky were Jewish. Sara was the token Gentile.

They were all wonderful, and wonderfully different. Joysanne was articulate and cultured, warm and shy. Joy Feldman was the only one who had already been in the company before the tour. The other eighteen-year-olds were hired when older members declined to make such a long trip (which also included Osaka and Manila). So Joy was a bit older, wiser, and sassier and called me Uncle John. However, when my entry to their dressing room one night caught her less than fully clothed, she told me to wait: "You're not really my uncle!" Judy Friedman was the smallest, with a shy smile and wonderful humor. She was a gifted pianist as well as dancer. A weight problem led her to leave the ballet and go into medicine and psychiatry not long afterwards. Sara Letton was absolutely outgoing and free living. Vicky was the quiet, beautiful one, who, as I gazed dreamily at Joysanne, was gazing dreamily at me.

As the end of the season approached I knew that I was going to New York. I asked the conductor for advice. He told me to come and study with their flutist, Frances Blaisdell. I also asked for a recommendation – "You write something and I'll sign it." That was not what I had in mind so I didn't follow through. Roy said that if I could find a way to get there I could stay with him in New York. He was such a good friend, and loved me in a way he knew I couldn't return. Joysanne and I on the other hand, chaste as our relationship was, felt we were deeply in love, and at bottom this was the real impetus for my decision to leave. Mick and I went out to the airport to see them all off, and suddenly they were gone.

I was emotionally and physically exhausted and went home to my mother's for the break before my final term. I began writing to both Roy and Joysanne and went to the U.S. Consulate to see about claiming my passport by right of birth, presenting the registration filed by my father at the U.S. Embassy in Brazil. They asked me to fill out a questionnaire and then informed me that two of my adult actions, serving in a foreign army and voting in a foreign election (both of which were compulsory under Australian law), were grounds for loss of U.S. citizenship.

I protested my innocence of willful wrongdoing and was allowed to swear an affidavit to this effect which would be sent to Washington for review. If loss of citizenship was confirmed I could be admitted as an immigrant, not under the Australian quota, which was essentially zero, but as a Brazilian.

I began rationalizing a departure earlier than my imminent graduation would permit. By now I had no respect for the degree I would be awarded or the institution that would award it. I had grown intellectually during these four years and broadened my horizons dramatically but did not credit the conservatorium for that. My flute lessons were largely routine, and I realized more and more that I needed different guidance. I had been studying with Mr. Barklamb for a decade. My history teacher was a Catholic priest who felt obliged to slant our education. Verdi, for example, was a genius, which was OK, but Wagner was the devil. I recall a youth concert that my fellow students stayed away from in droves because the program contained the *Siegfried Idyll*. His final exam paper proposed, as one of the questions, a discussion of the relative merits of these two composers. I wrote for the entire time on the genius of Wagner without mentioning Verdi at all. I also just wanted to be with Joysanne. What in retrospect was such a small amount of time seemed a great number of days and hours at this young, manic-depressive stage of my life.

Back at Trinity it suddenly seemed so easy – just go! Everyone descended on me – my mother, the warden, Mr. Barklamb, and Joysanne. She had returned to New York and, after reauditioning for Balanchine, had been formally taken into the company. On opening night of the fall season she hurt her ankle and was out for the duration. Her own depression and inactivity colored her letters dramatically as she urged me repeatedly not to leave school and eventually not to be so sure of our future together, despite our current feelings.

I asked Mr. Barklamb for a recommendation for Juilliard. This had been one of my hopes the previous year, but I had given up upon learning that I would have to present myself in person to be considered for scholarship aid. At that time the idea of a round trip to New York to audition was unheard of. He wrote that I was a "talented flautist with outstanding natural technique. Although tone and articulation are by no means inferior these no doubt will be greatly improved by further instruction than I can give. A lad of gentlemanly instincts – has had the highest education that this country can give – cultured, artistic and keenly developed intellect – absorbing ambition to become a successful flautist. Decision to take this step hastened by association with New York City Ballet during its recent visit – ten more weeks of study would have given him...."

He even wrote to Joysanne to beg her to dissuade me. She gave me all the arguments: not giving up in the middle of something, the current recession in the US, the need for a college degree to achieve anything. They were all correct, of course, but I was headstrong and I had made up my mind. While it seems silly in retrospect, it was a decision I have never regretted. Indeed, my regret for the next several years was that I had not gone sooner.

The decision made, I went to a travel agent to learn about fares and flights and back to the consulate to learn my fate. No word. Impatient, indeed frantic, I said to forget the citizen part and just let me immigrate. Well now, they couldn't do that until they heard from Washington. I was stuck. Could we speed up the process? Well, if I wanted to pay for a telegram, they would send it. Success, or rather failure; word came back that I was no longer a U.S. citizen. I felt I had been unfairly treated in the circumstances and almost forty years later, on my petition, the State Department agreed, and reinstated my birthright. Ironically, my younger brother used my experience as a way to avoid the Australian draft, and I belatedly learned that I could have used my Australian service to avoid the U.S. draft.

However, at the moment I just didn't care. Now they could start the immigration process. First I had to deal with the question of sponsorship or other assurance that I would not become a financial burden on the state. Yes, a bank account with a certain balance would serve. After writing letters to Joysanne and Roy and looking at the possible options, I learned that my mother still had a bank account in Rochester, though it only held a token balance. At this key moment my friend Jim Grimwade lent me several hundred pounds, which we wired to Rochester. In due course a bank statement came back, and somewhat grudgingly the consulate accepted this proof of solvency. I think they just wanted to get rid of me.

As I was fingerprinted and processed, each day's wait was an agony. I was sure that as soon as I saw Joysanne our relationship would be completely restored, and I had a studio photo taken to send her. September had gone into October, into November. I had officially dropped out of school and Trinity, and had sold everything I owned to buy my ticket.

Living at home with my mother, I played for the opera, a part of the VSO's job. I had already had some exposure to this world. I had seen visiting companies perform *The Marriage of Figaro* (in Italian when the Italian leads were on stage, English when they weren't), *Don Giovanni*, *Aida*, and *Rigoletto*, and had more recently been hired to play in the stage band for the Victorian Opera's *La Bohème* and *The Bartered Bride*, the former on snare drum, the latter on bass drum. The *Bohème* experience affected me emotionally – not the stage band, but the night I finally went out front to see how it all ended. By the time the final curtain came down I was a mess.

Now I had the opportunity to play second and piccolo to Dick Chugg in *The Barber of Seville* and to Audrey Walklate in *Fidelio* (with Sylvia Fisher a memorable Leonore) and *Peter Grimes*. We all three played *Lohengrin*. The whole season was a great thrill for me. In the concerts that followed the opera season I played Mendelssohn *Italian*, Walton, and Bruckner *Fifth* symphonies

Head shot, Melbourne, 1958.

I made a tentative reservation on PanAm and waited for my visa. Finally it was ready, but, because of Veterans' Day, I couldn't pick it up until the twelfth of November. I confirmed my flight for the thirteenth. I made my final preparations and my mother drove me to the airport, where my family and friends saw me off. Our first stop was Sydney, then next morning the incredible tropical perfume of Fiji. We flew on to Hawaii – Nietzsche my daylight companion – and immigration control. I had a most unusual classification I was told, signifying that I had previously entered the country. My green card safe in my wallet, we flew on to San Francisco. After a late arrival, and a hurried change to TWA, we flew on to Idlewild (nervous because I didn't know this was the name of the New York airport). Night fell, and I stared out at the parade of glittering highway snakes and ever-growing light. On November 14, after forty hours of flying, I landed. Roy and Joysanne were waiting for me.

Settling in to New York

1958

Roy Tobias lived on the top floor of an unheated, brownstone walk-up on Fifty-fourth Street, west of Tenth Avenue. This dreary tenement in Hell's Kitchen was presided over by Mrs. Grimes on the ground floor. The quarter-floor apartment consisted of a living room facing south onto the street, with a stove, sink, and refrigerator making a kitchen just inside the entry door. In this area Roy installed a wood-burning Franklin stove in honor of my arrival. Behind the kitchen were two single beds in line against one wall, separated by a bookcase, and beyond them the bathroom with toilet and tub. From this drain I got my first whiffs of the peculiarly sour New York odor that I still occasionally smell on the street, emanating from some sewer. Roy's exquisite taste had done everything possible on a dancer's tiny salary to make all of this look elegant.

Roy Tobias

New York was overwhelming with its noise, fast pace, cars coming from the wrong direction, and currency in dollars and cents. The first days and weeks were a jumble of new, anxiety-creating experiences – shopping up the street for juice and cigarettes, going to Tenth Avenue to the supermarket, exploring other parts of the city. My first time using the subway was to visit Joysanne's home in Brooklyn. Roy showed me the entrance to the BMT at Fifty-fifth Street and Seventh Avenue, but I couldn't decide which direction was Brooklyn bound. Every time I made a decision the train doors would close too soon. Finally I acted quickly enough, but soon discovered I was on my way to Queens. Having paid my fifteen-cent fare I decided to stay on for the ride, and I was unfashionably late when I finally arrived at the Sidimus residence for dinner.

Joysanne's ankle, which she had sprained on opening night of the fall season, had not healed and she was in a cast. Mrs. Sidimus, a short, throaty-voiced teacher, was kind to me on this and later occasions. Joysanne and I would sit around her apartment listening to records. I would start to relax, till suddenly the wail of a siren in the street would remind me where I was.

One of the records Joysanne introduced me to was Leonard Bernstein's *Candide*. *West Side Story* was currently the big hit in New York, and she would tell me stories from her friends in the cast, how the intensity of their portrayals was affecting their off-stage lives. With Joysanne immobilized, kind (or sneaky) Vicky offered to show me around Manhattan. Apart from the usual tourist sights, she got us standing room for *West Side Story*. What a thrill it was to see this powerful, original show in its superb Broadway production.

With the ballet in rehearsal, I was on my own a lot, but I certainly had plenty to do. My very first project, after finding the Wall Street bank to which the money from my Australian account had been wired, was to buy a flute. My wooden flute was totally out of fashion here, and I needed my savings for a silver one. I looked in the Yellow Pages and found an ad for Weatherly Flutes: *"Flutes are my business."* Al Weatherly's shop was on Sixth Avenue at Forty-eighth Street. This avenue, recently lightened by the removal of the elevated line, was becoming more integrated into the city's glamorous midtown, with the construction of Rockefeller Center and ever-increasing skyscrapers. I walked up the stairs and into his shop and the start of a new life.

Al, who was to become a close friend over the next years, had a whole array of used flutes on hand, left on consignment and stored in his safe. The only choices at that time were Haynes and Powell. He explained the difference, how Mr. Powell had left the Haynes factory to start his own firm, and how Al himself had apprenticed to Powell and had participated in the making of his own instrument, number 480, which I was later to own. With a long waiting list for new Powells, used ones commanded a premium price, so my option was narrowed to Haynes. Al started playing the different flutes and my mouth dropped open – this was the finest flute playing I had ever heard, and he was only the repairman! What could the professionals be like? I was to find out soon enough but for the moment, five days after arriving, I went home with my $315 number 21482 and began practicing.

Al and Sue Weatherly

The next step was to contact Mr. Baker about the possibility of lessons. "Why don't you look in the phone book?," asked Roy. "Julius Baker would be in the phone book?," I replied in my naiveté. He was indeed listed, actually less than a mile away on Seventy-first Street. Trembling, I phoned and spoke to a female I assumed must be a maid, having never heard of an answering service. If I left my name Mr. Baker would return my call. "Julius Baker is going to phone me? No way," I thought. She insisted, and a half-hour later the phone rang: "This is Julius Baker" *Omigod!* He would like to meet me, why didn't I come right around? I nervously walked to his building and rang the apartment bell. The door was opened by this barrel-chested man with a wide smile and out-thrust hand. "Where's your flute?," he asked. "Uhh,...," I stammered. "Well, why don't you go back and get it?" I ran home and back, and so began my $25 lessons.

He played a rose gold Haynes at the time, and rose gold was a good description of his sound. It was not the pure, filtered sound of his record, but it was amazing. At this time in his life Baker was playing jingles and movies for a living and, outside of his teaching studio, you could rarely hear him play live. He could play louder than anyone and softer, but his recording mode was the in-between, where his sound was at its most voluptuous. A few years later, when he joined the New York Philharmonic after John Wummer's retirement, we started to hear rehearsal stories – "Where's the flute?" – "Can't hear the flute!" – from the dreadful new stage at Lincoln

Center. Some time after that, I was playing next to him, and was surprised by the roughness of his sound, it had changed so much. Then one night I heard the orchestra from the audience and out soared this gorgeous flute sound – this astonishing man had again made the necessary adjustment for the new environment.

His fat, stubby fingers gave the impression that he had been born holding a flute, his cheeks vibrated with his warm vibrato, and his thinnish lips spun the air into the flute and turned it into golden sound. I was later to hear an early recording of Baker playing in a Bach cantata. The flute sound was quite ordinary, so he had not indeed been born perfect.

Our lessons quickly got stuck on the first Berbiguier study, with its opening leap of a tenth. My embouchure was so undeveloped that I made my top octave by closing off my throat, and the high E came out as something of a thin squawk. "Not like that," he would say in endless repetition, "like this." I would go home each week and stand in front of the mirror for hour after hour, trying to stand like Baker, look like Baker, sound like Baker. Each week, thinking I had it, I would play. He would stop me and say, "No, John...." His style of teaching was by example; he couldn't, or at least didn't, say what I was doing wrong. I became more and more frustrated, and after a few months took advantage of the fact that he was going on tour with the Bach Aria Group to stop the lessons. I never lost the goal of trying to sound like him. Years later, when I had my act better together, I thought, *now I'm ready to study with him*.

Each lesson's highlight was playing a duet from Kuhlau *Opus 87*, the fast movements of which he would play at breakneck speed, leading from the second part. A fellow student later told me that he became so freaked out by the strain of this sight reading that he bought some duets, learned a fast movement, and put the music back in its bag. At the appropriate moment he whipped it out and led into it with great bravura. Of course Baker kept up with him, but the student felt good.

Sometimes Baker would play me something he had recently recorded – a Quantz trio with Robert Bloom, or some Telemann duets with one of the "better younger players," Jean-Pierre Rampal. I liked one of the performers more than the other on this latter recording but was afraid to ask which was which. He would talk about his teacher, William Kincaid. Everyone thought Kincaid had a great sound but, "I've spent my entire career trying not to sound like that – on a good day he was OK – listen to him playing in ...."

The ballet's winter season began two weeks after I arrived, and I was introduced to its cavernous home at City Center, a former mosque on 55th Street. Roy would get me a house seat, and I started to see all the ballets I had only been glimpsing before (Roy himself was a wonderfully elegant waltzer in *Serenade*), and I got to hear that great orchestra. Frances Blaisdell, one of America's first female professional flutists and one of its finest, was the principal; Murray Panitz was second; and Victor Harris played piccolo. The new principal conductor was Robert Irving, from the Royal Ballet. I met him at a party, and eventually auditioned for him, playing a Bach sonata and some *Nutcracker* (that being the music on the stand in the ballet pit). He only commented that I didn't play with much dynamic variation, and it would be some time before I actually got to sub with that orchestra.

The highlight of the season was Balanchine's new work to Kurt Weill's *Seven Deadly Sins*, with Lotte Lenya, Weill's widow, singing the role originally written for her, and Allegra Kent dancing her alter ego. Then came my first *Nutcracker*, with its magical growing Christmas tree and its snowfall with a recorded boys' choir.

Roy also introduced me to Broadway on his nights off with *The Visit* by Friedrich Dürenmatt, starring Alfred Lunt and Lynn Fontanne. I learned later, when we did the Gottfried Von Einem opera, that the play was actually called *The Visit of the Old Lady*, but Miss Fontanne had had that modified. The other play was William Inge's *Dark at the Top of the Stair*. I don't think I appreciated these as much as he had hoped. I thought people overacted and were not as refined as visiting English actors I had seen in Melbourne. But I was started on a journey that would make New York's theatrical offerings one of the good reasons to live there.

My first Thanksgiving took me out of the city to Roy's family in Philadelphia and my first look at American suburbia. Their charming old house (everything in America was old after Australia) and warm hospitality were a perfect introduction to this new holiday, from the mother cooking in the kitchen to the father raking leaves in the yard. Christmas was another new experience. I was used to the incongruities of midsummer heat and plum pudding, live eucalyptus and fake firs. Now it was the skating rink and the tree at Rockefeller Center, the Christmas show at Radio City Music Hall, the unbelievable windows on Fifth Avenue, and the crisp, cold air. I had promised to phone my mother and placed the call from the apartment. In Australia I was used to the operator coming on the line to say that time was up, so I chatted on with nothing really to say, till Roy finally suggested I had better get off. With tax, the bill was $110 ($775 in today's money).

Joysanne had a good friend, Paul Fein, who was the timpanist of the Juilliard school orchestra. She arranged to meet me there and introduce us, in the hope that this would lead to further contacts for me. Juilliard was at that time uptown on Claremont Avenue, where The Manhattan School is now. I took the wrong train and got off at One-hundred-sixteenthth Street in Harlem, instead of Broadway. Unperturbed, I walked through "black" streets and across Morningside Park. Just as Al Weatherly had been the finest flutist I had heard, I now discovered that the Juilliard was quite the best orchestra. The principal flutist was Harold Jones, from Chicago, currently Juilliard's star. Later we became good friends and tennis opponents, and even later I subbed for him in the Broadway revival of *On Your Toes*.

I also visited Local 802's offices on Fifty-second Street to inquire about joining the musicians' union. I discovered that the first necessity would be an "Intention of Acquiring Citizenship" form, which I could apply for from the Immigration and Naturalization Service after six months of residency. Within six months, however, I had to register for the draft, and six months after that they would be able to conscript me.

My supply of money dwindled with the year. Partly it was that necessities were more expensive than Melbourne, and partly it was that I hadn't yet sensed the value of the money itself. A quarter here and a dollar there didn't seem to mean anything.

My relationship with Joysanne also dwindled. She made it clear that we had no future other than as friends, and I asked her not to phone me anymore. Joysanne went on to become a soloist with London's Festival Ballet and a Principal Dancer with the National Ballet of Canada. In 1985 she founded the Dancer Transition Resource Centre in Toronto. For her service in this area she was awarded the Governor General's Performing Arts Award for Lifetime Achievement.

I was practicing hard and immersed in the flute but knew that very shortly I had some important decisions to make. If I stayed I would have to give Roy back his privacy, I would have to start earning some money, and this pesky business of the U.S. draft was looming. The alternative was to go home with my tail between my legs.

Then came New Year's Eve, a dark night at the ballet, and Vicky's birthday. So, screwing up my courage, I asked her if she would like to go to a show, if she had no other plans. The only musical to which I could get tickets was the Jean Kerr/Leroy Anderson *Goldilocks*, with Don Ameche and Elaine Stritch. In one funny moment an Egyptian movie scene being shot in New Jersey is snowed upon. Outside, afterwards, it was indeed starting to snow – my first. I took Vicky home to Greenwich Village and walked back to the subway on a silent Grove Street, through the snowfall. A few years ago we saw a lovely movie called *The Hudsucker Proxy*, which opened with a New York night scene of quiet snowfall and a voice-over saying, "It was New Year's Eve 1958." It was just as I remembered.

1959

My first goal for 1959 was getting a source of income. One of Roy's friends who was an agent told him before I arrived that playing for a tour might be a possibility. I don't know what I thought – sometimes I fantasized that I would just walk into a TV studio and bingo! I now knew that the reality was quite different. I couldn't even find the bottom of the ladder I hoped to climb. Clearly I was not about to get work playing the flute.

So it was that, bright in the new year, I looked in the Yellow Pages and found an employment agency, the Albert Agency, a few blocks away. I presented myself, filled out a questionnaire, was interviewed, and advised not to mention the "musician" part as it would suggest impermanence to an employer. A card was looked at – the Waldorf-Astoria needed an elevator operator – a phone call was made, and off I went to the East Side, to this most elegant hotel on Park Avenue.

Uniformed, I presented myself to Jane, the starter at the east bank of elevators and Irish like most of the hotel service staff, and began my new life. She and red-headed Peggy taught me the business, and soon I was whizzing up and down, arm outstretched when closing the door, always polite, always neat. Now, what were those up/down lights together on fifteen every afternoon? Mrs. Appenzeller, a resident, liked a private elevator, and always gave a crisp new dollar bill to the operator. One day, Jane said, "Johnny (oh that Irish accent!), you get that." I was in! My own accent, educated Australian, didn't hurt. As a fellow operator said, "You've only been here a few months and you speak better English than I do." Of course he, like most New Yorkers, didn't know much about Australia, and probably thought I was Austrian anyway.

Actually, I spent the first months on the job trying to lose my accent. I was shy and didn't enjoy being singled out; and nobody understood me when I ordered a Coke. The American o's and r's were the hardest. I thought I got it pretty well – certainly none of the visiting Australians picked me as one of their own. But I was – am – always from some other part of the continent to an American – maybe Boston, unless I'm in Boston, or maybe Canada. Years later I was in a taxi in Washington and, after a half-dozen words of direction, the driver asked what part of Australia I was from. It turned out he had been the driver of an Australian officer during the war.

With money coming in, it was time to find a place to live. Although Roy was far too much of a gentleman to say anything, I was in his way, and one of his friends firmly told me my time was up. I was not the only defector from Australia to NYCB. Another of the dancers had gotten very close to an Italian waiter in Melbourne, and had secretly married him before leaving. Already they were separated and Gianni Parente with his gorgeous cheekbones, wavy black hair, and suave charm was well ensconced as a waiter at the swanky Copacabana on the East Side. He needed a temporary roommate, so we took a room together on East Sixtieth Street, near Bloomingdale's. It was an easy walk down Lexington to work, and the price was right. Cooking was not allowed in the room, though we had a hidden hotplate. Neither our personalities nor our interests meshed, but neither did our schedules, so we rarely saw each other. By summer a single room had opened up, and I took it. For the first time in my life I was actually alone. The room was tiny, just twice the size of its single bed. It had a chest of drawers and a skylight, which too often I forgot to close when going to work, returning to a wet bed.

A new New Yorker.

At work I had been offered a new night job, running the ballroom elevator. What a great job it was! Basically I brought the patrons up at the beginning of the event and down at the end. In between, I could listen to the entertainment provided – The New York Philharmonic, Count Basie, Ella Fitzgerald. It was an education. I also discovered that the Waldorf had kitchens and that you could help yourself. I then went on to the midnight elevator shift, and finally, by fall, I became a package boy. This came with a considerable reduction in salary, but the prospective tips would more than counter that. Being back on a day shift also meant I had to find a studio where I could practice. I could get away with daytime practice in my room, but never in the evenings when the other residents were home.

Most of our work was delivering packages to residents of the Waldorf Towers. These included President Hoover, who said a few kind words, General MacArthur, U.N. Ambassador Lodge, and numerous other social and industrial leaders. Packages from the outside were delivered to the package room only, and then, via our services, to the hotel guests. When visiting South American dictators were in town, packages from all the Fifth Avenue stores to their wives came nonstop, and so did the tips. Conventions offered ample opportunities for theft. My boss, who probably should remain nameless, solved his cash flow problems via a resident who had regular grocery deliveries. My boss would pay for these by presenting a chit to the cashier against the resident's bill, and then passing on the cash to the outside deliverer. If he needed a few extra dollars, he just signed and presented a chit. Clearly the resident never checked.

With these two essentials (money and shelter) taken care of, I was able to focus on the next problem, finding a flute teacher who could better help my tone problems. Al Weatherly suggested Claude Monteux. Claude, the son of conductor Pierre Monteux, was an intelligent, articulate, humorous, unpretentious, wonderful human being and musician, who was currently living in New York, as a freelancer. My first lesson was a revelation. I played something and he simply said, "You're doing this and this, and you have to be doing this and this." It was the first time

Claude Monteux

anyone had provided such information, and from the first lesson I made progress. Within a year our lessons had become routine. He would assign me pieces, approve my work, and assign more. However, his integrity could not allow this to continue. He told me he had taught me all he could, then made up a list of contractors with their phone numbers, made calls where he could, and wished me good luck. This was not the end of our relationship, which continues to this day. He helped me get work as long as he was in the city. Afterwards, when he moved to Dutchess County to pursue his conducting interests, he helped provide work for my quintet.

In the early part of the year, I began paying back my loan from Jim Grimwade. I bought a flute from Al Weatherly for my friend Nikki Seymour in Melbourne. She in turn sent the payment to my mother, who wrote a check to Jim. Australia's import duties and currency restrictions fostered such shenanigans. Later in the year I decided to send my matching wooden Rudall Carte flute and piccolo to Australia for sale, certain I would find no buyer in New York. Weatherly did a superb job of renovation; the black wood became brown with a lovely grain, the "German silver" key work was plated, shims took up the lost motion in the rods, and new screw-in pads replaced the old glued ones. I sent the set home with my visiting brother Frank, and my mother sold it for what I had paid for the overhaul. The argument for the low price was a crack in the flute head-joint which had been there since I bought it. As the head was metal-lined it made no difference. Now those instruments would have considerable value. I wonder where they are.

I also tried to make contact with my half-sisters, as well as my cousins in Bellefonte. Sister Kathryn was the closest; she lived in Easton, Maryland, where she had a pony farm. In April I used some days off to take the train to Wilmington, where she met me. It was the strangest thing, meeting my sister for the first time as an adult. She was twenty-five years older and had a daughter not much younger than I. We had a very pleasant visit, catching up on our lives and our different perspectives of our father. I enjoyed watching her school the ponies and getting a lesson myself. I visited her husband's saw mill and spent an evening with my niece Pam in town. I drove back to the train with a load of timber, desperately trying to understand the driver – my first experience with southern black speech.

I saw Kathryn only once more before she died. She had been befriended by a wealthy horse-owner who invited her to visit his estate in France. She stopped in New York on the way home, and we spent a lovely evening together. She was a most interesting person. After leaving Australia at the age of fifteen, she and her sister Jocelyn had found their way into show business, becoming Broadway "hoofers." In this way they had made their way to California, where Jo had married Herbie Weire. Kathryn was not a beauty when I met her, with short hair, weathered face and generally horsy look, but she still had lots of character, and I enjoyed our brief acquaintance.

In the spring I mustered up the courage to audition for Tanglewood, summer home of the Boston Symphony. Joysanne had sent me letters from there the previous August, describing its idyllic setting and wonderful music programs. I played for the symphony's principal, Doriot Dwyer, in a studio in Carnegie Hall. This arrangement was much less formal than such auditions tend to be today. I recall that when she asked me if I knew a particular Strauss solo, I replied that I didn't, but I knew the (much more difficult) solo from *Sinfonia Domestica*. She seemed delighted by my effort, and I duly received notice that I was accepted as a student in the Orchestra and

Chamber Music Program for the coming summer. I was thrilled, but after much deliberation decided that I could not handle the financial side and turned down the offer.

In retrospect this was big mistake; somehow I should have borrowed the money. I always felt that my career suffered from not having gone to school in America and having the opportunity to meet and know on a first name basis the movers and shakers of the music world. Tanglewood would have given me just such a chance to meet not only my fellow students but conductors, and members of the BSO. Later, this experience enabled me to keep one of my own students from making a similar mistake.

In January I had registered with the draft board, and in May declared my intention of becoming a citizen. This registration enabled me to join the musician's union. I spent the rest of the summer and fall wrestling with the question of what to do if and when I was drafted. I had heard that they grabbed the immigrants first, so I expected I would not have long to wait. My mother and all my friends at home were urging me to leave the country, to go to Canada if that was all I could afford. I was wondering whether the opportunity to be in an army band or orchestra might not be the worst possibility for my near future.

A big part of my quandary was that I was in love. Vicky was on tour with the company at the Hollywood Bowl and Ravinia, and the separation had clarified things for both of us. When she came back, I became an ever more frequent visitor at her mother's house, providing late summer entertainment for her sister Jenny and stepsister Nancy as they watched us necking on the back patio.

Victoria Simon as a Candy Cane, 1954.

Vicky and Jenny had grown up in a sequence of apartments in Greenwich Village and now lived with their mother and stepfather and new brother Stephen in a townhouse on Grove Street. Their parents had separated when they were young. Their father, Robert Simon, a founder of Crown Publishers with his partner Nat Wartels, was a very gentle, warm, soft-spoken man, educated not only in literature but in all the arts. His family had come from Europe to New York in the 1880s, and his mother could talk about the open farmland north of Chelsea when she was young. His second marriage had been to the travel writer Kate Simon, and he was currently moving towards his third marriage. He seemed drawn to strong women who then became frustrated by his soft nature.

The first of these strong women was Vicky's mother, Beatrice. She had also grown up in New York, one of two daughters of Russian immigrants. A beautiful, artistic, and outspoken person, she and her second husband, Philip Jones, were active in leftist politics. Phil was a partner at the law firm of Wolf, Popper, Ross, Wolf and Jones, representatives of most of the Communist countries.

Vicky, who looked very much like her mother and even more like her grandmother, had started dancing when she was eight, studying from the beginning at Balanchine's School of American Ballet, then on Madison

Avenue. She had gone to the High School of Performing Arts, of *Fame* fame. After completing three weeks of college at NYU in the fall of 1957, she was accepted into the New York City Ballet as an apprentice, then joined fully for the Pacific tour. She had first danced with the company as a Candy Cane in the original production of Balanchine's *The Nutcracker* in 1954 and would go on to become a soloist before retiring in 1965 to start a family.

As a visitor on Grove Street I had an awful lot of learning to do. Apart from U.S. politics and Jewish traditions, I was introduced to unsalted butter and rare meat. I knew nothing about food when I arrived, having grown up with old-fashioned English cooking, which included beef or lamb cooked until it was distinctly gray. For some months Bea would patiently serve me the end cuts. She was a great cook in many cuisines, and her dinners were always events.

She and Phil were also considerable collectors of art. One of my favorite pictures was a portrait of Bea with Vicky when she was a toddler. Bea had been approached by a neighbor asking if she could paint Vicky. The resulting portrait, showing a sad mother with a curly headed child on her lap seated on a park bench, became part of an exhibition at the Metropolitan Museum before Bob Simon bought it for his wife. Many years later Bea give the picture to Vicky who wondered if the painter, Lily Harmon, was still alive. We were talking about the picture with dinner guests when Leslie Ellen, an editor at Simon & Schuster, said that they had published Lily Harmon's autobiography, and that she lived in Manhattan. After reading her fascinating story we looked in the phone book and found a listing on Central Park West. Vicky wrote a lovely letter, signing it, unusually, Victoria. A few days later the phone rang and the eighty-year-old painter said, "You used to be Vicky." This dynamic violet-eyed lady came around to see the painting she hadn't seen in fifty years. Her first comment was, "I can't believe I put the dog in it," followed by, "It's really very dirty you know." She arranged to have it restored, and her memory proved to be quite accurate as the smoke-covered pinks and lemons reappeared.

Mother and child - Lily Harmon.

By the fall I had realized that Vicky was worth my having to deal with the likelihood of being drafted, and I proposed marriage. She accepted, but Bea was adamant. No daughter of hers was marrying an elevator boy!

The ballet's winter season began in December, with Vicky busy rehearsing new productions for the post-Nutcracker part of the season, which would run through the first week of February. I became a regular "stage door Johnny" when I wasn't out front or in the wings. Afterwards we would all go to the Carnegie Tavern up the street.

While waiting for Vicky after one performance I met a charming violinist, Max Ellen, who was waiting for his ballerina wife. Max's mother was a Viennese émigré. By a remarkable coincidence, she was a close friend of the Weire brothers and so knew my sister Jo. Max had served in the army at a very young age at the end of the European war and was now freelancing in the city. He had studied at what was then Hartt College. Now he worked the clubs and restaurants, and at NBC. He went on to make his living in the small circle of regular commercial players, both playing and contracting. In this latter capacity he was kind enough to use me on the few occasions when he needed a classical flutist.

New Year's Eve was the traditional interruption of the Nutcracker run and Vicky celebrated her birthday dancing *Divertimento #15*, *Medea*, and *Western Symphony*. As I watched conductor Robert Irving and composer Hershey Kay dressed up as cowboys for the latter, I had no idea how my life was about to change.

Vicky in Divertimento #15 (Photograph by Martha Swope).

A New Life

1960

As 1960 began, Claude Monteux started offering me some of his performances and lessons when he had conflicts. The first, in mid-January, was to play some school concerts with a soprano and a harpist in Baltimore. I was just back from that trip, taking my weekly lesson, when the phone rang. Joe DeAngelis, Personnel Manager of The New York Philharmonic, was calling. Was Claude available for next week's concerts? No, he wasn't; he was working with Igor Stravinsky, recording the *Rite of Spring*. That was one of De Angelis's problems. The city was in the middle of a flu epidemic, one of his own flutists was sick, the Stravinsky had grabbed five flutes, the Philharmonic was doing the Mahler Ninth and needed five flutes themselves. Did Claude know anyone at all who was free? Claude handed me the phone, and in a daze I wrote down the necessary information.

My boss at The Waldorf, Mr. Thomas, had been encouraging me to train as a hotel executive, and was not about to give me a week off – particularly if he knew the reason. So I quit my job and went to hire a set of tails. I was a musician again.

Incredibly, I was on the stage of Carnegie Hall in all its cream, gold, and red velvet glory, with the legendary principal flutist John Wummer off-stage playing long-tones into the wall; Music Director Leonard Bernstein backstage saying a friendly hello; the aging, bald Dmitri Mitropoulos conducting my debut in Mahler's great *Ninth Symphony*. The second flute was Bob Morris, third was Paige Brook. Frances Blaisdell was substituting for an ailing Fred Heim. Much later I learned that this season's Mahler concerts (this was program four of their Mahler Festival) constituted the revival which put Mahler firmly in the Philharmonic's repertoire.

Thursday evening I got into my outfit, which had come equipped with dress shirt, studs, wing collar, and bow tie, for the first concert. Upstairs in the orchestra's dressing room I walked around trying to look nonchalant. One of the members came up to me asking, "Who are you?" Following my reply, he said, waving at my attire, "I thought you must be out front." As I looked more carefully at everyone, I saw to my great embarrassment that they all wore regular white shirts with clip-on bow ties. I survived the evening, and for Saturday night (Friday afternoon, my birthday, called for less formal attire) came properly dressed. Otherwise it was a remarkable week, and, I hoped, an auspicious beginning.

One Hundred Eighteenth Season

New York Philharmonic

Leonard Bernstein, MUSIC DIRECTOR   1959 - 1960
                                                            Carnegie Hall

6085th, 6086th, 6087th, 6088th Concerts

Thursday Evening, January 21, 1960, at 8:30 ("Preview")
Friday Afternoon, January 22, 1960, at 2:15
Saturday Evening, January 23, 1960, at 8:30
Sunday Afternoon, January 24, 1960, at 3:00

DIMITRI MITROPOULOS, Conductor

MAHLER FESTIVAL — PROGRAM IV

Commemorating the 100th Anniversary of Mahler's birth and the 50th Anniversary of his first season as Music Director of the New York Philharmonic

WEBERN   Passacaglia for Orchestra, Opus 1

MAHLER   Symphony No. 9
                Andante comodo.
                Im Tempo eines gemächlichen Ländlers.
                (In the tempo of a comfortable Ländler.)

INTERMISSION

                Rondo. Burleske.
                Adagio.

Steinway Piano   Columbia Records

Two interesting things came out of this experience. Without my thinking about it I had set myself up for unemployment insurance. As far as the state was concerned, I had not quit my job at the hotel; I had moved to another job where my employment was terminated after one week. Secondly, Vicky's mother who had said that no daughter of hers was marrying an elevator operator, now said that an unemployed musician was a different matter.

Our wedding day, February 10, 1960.

Vicky's winter season was to end February 7 with a performance of Balanchine's new *Theme and Variations* to music from Tchaikovsky's *Third Suite*. So, with a three-week layoff ahead, we set our wedding for the tenth. We found an apartment on Seventieth Street between Columbus Avenue and Central Park West, the front half of the top floor of a brownstone and a five-flight walk-up, for what I thought a very expensive $110 a month. As the area had yet to be gentrified by its proximity to the future Lincoln Center, I suppose it was really quite reasonable. Vicky's father gave us a grand gift of $1,000, which disappeared with alarming ease as Vicky and her mother shopped for basic furniture. Bea and Phil provided all sorts of things like china and silver and unneeded rugs and tables and posters from their house.

Having obtained the necessary license beforehand, we made our weekly visit to the unemployment office and went to be married before Judge Henry Clay Greenberg in his Central Park West apartment, in the presence of Vicky's immediate family. Afterwards was a reception at Bea and Philip's with their friends and family, and then dinner at Voisin in the East Sixties with Bob Simon, his mother, Bea, Philip, Jenny, and Stephen. Oh, and I never smoked another cigarette from that day.

Bob had spoken to the only professional musician he knew, a cellist, Arthur Aaron, who said he would try to use me in one of the orchestras he hired. As a result of this help I began my life as a New York freelancer by playing at Cooper Union – the first of many concerts I played for Arthur over the next years. Claude was also able to get me hired as his second in another group, The Connecticut Symphony, whose conductor was the revered Jonel Perlea.

Perlea, a Czech, had been an admired conductor at the Met among other places, but his success was limited because he lacked the political ability to smile when necessary. Now, after a stroke had left his left side immobile, he was teaching at The Manhattan School and conducting wherever he could. He was a great musician, and made more music with the gesture of an eyebrow and whatever he could do with his right arm when he wasn't turning pages than most conductors with whom I have worked. He was obviously in pain and frustrated by his limitations, and could be quite nasty. But the results always spoke for themselves. I recall a particularly elegant *Baisée de la Fée* and, a few years later, at Carnegie Hall, a concert version of *Lucrezia Borgia* by Donizetti.

That concert is better remembered as the U.S. debut of Monserrat Caballé. The way she floated her pianissimos in a rising phrase all the way to the back of the family circle was astonishing. When she ended her opening cabaletta I thought an explosion had gone off in the hall. The entire audience was on its feet in a tumultuous roar.

I started to meet New York's famous musicians, different ones at each concert. The first concert had a wonderful oboist, the second an even better one, and the third.... The third was Lennie Arner, a great artist, and someone whose path became entwined with mine in not altogether pleasant fashion, and who will get further mention in my story. I met another longtime colleague-to-be, the bassoonist Loren Glickman, when Claude sent me as a sub for some chamber concerts. On the humorous side, I was hired to play piccolo in a band on Staten Island for a Sunday afternoon concert. The intonation was so dreadful that the concert was half over before I realized that my part was for piccolo in D♭. I didn't go back to Staten Island.

The way the freelance business worked, you would be approached by someone new at every engagement – assuming you didn't screw up. He would ask you who you were and write down your name and phone number. You were at the bottom of another contractor's list. All you needed now was another flu epidemic.

In April, I started subbing with the Symphony of the Air, a cooperative venture by the members of Arturo Toscanini's former NBC Symphony. I played and recorded a concert with the soprano Eleanor Steber, then in her prime, and next came my first experience with conductor Leopold Stokowski. The principal flutist was Murray Panitz, who was to astonish us all when he gave up New York freelancing to become principal with Philadelphia. Murray gave me some good advice before the first rehearsal: "Don't cross your legs!" I sat, legs uncrossed, as he dazzled his way through *Peter and the Wolf* with Captain Kangaroo narrating. After this were two concerts with choral groups where I met Sam Baron who was playing principal flute for the Bach *B Minor Mass*. At this engagement the horn player Ralph Froelich bowled me over, the way he just sat there forever, then coolly played his sole, magnificent solo.

Rehearsing with Roberta Peters.

With summer came outdoor concerts in Central Park and in Connecticut. The latter were the most interesting, with such stars as Bob Hope and Roberta Peters, with whom I did my first mad scene from *Lucia di Lammermoor*. Woody Herman conducted another pops concert and, unskilled as a conductor, ran into trouble with George Gershwin's *American in Paris*. The concertmaster had wisely given him a violin part to conduct from, but he still had difficulty with the beat patterns. Finally we cut all the slow rhapsodic sections and played just the "swing" parts. His beat went down-up like a piston; if we came to a three-four bar he just continued down-up until things got back on keel with another three-four bar.

Another interesting site in New York was a park by the river on the Lower East Side, where Arthur Aaron began using me that summer. Of the concerts I participated in over the next few years, I recall one conducted by Skitch Henderson, where the slow movement of the Gershwin *Piano Concerto* was dominated by Skitch's trumpeter, Doc Severinson. At another, conducted by Robert Irving, I played second to the wonderful Andy Lolya in Smetana's *The Moldau*. Andy took over from Murray Panitz as principal at NYCB and had a distinguished career there until his death in 1999. Later I played my first *Volière*. One of the pianists was

Lucy Brown, who began talking about her brilliantly talented niece, Paula Robison, new in town and studying with Baker at Juilliard.

In the spring I had played an audition for George Koukly, a funny little Russian bass player who was the contractor for the mighty impresario, Sol Hurok. Koukly was putting together an orchestra for a tour by the Royal Ballet. He seemed satisfied with my playing and asked whether I was prepared to accept the second-flute chair. With great bravado I said I was only interested in playing first. (I later discovered that the person he hired for second had been asked the same question and had been agreeable, and she was actually the stronger player.) In May I signed a contract to play first flute for the entire season from September 11 until January 29 the following year. The rehearsals and first four weeks would be at the (old) Metropolitan Opera House, followed by a tour of the United States and Canada. I was starting to feel as if my career was back where it had left off two years earlier. But for all I had learned about tone control from Claude, I was unable to put it into practice under pressure. Indeed I was to find that I would need a full five years to achieve that.

With things starting to look rosy, I was suddenly brought back to earth at the end of June, when I was ordered to report for my army physical in two weeks. Vicky was away on tour with the ballet and, after a late night of partying, I arrived at the Induction Center on Whitehall Street at 7:30 A.M., bleary-eyed and hung over. I proceeded down the line being inspected, prodded, and sampled until I arrived at the classroom where the IQ test was to be administered. The instructor droned on with his instructions. My ears pricked up when he asked if anyone, for any reason, felt that he would not be able to do his best. Well, I by now had a splitting headache, which might (or might not) be caused by the conjunctivitis for which I was being treated this summer. Anything was worth a try I thought, so I explained my problem and was sent out of the building to report to their eye specialist. He confirmed the infection, but gave me a clean bill of health, which I took back with me. I was put back somewhere into the line. I duly reached the end, without, however, being ordered to fill in a page of health questions such as "Do you wet your bed?" I mutely handed my form to the NCO in charge who looked it over, selected a stamp, stamped the back page, and indicated the officer by the exit door. I snuck a look at the stamp as I waited – "knows insufficient English to answer these questions" – ah, the joy of being Brazilian! I went home with a form signed by the officer stating that I had been "found not acceptable for induction under current standards," and in due course I received my 4F classification. I was saved.

At the end of August, Bea and Phil took us with them to visit Stephen at his summer camp in the Adirondacks. Everything for me was still a new experience, and this one included the fabled Saratoga Race Course where we saw Bob Irving's horse run.

Next came Vicky's fall season, and the Royal Ballet for me. At the summer concerts in Connecticut I had met a very gifted clarinetist, Fred Loeb, who became a good friend. He invited Vicky and me to his apartment for dinner where we met his wife Dolores, a horn player, and bassoonist Dick Lawson and his wife, Lynn. Fred, Dolores, and Dick were doing the ballet tour so I didn't feel alone when rehearsals started.

With Fred Loeb in Connecticut, 1960.

The first day was *Sleeping Beauty*, and we were set up in one of the theater foyers. The principal conductor, John Lanchberry, was in charge and I was very nervous. My second was Marilyn Laughlin, a recent Juilliard graduate who became a good friend over the next months; piccolo was Harry Moskowitz, a seasoned professional who would be playing only the New York season. I got right off to a bad start. One of the variations in the prologue has a flute solo. Unfortunately this variation is the same tempo as the previous one in which the flutes don't play; not seeing the *tacet* indication I started in on my solo, making obvious to one and all that I didn't know the music. I ended the rehearsal thoroughly exhausted, and somewhat depressed. Although confident of my fingers, I spent the entire engagement nervous about slow solos and intonation.

The latter became my biggest problem. I discovered that my time away from playing ensemble, especially solos in an orchestra, had made me hear the faulty intonation of my Haynes as accurate, and I had to try to adjust my ears. A further problem was that the headjoint was too long to be able to play a high enough pitch. When I finally realized this, I had to find someone to do the necessary cutting.

Opening night, with Margot Fonteyn dancing the "Rose Adagio" and concertmaster Frank Gittelson playing the violin solos exquisitely, was brilliant, and my "Bluebird" solo went fine. I had played at different times some parts of *Sleeping Beauty*, but it was a thrill to play the entire score, and in such a wonderful situation. Here I was in the pit of that famous house looking out at the glittering scene, just as it had been photographed from the stage and placed on the dust jacket of the book of opera plots my mother had given me ten years earlier.

The season developed – complete *Swan Lake*, *Giselle*, *La Fille Mal Gardée*, *Ondine* (a new ballet for Fonteyn to music of Hans Werner Henze), and a mixed bill of *Les Sylphides*, *Les Patineurs*, and a *pas de deux* such as from *Don Quichotte*. In the middle of October we took it on the road.

This would prove to be Hurok's last train tour – the next would be by air. We assembled at Penn Station and were shown our assigned canvas-curtained berths in the Pullman car. By the light of the setting sun, we headed north along the Hudson River for our opening in Lansing, Michigan. The minimum stay in a city was half a week. Usually we played for a week and for the bigger cities like Chicago, two. I felt I was being paid to take the grand tour. Normally the trips were overnight, following the close of the engagement, though we also had a lot of daytime travel when the trips were longer. These were the times when one got to see the stars like Fonteyn and Soames relaxed and enjoying company. It was one of the few situations where they couldn't be working.

In the orchestra the great raconteur was concertmaster Frank Gittelson. He was a large, spectacled, elderly man with a goatee, who was one of the best violinists around. He was touring specifically at Fonteyn's request. He was a gourmand whose dining advice was sought for each new town. He had poor digestion, however, and had to sleep sitting up in the parlor car.

Dick Lawson and I were roommates, until he developed appendicitis in Los Angeles and had to leave the tour to recuperate. In spite of the good times that we were having, Fred and Dolores Loeb were drifting apart. Fred spent the rest of his life alone, living for his gambling, drinking, smoking, card parties, and touring with ballet companies, and never receiving the credit his artistry deserved. His night of glory was the recital he presented with his many friends at Alice Tully Hall in Lincoln Center several years later. He was loved and respected by so many.

From Lansing we went to Cleveland and began the trip west: St. Louis; Denver, where we found the ultimate cheap hotel ($4) that was the goal of every touring musician (how to avoid spending one's per diem); Seattle; Vancouver; Portland; and San Francisco, my first real thrill apart from the views of the Rockies. Here we played the War Memorial Hall and took in all the museums and sites, from Chinatown to Golden Gate Park, Fisherman's Wharf to The Peak. We ate like kings, including Gittelson's recommended Blum's for ice cream sundaes.

After a side trip to Sacramento, we reached Los Angeles where we played the Shrine Auditorium. I had told my sister Jo that I would be there, and she invited me to visit the Weire ranch in the San Fernando Valley and join Herbie and her and their children for Thanksgiving. She and Herbie were leading separate lives now – he was on the road so much of the time anyway – but they seemed to have an amicable relationship. Jo, tall and thin, worked for the post office, and was far from the woman in the glamorous photo that had sat on a table in our house in Australia. We had a good time catching up on things. They showed me the movies they had taken when the brothers had visited us in Melbourne. I visited Harry and Sylvester at their homes and had a pleasant time all round.

Back in Los Angeles I visited the brothers at MGM, where they were filming their weekly TV sit-com. It was for me another storybook experience, to walk down the much-photographed streets of the lot and into the cavernous space where their set was constructed. I watched them at work for a while. I hadn't known how few lines at a time they had to learn, how much re-taking was done, how shots were made from a variety of angles and distances, to be spliced together later.

After a side trip to San Diego, where I fell in love with the zoo and became homesick at seeing the Australian fauna, we began the long trip back across country again to Houston and New Orleans. The latter had been looked forward to by my colleagues as the gastronomic high point of the trip, and, inexperienced as I still was in this area, I was getting pretty excited myself. It was an amazing week of indulgence: Brennan's for breakfast; oysters or shrimp with beer for lunch; Galatoire's or Antoine's for dinner. We also played ballet.

Travelling northeast through Birmingham and Atlanta, we arrived at Washington, where I had a brief reunion with Vicky. She had taken the train down after a Sunday night performance to spend her day off with me. Unfortunately this coincided with the worst snowstorm of the decade, and her train crawled into the station about twelve hours late. *She* went back to New York, and *we* headed off to Chicago – another great city that had featured in my childhood, as the birthplace of my brother Frank. It was cold. I had never experienced this kind of bitter dry cold that went straight to my bones. With Dick Lawson's help I bought my first hat, a Cossack-style, sealskin beauty. We started heading north: Rochester, where my brother Richard had been born (at Niagara Falls they had a photo of the winter of '38 when the falls froze over – the year the Wions were there, straight from sunny Rio!); Detroit; and back into the Empire at Toronto. Here we played the new O'Keefe Center.

The stage crew had trouble with the lift that raised the pit into playing height. After considerable delay they finally got it moving, then couldn't stop it. All of a sudden the bedraggled, tour-tired orchestra was at stage level, being assessed by the opening night socialites. Touring musicians quickly learn just what they can get away with in terms of dress; if you are in a pit you don't need to wear black socks, or even matching socks. Al Weatherly told me a lovely story of his own experience on tour. He had discovered the trick of wearing just a false shirtfront under his tuxedo jacket, to save on laundry. It worked just fine till the sweltering night when the contractor sent word around the pit for everyone to play in his shirt.

Touring musicians develop a great camaraderie, living and working together so intimately. It is quite normal to have a practical joker. Our piccolist for the tour, elderly, pencil-mustached, elegantly dressed with silk scarf and black fedora, Emile Denti, told how my predecessor, Phil Dunigan, had once phoned him at four in the morning. Pretending to be hotel staff, he inquired if Mr. Denti had left a six o'clock wake-up call. Yes, he had. "I just wanted you to know you have two hours to go."

From Montreal, another eating town, to Boston, where we played in the arena normally used for ice hockey. They just put wooden boards over the ice and we froze. Well, *Patineurs* was appropriate anyway. Through New York to play Philadelphia and Baltimore, and at the end of January it was over.

It had been a truly wonderful experience, but I knew I had some serious work still to do to raise my flute playing to the level needed to succeed. That meant a new teacher, and Marilyn Laughlin suggested Kincaid. "That's what all Baker's students at Juilliard do on the side," she said. Koukly made it quite clear that my insecurity of intonation would prevent him from hiring me for another tour. That meant buying a new flute and a tuning machine, and being tougher on myself – and quickly.

1961

Immediately after getting home from the Royal Ballet tour, I went to the Haynes showroom on Fifty-seventh Street and bought a silver flute, my first new flute ever. I also phoned Mr. Kincaid who agreed to hear me play in his room at the Wellington Hotel, where he taught every second week. When I presented myself, a tall, ruddy-faced, white-haired gentleman opened the door. He had made it sound as if this were an audition – he had so many people wanting to study with him that he couldn't promise anything. So I was delighted when he agreed to take me as a student. (In retrospect, I imagine he was just protecting himself in case someone totally inappropriate showed up.) So began my year of $15, fifty-minute lessons.

William Kincaid

By that time he had his teaching routine down to something of a formula, but this routine was just what I needed. We started with Maquarre *Daily Studies*, which he made me play by ear after learning each C major/A minor sequence. We worked through Andersen *Opus* 33, as written and at the octave where playable. And he took me through standard repertoire. I bought new copies of these works so I would have his written comments on the music. Of particular interest was the Griffes *Poem*. His revisions and corrections had absolute authenticity as he described arriving at his own lessons with Georges Barrère, to find his teacher and Griffes working on the *Poem* together.

Al Weatherly had played me some of Kincaid's legendary recordings under Stokowski, particularly *Afternoon of a Faun* and the conductor's arrangement of a Chopin mazurka, but it was still a thrill to hear him play live. When he played his platinum Powell during lessons, my major impression was of solidity. The tone, up close, did not have the purity or shimmering ease of Baker's but a certain heaviness. Yet he had an absolute evenness of tone and legato between all notes. The vibrato, which he had taught himself, was comparatively slow, and very evenly produced. He had originally played with a faster, less controlled vibrato.

His breath control was legendary. I loved the story of his final concert with Philadelphia. He was being forced to retire at age sixty-five, and conductor Eugene Ormandy was supposedly delighted, there being no love lost between them. At the rehearsal of *Tales from the Vienna Woods* Kincaid played the cadenza, only to have Ormandy ask for less liberty – it's not much more than a trill after all. At the concert Kincaid began the trill, and trilled and trilled and trilled as the conductor's arm got higher and higher in preparation for the resolution. At its absolute height, Kincaid abruptly resolved the trill, leaving an embarrassed conductor awkwardly off balance, floundering to get the orchestra going again. If true, it must have been quite a moment.

So, if Monteux taught me how to produce a sound, Kincaid taught me technical security. At the same time I bought a Conn Strobotuner and worked daily at intonation. The machine had to have its dial turned for each note, so it was no help with intervals, but it was an invaluable aid for holding a steady pitch and tuning octaves.

The final decision I made as a result of the ballet tour was that such touring was not the way I wanted my life to go. It was a great experience; it gave me a chance to see the country, and it provided a bit of a financial cushion. For a young man without obligations, the salary was considerable. But I looked carefully at the players twice my age or more, with families back home to support, and shook my head. I chose the alternative, which meant sitting by the phone in New York and being available for anything and everything that was offered there.

The offers weren't a lot at first, and we relied heavily on unemployment insurance and Vicky's salary, but slowly things developed. With Frances Blaisdell having gone to California to live, Murray Panitz and Andy Lolya were now playing at the ballet, and I started doing some subbing there. Josef Marx, the oboist, also had begun to use me.

Josef was a fascinatingly brilliant man who lived in a rambling apartment at Eighty-sixth and Broadway, where he had regular Saturday chamber music evenings. His broad interests ranged across the centuries, and music would be pulled from one of dozens of cartons that littered every horizontal surface. It could be a Zelenka trio, or a Cambini quintet, depending on who showed up, or we would make up an orchestra for Seymour Lipkin to play a Mozart concerto. Josef's publishing company, McGinnis & Marx (McGinnis was his wife's name), published new American composers and reissued forgotten European ones. Much of the oboe music written at that time was written for Josef. He was a wonderful musician, but not particularly interested in making a pretty sound on his instrument. As someone joked, he didn't play the oboe, he played the jomarx. During the day, he ran a retail music store of a kind that no longer exists in New York. You could browse through drawers filled with the most complete range of published wind music. Among the more interesting concerts I played for Josef was a *B Minor Mass*, a week of Gilbert and Sullivan over Easter, and Elliott Carter's *Quartet* for harpsichord, flute, oboe, and cello. Josef was a feisty man who years later won a court case against his landlord only to die in a taxi on the way home.

In July I was hired to play at the Empire State Music Festival in a tent at Bear Mountain State Park. The season included two operas, *La Bohème* and *Madama Butterfly*, for both of which I played piccolo. The principal was the Metropolitan Opera's Jimmy Politis. I couldn't have had a better teacher.

Jimmy was a terrific, no-nonsense flutist – brilliant and absolutely crazy – and a big drinker. He developed a prototype for a new flute where metal keys, when closed, filled the hole in the tubing, as if there were no break. A plastic flange closing against the outer surface of the tube created the seal. He was able to get a flute with one key built to test his theory that the tone would be improved, but failed to get the necessary financial backing to produce a complete instrument. Our paths crossed over the years, and he always had a helpful tip for me about some opera I was about to play for the first time. I had just started working as his alternate at the Met in 1976 when he went to hospital with terminal cancer. I was very sad when I visited him for the last time, and listened to his stories of playing for Herbert von Karajan. Berlin had an opening at that time, and he said how much Karajan had enjoyed his work; maybe he would apply. Then the reality of his situation came over his face and he said, "Well, a bit late for that."

James Politis (Photograph by Louis Melançon, courtesy of the Metropolitan Opera House).

Among the orchestral concerts at Bear Mountain was one conducted by Eugene Goossens. Goossens had been the conductor in Sydney when I was growing up and had been forced to resign when customs officers, acting on a tip, opened his briefcase after a trip abroad and found some scandalous (by Australia's Victorian standards) photographs relating to witchcraft or some such thing. A lovely postlude to that was when the same officials, acting on another tip some time later, opened the briefcase of the visiting conductor, Malcolm Sargent, and found it filled with photos of Eugene Goossens.

Goossens's program included *Scheherezade*, in which I was wowed by Eli Carmen's bassoon cadenza. Not so Goossens, however. He asked for something different, and Eli just turned off. I was developing such respect for these New York players. Eli, who played principal at NYCB, was a total master of his instrument; he was warm-hearted, but a tough cynic and another heavy drinker. He died tragically when his tenant's car ran over him in his yard and ruptured his spleen.

One of Broadway's hits this year was Alan J Lerner and Frederick Lowe's *Camelot*. The flutist was Lois Schaefer, on leave from her position as principal with the NYCO. In August she asked me to play her vacation week. I made a sufficiently good impression so that when she had to return to NYCO in the fall I took over for her, and stayed until the show closed fifteen months later.

The brilliant cast at the Majestic was led by Richard Burton and Julie Andrews, with Robert Goulet as Lancelot, and included such luminaries as Roddy MacDowall and Robert Coote. The conductor was Franz Allers, a Viennese who had an orchestra of some of the city's finest musicians. The wonderful score was orchestrated by Robert Russell Bennett, and was filled with the most lovely colors. A revival years later was disappointing at least in part because the orchestra was reduced and key instruments eliminated.

Franz never let the players relax into sloppiness. Two years into the show he called an orchestra rehearsal. He was always sending down notes to individual players during the performance: "After letter A in 'The Merry Month of May,' more like Brahms *Third*."

Among my colleagues was bassoonist Connie Merjos, who bragged that he never took his instrument home and that his kid didn't know what he did for a living. Mostly he gambled – at the track with Melissa Hayden's husband, or at the theater in the backstage poker game. He would arrive early, put his bassoon together, and play poker until curtain time, entering the pit after the conductor to take his seat in the entrance-way. One night things didn't sound quite right and, shaking his instrument, he heard a rattle. He had managed to get his reed-making tools into the bore as he put it together.

Next to me was oboist Lennie Arner, whose playing I admired from the first time I heard him. He was another brilliant man who could speak eloquently on any number of subjects, equally erudite on the stock market and Chinese jade. We had a great time until the night I, not knowing the meaning of the word, called him a fink. I thought it was just an expression you joshed someone with. He said, "Don't you ever call me that," and didn't speak to me for the rest of the run. Why I didn't apologize I don't know. Perhaps I was embarrassed and just hoped it would go away.

I did an enormous amount of reading in the pit between numbers. I eventually had my part memorized, so I was able to maximize my exposure to literature. It didn't matter if it was *Crime and Punishment* or *The Rise and Fall of the Third Reich*, the segues were seamless. Not looking at the music also meant I could look at the audience while playing. My most vivid memory was the night the astronauts came. Gus Grissom sat stone-faced through the whole show.

While playing the Bear Mountain tent in July, I had met oboist Charlie Kuskin, who drove me there and back. We got to be great friends. He was manic, but I loved his wry sense of humor. He arranged for me to audition for his woodwind quintet, the Concord, which mostly played school concerts for Young Audiences, an organization run with a tyrant's hand by Carol Morse. The group's leader was the clarinetist, Emery Davis, son of band-leader Meyer Davis. Emery lived on my block, and I learned that I had been accepted when I heard him shouting up from the street below my window as I was practicing.

Vicky (Photograph by Martha Swope)

The rest of the group consisted of bassoonist Mark Popkin, a physicist whose day job was at the Brooklyn Navy Yard, and horn player Bob Abernathy. So, concurrently with my evening shows, I was being driven all over the five boroughs two or three mornings a week to play a pair of children's concerts. It was a fine group, and we had a successful routine that made us quite popular.

We fooled around a lot of course – for example, seeing just how fast we could play the first of Ibert's *Three Pieces*. (Jacques Ibert sometimes became the American composer Jack Seibert if it seemed appropriate.) Mark was a terrific arranger, and we were always experimenting by reading something new.

So the year ended with my being gainfully employed, and generally on top of the world. Al

Weatherly sold me his Powell number 480 that he had helped build, I purchased a beautiful wooden Haynes piccolo, and my lessons with Kincaid were going well.

Vicky was starting to move up in the hierarchy of the ballet also. Balanchine began to take an interest in her and choreographed a solo variation for her in his new ballet using music from Glazounov's *Raymonda*. The premiere was in December and she was great.

1962

Although this year was framed by daily performances of *Camelot*, regular school concerts with the quintet, and lessons with Kincaid, my life had other dimensions as well. We were able to use our new affluence to move to a larger apartment, for example, and I put my *Camelot* savings into a rebuilt Steinway, now that we had a place to put it.

Our new home was at 334 West Eighty-seventh Street, just off Riverside Drive, a ground-floor apartment in a pre-war building. Not only were the rooms bigger, but we had a small second bedroom that doubled as study and guest room, and a dining alcove. And we didn't have all those stairs to climb. The space became available when a gay couple split up, and they had left it fully furnished. Much of this furniture, though elegant, was not to our taste – lots of green velvet – and we sold it before moving in. But the chandelier in the mirrored dinette stayed and is still with us today. So is the Steinway.

I had become friendly with a flutist named Bill Watson, who had arrived in New York after spending some time getting experience in German orchestras. He was an intelligent, quick-witted person with great imagination and a wild sense of humor. We had great times bluefishing, and playing bridge with our wives. Bill would go on to many other careers, as an administrator and as an inventor, and took some really hard knocks as his confidence in his playing waned. But at this time we were friendly rivals.

He phoned one day to say that Leopold Stokowski was forming a new orchestra of which he was to be the principal flute. Stokowski had told him he could pick his own section, and Bill wondered if I would be interested in playing piccolo. The American Symphony was to be a new twist on an earlier youth orchestra project of Stokowski's. This time he would have seasoned players sitting next to talented young people throughout all the sections. It was rumored that Baker would be the principal flute. Then funding didn't come through, or disappeared. Whatever the story, by the time the first season began in the fall of 1962, the orchestra had few really top pros – in the winds, only clarinetist Bernie Portnoy.

Bill explained that I would have to audition for Stokowski, but it would only be a formality. He explained Stoky's audition book – what he would ask me to play, etc. I phoned the maestro and arranged an appointment at his Fifth Avenue apartment. When the elevator door opened I was already in his sprawling abode, high over Central Park. The beady-eyed eighty-year-old man with his wispy long white hair and phony accent took me to a small studio and took me through the audition material, just as Bill had said. Then he led the way into his living room and sat me on the opposite side of his huge desk overlooking the park. "I am not sure if you know why I have asked you here today. I am forming new orchestair [as he always said]. You are very fine flutist and I would like you to be my first flutist. Unfortunately I already have a first flutist – [looking through his book] William Watson. Do you know him? I can offer you second flute or assistant principal and piccolo." I fumbled for answers all through this rather bizarre experience and opted for the assistant/piccolo position. The next piece of my life was in place.

Vicky was going on a U.S. tour for six weeks over the summer, so I decided to take my vacation from *Camelot* and make my first trip to Europe. Arthur Lora, a Juilliard teacher and former principal of the NBC Orchestra, would take over for three weeks. I flew to London in the middle of July to join my school friend Tony Casson. I would have a week seeing the sights there, then he would take his own two weeks off from his job with LEO computers and we would go to Italy and Paris.

We had a wonderful adventure. The London tour was extended by a long day's drive taking in Oxford, the Cotswolds, Tunbridge Wells, and Stonehenge, courtesy of Casson's sister, Penny. Then the two of us were off on the train, cross-channel ferry, and train to Paris, practicing our high school, "*Pardon, s'il vous plait .... Merci, madame,*" wherever possible, and straight through overnight to Italy.

We traveled by train third class where other passengers offered slices from their salami, a piece of fruit, a crust of bread, and we struggled to make some kind of conversation with no verbs and a few Latin-like nouns. The popular American book at the time was *Europe on $5 a Day*. Casson thought this was a great joke – who but Americans could afford that much! We would walk from trattoria to trattoria looking for the cheapest *menu turistica*, a hundred lire making a big difference in our budget. We managed to miss a lot of things en route to Venice. We got off at Milan but the *Last Supper* was *chiuso*. The Palladio in Vicenza was *chiuso*.

My low point in Venice was when we were taking the vaporetto to Santa Maria della Salute. I didn't realize that Casson had debarked, and I jumped for shore as the boat pulled away from the pontoon. I found myself fully immersed in the Grand Canal with Casson yelling, "Throw me the Michelin!" We sat on the church steps while I emptied out my wallet to dry its contents. We saw the wonders of Venice, Florence and Rome without further mishap, and circled back to Paris to camp out on the floor of Keith Humble's newly acquired apartment on the Left Bank.

With Casson back in London, Keith took me to see the sights, including Versailles. More important, he took me to the street markets down Rue Mouffetard where I watched him shop, then home, where he prepared chicken with forty cloves of garlic. I caught up on all he had done since leaving Australia. He had been one of the few people to congratulate me when I left Melbourne, and we had exchanged a few letters. He had started a music series at the American Student Center, where his programs of avant-garde music were becoming an important part of Paris cultural life. He talked about these concerts and about his friends, the soprano Ethel Semser and her painter husband Charlie, tenor Bob Gartside, and the expatriate Aussies, jazz-man Johnny Dankworth and composer Don Banks. He promised to write me a piece.

In the fall, NYCB went on tour to Hamburg, Germany and the Soviet Union. This latter was part of a cultural exchange program and was a big deal at the time. In addition to the political ramifications, Balanchine was going back to Russia for the first time since he had left at the age of twenty.

I was at home practicing when I received a call from Balanchine's assistant, Barbara Horgan. Vicky had been in an accident in Hamburg. Apparently she and Jacques D'Amboise had been waiting for a streetcar when one had swung around a curve and the front, protruding away from the tracks, hit Jacques, whose body had hit Vicky. She had been taken by ambulance to the hospital, where she had her gashed upper lip stitched. She would need further cosmetic surgery. She also lost her front teeth, which would have to be reconstructed. I phoned her parents, and we all spent a few trying days waiting to get more information. It turned out that she was in good hands and would be patched up well enough to join the company for the Russian season.

I was no sooner over that shock than the Cuban missile crisis erupted during the NYCB Moscow season. Sitting in the pit playing *Camelot* that week was a trial – it was bad enough that the future of the world was at stake, but the timing was really poor. The NYCB tour was a great artistic success despite all, and in due course my scarred beloved came home for a more than usually thankful Thanksgiving.

The American Symphony Orchestra began its inaugural fall season of three Carnegie Hall concerts in October, with a similar spring season to follow. I played piccolo for this and the two following years, the "assistant principal" part failing to materialize. I was fortunate to have this experience in which I got to play most of the basic repertoire, and it culminated in April 1965 with the first performance of Charles Ives's *Fourth Symphony*.

Stokowski was an absolute autocrat, even in these twilight years when he seemed fragile. You couldn't question him, no matter how right you might be. If you said something, he countered. If you responded to that, he countered again, but then you probably wouldn't be playing the next concert. He *had* to have the last word.

He was always on the podium long before the start of each rehearsal, and he expected everyone to be in their seats practicing a half-hour before as well. I once watched him fire a violist. She came hurrying through to her seat, not late for rehearsal but late for the half-hour practice. He watched to see where she sat, then picked up a pencil and drew a line through her name. No word was spoken. I learned that it didn't matter how you played but whether you watched him. I could be playing a good projecting tone but with my eyes on my part, and he would stop the orchestra and say, "More piccolo." If I looked him in the eye he never said a word. I was always sure to stare at him if I had a solo that was hard to project.

He also expected us to be on stage all the time, regardless of whether we had a part. If we were playing a symphony with double winds, he could point to you at any moment and expect you to double the first part – even at the concert. We took one program to Washington where the concert was televised and shown in two parts. The second half was the Tchaikovsky *Fourth*, where I certainly had my hands full after the first two movements. But during the first half of the concert I didn't have a note to play; I just sat there, always in the camera angle.

His background as an organist had led him in the direction of great orchestral color during his tenure in Philadelphia, and he had learned from those master players just what varieties of color were possible. We were rehearsing *Götterdämmerung* funeral music, and he asked the brass to play softer. He stopped them repeatedly, insisting, despite their grumbling, on even less. He said, "I don't care if you put your instruments between your legs or cover them up, but it must be softer." The concert was unbelievable magic. Most conductors would have given up after a try or two, but he knew what was possible and insisted on it.

One of our first concerts celebrated his eightieth birthday, along with that of our guest, Lauritz Melchior. On the program was the Brahms *Second*. Stowkowski shuffled onto the stage, all made up and looking frail. The performance was quite dreary. We did a repeat on Long Island, where he had started the concert by chastising the audience for not being quiet. When he started the Brahms he was like a different man. The tempi were different, everything was vital – he was a young man. I thought, "Wow – this is what it must have been like in Philadelphia!"

In another concert we played *Petrouchka*. This score exists in two versions, where certain sections are notated differently. He conducted one version, but not the one the orchestra had on their stands. He would not hear a word of any problem. He was at his worst in situations like these. He was not good with pieces with complex beat patterns, following rather than leading with his stick. That didn't matter if the orchestra knew the piece well, like his Philadelphians, but in our case with *Petrouchka*, and later *Sacre du Printemps*, it was the blind leading the blind.

At one concert we played a charming symphony by Henry Cowell. One movement was in five-eight and was conducted in alternating two's and three's. In the concert, Stoky got confused between the two and left out a beat. The experienced players ignored him and kept playing as written, but some of the others jumped. The movement, which was supposed to dissolve into silence with a series of carefully placed chords, disintegrated instead into chaotic bleeps and blops. Totally unfazed, Stokowski just kept beating till he was sure all such noises had stopped, then turned the page for the next movement.

I was fortunate to have a very good piccolo, through good luck. The instrument I had bought from Haynes developed a crack in the head-joint soon after. I took it back to have the head replaced. One night between numbers at *Camelot*, I was staring at my piccolo as it sat on my stand, and the light caught a mark on the head-joint. I picked it up and looked carefully. Two marks. This was not a new head. They had marked the extremities of the crack with a scribe and filled it in with something. Next day I went screaming to poor Mrs. Davis at Haynes. Terrified, she went to the vault and took out all the piccolos: "Please, pick one!"

I was certainly getting the lowdown on how to play orchestral piccolo, dealing with the low solos that are supposed to sound loud, and the high ones that aren't. Apart from the three big Stravinsky scores and *Daphnis and Chloe*, we did the Shostakovitch *Fifth* and *Sixth*, which were a workout. I recently heard a performance of the *Sixth* at Carnegie Hall. As I sat watching the young piccoloist play the extended solo in the slow movement so beautifully I thought, *where did I get the nerve to sit on that stage and play that solo?* We also did a Mahler symphony each season, including the unfinished *Tenth*. I had a real problem at the end of the slow movement of this symphony, where the piccolo doubles the rising violins. The higher we got, the flatter I got to them. Paul Ingraham, the first horn, took me aside during the break and said I had better figure out something. In desperation I finally fingered the whole passage a half step higher and lipped it down into tune.

My year ended with *Camelot* on its last legs. The stars had all long gone, Franz Allers had a new show, and they were asking us to check the new parts prepared for the national tour. After the holidays it closed. The other *Camelot*'s days were also numbered.

1963

With the closing of *Camelot* I had a sudden drop in income and a corresponding increase in free time. One of the first projects to fill the void was preparing a taped performance of Harvey Sollberger's new quartet for four flutes, under the supervision of composer Charlie Wuorinen. It turned out to be a real challenge, particularly making all the quickly staggered entries. We joked that these were the kinds of entries we were always trying to avoid in the real world.

In February, things started picking up, and by the season's end in May I was a busy freelancer, even if I didn't make a lot of money. The ASO's season expanded with some extra concerts. I was teaching a handful of young students and continuing with the Young Audiences quintet concerts. I subbed at the ballet and, back in the Majestic, at a brilliant production of *School for Scandal* with Ralph Richardson and John Gielgud. Joe Marx used me for a *Saint John Passion* and a *Saint Matthew Passion*. I was hired for another Connecticut Symphony concert. And I played my first Westchester Symphony concert with conductor Siegfried Landau. For this I was hired by Secundo Proto, the feared contractor of The New York City Opera orchestra, among others.

All these contractors held great power. Musicians had no recourse if they suddenly found themselves not used. We learned to show up on time and to keep our mouths shut. The more successful freelancers also learned how to lie. To make any kind of a living one had to be working all the time, but the rehearsals for the different concerts kept conflicting. A Julius Baker might arrange a sub for a rehearsal, but generally speaking contractors didn't want to hear that someone could play everything but the first hour of one rehearsal. Contractors were not averse to having a crony phone to offer sympathy when someone called in sick. One colleague was fired when it was discovered he was not sick but playing a jingle.

One of my own experiences actually involved subbing for Baker the following fall. Robert Russell Bennett, who had orchestrated Richard Roger's *Victory at Sea*, was scoring music for a TV series on the Korean War. I wasn't in the league of subbing for Baker, but I got lucky when his regular sub, Jimmy Politis, needed a sub for one session. When I eventually got my check from Julie it was for the net amount after taxes. He wouldn't understand that I didn't earn enough to pay taxes and that he had to pay me the full amount, then use that as a deduction from his own income. His wife Ruth was able to straighten it out, but Julie still wasn't happy.

The conductor Dmitri Mitropoulos had died not long after the 1960 Mahler concert that had started me off in New York. I was now hired to play the memorial concert, where the Symphony of the Air was conducted by many of his colleagues, including Karl Böhm and Fausto Cleva. The latter conducted some of the Verdi *Requiem*, and I naively went during a break to ask him if the piccolo part was really supposed to be way up there. I thought it must be a misprint. He smiled and said ruefully that indeed it was. I was glad it was a private conversation.

Several years later, at another Mitropoulos memorial, this time with the Philharmonic, I worked for the first time with Leonard Bernstein. On the program was the first movement of the Mahler *Fifth*, which starts with an unaccompanied trumpet solo. Bernstein, with eyes closed and anguished expression, made an enormous circle with his arms and, somewhere in the middle, Bill Vacchiano, the trumpeter, just came in. I couldn't believe it. It was a curious event all round. The principal speaker, Aaron Copland, kept talking about Bernstein instead of Mitropoulos.

The spring of 1963 saw the first Mitropoulos Conducting Competition. For a week the Symphony of the Air was hired to sit on the stage of Carnegie Hall while some forty young conductors showed their skills. I was hired to play first, largely due to the fact that more respected players were unable to commit to such a large block of time. Next to each stand was a foot-high stack of music, basically the entire symphonic repertoire. Each conductor had ten minutes and played sections from three pieces of his choice. The pieces were announced, and we scrambled to find them as the conductor was introduced – no pauses, and no time for questions. My education had not prepared me for this, and there were just too many pieces (like the Brahms *Third* and even the *Leonore* Overture) that I had never played, and didn't really know. I did not make a good impression, and it was some time before I got to play first again. But did I learn a lesson! I vowed never to be unprepared again. I began to borrow recordings and scores from the library and to copy out difficult solos in this time before excerpt books. Orchestral excerpts are an integral part of my teaching now. The winner of the competition, decided among three finalists in a concert the next week, was a mature Claudio Abbado. As a part of his prize he became an assistant to Bernstein at the Philharmonic.

While all of these things were going on in my life, I learned that Marcel Moyse, the great French virtuoso and pedagogue, who had settled in Vermont in the fifties, was coming to New York each weekend and teaching on Saturdays at his son-in-law's apartment on West One-hundred-fifty-sixth Street. After canceling a couple of appointments because of engagements, I finally presented myself before the master.

He sat back in an armchair puffing on his pipe as I played. After a silence he said, "Meester Vion," in his heavy accent, "I get very little satisfaction listening to you play the flute" – a long puff on the pipe – "and I theenk" – puff – "if I were not a flutist" – puff – "I would get no satisfaction." I could either walk out the door or say, "Yes, sir!"

Opting to stay, I then got a greater lesson in music than I could ever have imagined. He had only to touch me on the arm for me to glimpse the expressive power of music, to start to comprehend that I was just playing the flute, not expressing anything through it. We went on through the end of the spring, whenever I wasn't working, as he explained Mozart, specifically the *D Major Concerto*, the phrasing, the articulation, the meaning. Then, unimaginably in retrospect, our paths diverged. We both had summer plans in different parts of the world, and the following fall I didn't call him.

My summer plans had been brewing for months. I was going home, and I was taking my bride with me. As we investigated, we learned that the cost of an around-the-world airfare was only fifty dollars more than the cost of a round trip fare from New York to Melbourne. I had all the time in the world, and Vicky was prepared to take a leave from the summer touring, so we headed off to London in early May. The first part of the trip consisted of introducing Vicky to everything I had seen the previous year. I also had a number of school friends settled in London to introduce her to. Then on to Paris, where Keith and Jill Humble entertained us royally, and found extra padding for us to sleep on their living room floor. In Italy we stopped in Venice, Florence, and Rome. Then it was on to uncharted territory for us both. Our first stop was Athens, where tourists were still allowed to walk through the Parthenon. Then across to Cairo, where we saw the pyramids and were hustled for a few dollars worth of perfume. By Istanbul things were becoming really strange as we were exposed to an unfamiliar culture, religion, and history.

In the Pakistan airport I must have picked up a bug, and our stay in India became a bit scary. Our itinerary was the triangle of Delhi, Jaipur and Agra. After getting inured to the extreme poverty, we were overwhelmed by the historic buildings of Old Delhi. By the time we reached Jaipur I was running a high fever. Our hotel was the former palace of the rajah. Our enormous room had a slowly revolving fan in the center of the twenty-foot ceiling and way over at the window, a small air conditioner. The bathroom was all marble, delightfully cold against my fevered body. I tried to eat in the formal dining room, as turbaned Indians served a traditional English meal, from soup to dessert, in the sweltering heat. We had the indoor pool to ourselves, unless that was a boy peeking through the skylight. Then to bed in our stifling room, as

I moaned and stirred restlessly, while Vicky kept putting cold towels on me and worried that I was dying. We never did see Jaipur, and somehow she got me onto the plane to Agra. The temperature was still in the hundreds, as was mine, as we visited the astonishing Taj Mahal. The next morning my fever broke. It rained, and in the early cool of dawn we were driven to see the abandoned city of Akbar the Great, Fatehpur Sikri, passing villages where people were drawing water and washing at the communal well.

Our next stop was Bangkok (before it was overrun with tourists, and still looked like *The King and I*). We visited temples and palaces and floating markets, and laughed with the saffron-robed monks when the rain poured down. The planes seemed to be getting smaller all the time, and the old DC3 sitting on the airstrip to take us to Angkor Wat in Cambodia did not inspire confidence. Then William Holden and Capuchine boarded, and we knew we would be all right. We all stayed at the hotel next to the temple grounds, and I used my high school French to act like an ugly American (or Australian) when it turned out that the hotel had no hot water. The pipes and faucets were there, but a heater had never been installed. We were awed by this Cambodian civilization that had actually been forgotten until the twentieth century, when the temples had been hacked out of the jungle by the French. The Khmers had been overrun by the Siamese in the fourteenth century, and when the irrigation system failed, the city was abandoned. Those temples that had been cleared stood silent, surrounded by grass instead of water. Where they had not been cleared, the roots of giant banyan trees grew down over the colossal four-faced Buddha pillars. Our experience among these cultured people made the human horror and physical destruction that later swept over this area all the more appalling.

A long night flight took us over Vietnam, a country we had been advised not to visit due to some local unrest. At the time only a handful of American advisors were in this country, and the pilot's direction of our attention to shell-fire on the ground received only passing interest.

Hong Kong was our last stop before Australia, and after surviving the seemingly perilous descent between the mountains, we enjoyed the city immensely. We had been on a very tight budget, and now felt we could splurge a bit on custom-made shirts, dresses, and shoes. The surging throngs of people everywhere, the shanties built on every slope, the ceaseless activity on land and water were an unforgettable experience. Then it was another long flight through the night and the growing excitement of going home.

I felt as if I had a touch of malaria when we arrived and spent a few shivering nights. Maybe it was the end of my Indian virus. Anyway, after negotiating the introductions and family reunions – two new wives and several nieces and nephews since I had left – we settled into my mother's new house, and I started making dates to see my old friends. In New York we were always squeezing in one more activity before it could get away but here I had to adjust – well tomorrow I have to shop, and the next day is no good... how about next weekend?

Slowly things fell into place. Casson was back from England, Mick Long and Jim Grimwade were married. I took Vicky to meet Les Barklamb and his wife Jessie, and introduced her to "footy" (Australian football). Then word came that Dick Chugg was sick and unable to play in the orchestra; he had been fighting cancer most of the time I had been away. His second, Jim Hopkinson, would move over, and I was invited to play second, which I did for the next five weeks. Very sadly, Dick died during that time and was mourned by the whole orchestra. After more than thirty years as the principal of the VSO, he would not be easily replaced. We left his chair empty for the next concert. His wooden Radcliff system flute with its silver head would sing no more with his fluid eloquence. He was just sixty-one.

The return to New York was quicker, but no less magical for us as we stopped in Tahiti. The airport extension had not yet been built, and tourism was limited. Our DC8 had a spare engine strapped to the body, and our luggage was placed in a fumigator on arrival. The airport sign politely reminded visitors that tipping would be considered offensive. Papeete was a bustling seaport and home to the French Foreign Legion since the loss of Algeria, but the road around the island was pure Gauguin – quiet little villages of palm frond cottages and laughing people. For total magic, we took a boat across to the neighboring island of Moorea, which was the inspiration for James Michener's *Bali Hai*.

As we docked, we were met by locals and taken to the island's hotel with its thatched cottages by and over the brilliant turquoise water. The owners were Americans who had dropped out of "the rat race" in California after visiting Tahiti. They were extremely friendly and gave us bikes to use around the island's single dirt road. We did so, avoiding ruts and fallen coconuts, till we came upon Cook's Bay, where the famous navigator had moored. Now plantations fill the hillsides, launches are moored in the water, a village has grown at the head of the bay, and people are everywhere. But then it was absolutely silent, absolutely perfect; we were absolutely alone.

Back in New York, Vicky went right into her season – the last for NYCB at City Center before moving to its new home in Lincoln Center – and I waited for October, when the concert season would begin. At the American Symphony, Bill Watson had been released by Stokowski, and the new principal was Jayn Rosenfeld. Neal Zaslaw, who was to become a leading Mozart scholar, remained on second. The Carnegie series was expanded to eight Monday night concerts.

I was playing for the Westchester Symphony regularly now, and had the opportunity to play alto flute in *Daphnis and Chloe* and principal in *Petrouchka* over the next seasons. I was also starting to work for Richard Korn's Orchestra of America, and Thomas Sherman's Little Orchestra. These two were wealthy men who used their money to hire orchestras to conduct. I was later to have a pleasant tour with the Little Orchestra playing, among other things the Bach *Fourth Brandenburg Concerto* with Paul Boyer, an elegant flutist from Philadelphia, who is now the maker of exquisite furniture. Although Mr. Sherman was a wonderfully educated, articulate, and sensitive man, and a good musician, he was not really a trained conductor, and his inelegant beat often got him into trouble. The worst was a concert performance of Berlioz' *Benvenuto Cellini* at the Brooklyn Academy, where he couldn't handle the precise movements needed to place the chords in the recitatives. Berlioz sounded more like Schönberg by their end, and our music stands became screens to conceal our chuckles. The Carnegie Hall repeat was more successful.

The year ended at the Brooklyn Academy, with Hollywood conductor, Franz Waxman, leading a charming performance of *Hansel and Gretel*.

1964

For all that I had been increasing my contacts, I still only worked when things got busy and jobs filtered down. This meant that the year started very quietly until the American Symphony season resumed in the last week of January.

In February, I was offered an Off-Broadway anti-war musical called *Dynamite Tonight*, with lyrics by Arnold Weinstein and music by William Bolcomb. The contractor and conductor was composer Charles Turner, who had written a beautiful ballet for NYCB called *Pastorale*. I was released from the next ASO concert and began rehearsing *Dynamite*. The orchestra consisted of only five players, so it was an intimate process. The show was being produced by The Actors Studio and was being overseen by its director, Lee Strasberg. In the cast were Barbara Harris, Anthony Holland, Gene Wilder, and George Gaynes. As rehearsals went on, it became apparent that this was an opera, and one with a terrific score. In fact, many years later when Bolcomb was well known, I mentioned this to Beverly Sills as a possibility for City Opera. She went so far as to get the score, but told me that someone currently held an option on the show.

Opera, of course, did not mesh with the idea of a commercial hit, and over the next weeks different directors were brought in to "fix" the show. Finally, Mike Nichols took over, working in an improvisational style with the actors in an attempt to make the show funny. It closed on opening night and I went back to freelancing.

Somewhat discouraged by the way things were going, I applied for the principal flute position in Melbourne, open since Dick Chugg's death. I couldn't get a clear answer, and in June played for the Australian Broadcasting Commission's music director when he came through New York. What I didn't know until much later was that he was in the process of hiring a Czech flutist, Arnost Bourek, something that the union would not let him do until satisfied that no Australians were qualified for the position. So my spring season wound down at the end of April with no prospects for advancement in sight.

A bleak summer of a few park concerts, and the odd trip to the Concord Hotel in the Catskills for a pops concert, was livened only by the World's Fair at Flushing Meadow in Queens. It offered some opportunities to play, and even more time to gawk. In August, I got a phone call from a horn player, Bill Brown, who was forming a wind quintet. I had been recommended by Art Bloom, a clarinetist whom I had met through Joe Marx, who would himself be joining. The two of them had been founding members of the Dorian Quintet, and now wanted to upstage that group. The two other members were to be oboist Bert Lucarelli and bassoonist Alan (Lanny) Brown. After several meetings and much discussion, the Lark Quintet was formed.

The Lark Quintet.

Bill Brown, the leader with grandiose ideas, was the principal horn of the New York City Opera. Art Bloom was mostly active in the contemporary music scene – much of the new music at this time was written for him – and a would-be conductor. Bert Lucarelli had recently arrived from Chicago, where he had been a protégé of Ray Still and Robert Bloom. Lanny Brown had studied at Eastman and had worked with the Rochester and Pittsburgh Symphonies before coming to New York.

One of our first chores was to have a publicity photo taken, and Bill arranged for us to use the Belgian Village at the

Worlds Fair as a backdrop. We sat and stood on the old-world steps, and smiled or were serious, and played or held our instruments in all combinations until the photographer was happy. We chose our debut program and booked October 20 in Carnegie Recital Hall, with a run-through the previous week at a museum. We would play an arrangement of some Jean-Philippe Rameau dances, the first Anton Reicha quintet, Gunther Schuller's quintet, and end with the Carl Nielsen quintet. Serious rehearsing began at Bert's apartment, followed by serious drinking. This group of individuals had a lot of sharing to do, and it took a bottle of Scotch after each rehearsal to do it.

A nervous ensemble took the stage that October before an enthusiastic audience of friends and family, but we were pleased by the results. To our great disappointment, the *Times* did not send a critic, and the only review to appear in print was not particularly complimentary – though we got good mileage from the heading, "Exuberant New Wind Ensemble." The Nielsen was not mentioned – the reviewer had probably left already – and the only other piece he liked was the Schuller. Ironically, Gunther had come to the concert, and while taking a smiling bow and shaking our hands, had quietly said, "We really should talk about this before you play it again."

In the fall, through Art Bloom's contacts, I began playing some operas. Art had studied in Italy on a Fulbright and was experienced in this area. Sometimes we played at the Brooklyn Academy, and sometimes in a small movie theater further into one of the boroughs. Sometimes we rehearsed, sometimes we didn't. As we were on the subway to one of the lesser, unrehearsed *Bohèmes*, Art said, "There'll probably only be a dozen or so in the orchestra, but they all know every note inside out, so if you hear a second flute part coming out of a viola don't be surprised." The Brooklyn Opera might start out its season with three rehearsals for an opera, but it always ended with no rehearsals. Among the rehearsed operas were *Aida*, *Stiffelio*, and *Giovanna D'Arco* of Giuseppe Verdi. The conductor, Vince La Selva, was a great Verdi interpreter and always got an exciting, if rough, performance. I was always sorry that he didn't have a success at the City Opera. I think that he was so used to having no rehearsal time and hearing everything in perfection inside his head that he didn't know how to polish the material when given the opportunity.

My first *Carmen* was at the Brooklyn Opera, unrehearsed. I did as much homework as I could by listening to a recording and showed up for the performance an hour ahead of time to look at the part, but the music hadn't arrived. Gradually players arrived and warmed up and chatted – still no music. At eight o'clock we were told to go into the pit – without music. At ten-past eight the music was passed in through one door as the conductor came through the other and moved toward the podium. He took a long bow, turned, and gave a downbeat. Playing second to me was an elderly Italian, Oreste diSevo, who used every available intermission moment to play licks from different operas to me – he knew everything.

Fortunately, that included *Carmen*, for which the parts had not been marked to show the selected cuts for this performance. I would be frantically trying to keep up when he would lean over between notes and say, "No cut." Or he would lunge at my part and turn several pages saying, "Cut! Here!" I would never have survived that evening without him.

At Carnegie Hall, I also was becoming a regular at the American Opera Society, which gave concert versions of rarely heard operas with stellar casts. I played in Arrigo Boito's *Mefistophele* with Renata Tebaldi and Nicolai Ghiaurov, Ferruccio Busoni's *Doktor Faust* with Dietrich Fischer-Dieskau, Benjamin Britten's *Billy Budd* with Richard Lewis, conducted by Georg Solti, and an already mentioned *Lucrezia Borgia* with Monserrat Caballé.

I was hired as second flute for a bus tour around the Midwest and South with Thomas Sherman's Little Orchestra Society. The tour began with a concert in Scranton, Pennsylvania, the night before the Lark Quintet's debut. Lanny and Bert were also doing the tour, so we drove back to New York after the concert, re-joining the tour in Washington afterwards. It was a congenial group with which to spend three weeks, although we hit some pretty small college towns, where eating was basic at best and drinking impossible – one always carried a reserve bottle of vodka. We spent a tense Election Day, in Meridian, Mississippi, where three civil-rights workers had been murdered that summer. But we made some good music together. Apart from the *Brandenburg* mentioned earlier, the programs included *Siegfried Idyll*, Hugo Wolf's *Italian Serenade*, Alberto Ginastera's *Variations*, with a memorable horn solo from Brooks Tillotson, and a Mozart two-piano concerto.

My third and final American Symphony season also began in October, although I had to miss the second concert because of the tour. The Monday series had grown to ten concerts, and four of them were preceded by Sunday matinees. The orchestra was occasionally hired for additional work. One such concert at Carnegie Hall was the New York debut of Zubin Mehta. The highlight of his program was *Daphnis and Chloe*, which he did brilliantly. But even from the opening bars of the first *Leonore Overture*, one knew this was a man with impeccable rhythm. Before the *Daphnis* performance, he caught my eye backstage and asked me to be sure to play my piccolo part in the final dance very strongly. I was surprised, as I couldn't even hear it myself. Again, I was too inexperienced to know that it was the flutes who were supposed to be providing the color at that point; it was they who were hiding.

Another concert took place in the recently built Philharmonic Hall at Lincoln Center. The word was that it was an acoustic disaster – no bass, no quality to anything, and one couldn't hear other parts of the orchestra. Our first rehearsal bore this out, but it was easy to see the problem. The stage was built on concrete instead of wood. It had no proscenium – the top of the stage was the top of the hall. The stage was framed, sides and back, in blue-painted wire mesh; much of the sound made on stage went through the holes into the backstage area, never to be heard again. The hall would go through many alterations to improve the sound; the first was to spray all that mesh with glue to seal those little holes.

The quintet auditioned for Young Audiences in October and started to play children's concerts in November after the Little Orchestra tour. These turned out to be quite an adventure. None of us had a car so it meant we each had to make our separate ways by subway, bus, taxi, and foot, to the furthest extremities of the city for 9 A.M. concerts, and then collectively to the second, somewhat nearby, but not necessarily convenient, school. We very quickly realized that it would be a mistake to wait until all five of us had arrived – who knew when that might be? We developed a repertoire for smaller combinations and would spend time introducing each instrument. This usually worked pretty well, say three of us arriving on time and the group in full complement ten minutes later. One day, Lanny was the only one there at go-time, and he started in without hesitation. He had a solo bassoon demonstration for about twenty-five minutes before any help arrived, and the full quintet assembled only in time to play the final piece.

As we got to know each other's foibles, rehearsing became easier and more productive. I never liked to talk about the music and didn't see why any one else would want to either. Bert didn't practice his part and didn't vibrate at rehearsals, but at the concerts he was always great. Art had all kinds of personal problems and was usually late to rehearsals, if he remembered them at all. We quickly got into the habit of phoning him if he didn't arrive on schedule, and he could usually manage to get there pretty quickly, full of apologies. Bill was always on the phone. Once he stormed out in a rage because we pulled the phone out of the wall, being unable to get the rehearsal started any other way. But that was down the road a bit. And Lanny just sat quietly and let it all go by, apart from a dirty chuckle every now and then. Apart from Lanny's Young Audience solo stint, for which he was not quickly forgiving, our low point was one hungover morning, when we suddenly snapped to as Art, in his clarinet demonstration, where he always played the theme from *Appalachian Spring*, distinctly called it a "Pennsylvania fuck tune."

On a more serious level, the quintet was preparing a program for a December presentation at the New York Flute Club, which offered Sunday afternoon concerts for its membership. We added to our repertoire Samuel Barber's *Summer Music* and Heitor Villa-Lobos's Quintet, and rounded out the program with the sixth Rossini *Quartet* and the Beethoven Trio for flute, bassoon, and piano. In this we were joined by the wonderful pianist Howard Lebow, whose life was tragically cut short not long after in a freak car accident.

For the last three months of the year, finally, I was working nonstop and making about two hundred dollars a week (about thirteen hundred in today's money). But I could already see this was not the way for me to go. The variety was a real charge, but manipulating engagements created too much tension. I was afraid to turn down anything, because I never knew when I would hit a dry spell. That meant I had no time to spend money when I was busy and was too scared to spend any when I wasn't. Somehow or other I had to get a more steady job and more regular income. Australia had not worked out, and with Vicky doing so well at the ballet, leaving the city was not a viable option.

At that time orchestral auditions were handled differently than now. If an important principal position opened up, a few respected players would be invited to play for the conductor, and one of them would be offered the job. When Julius Baker went into the Philharmonic he didn't audition, his reputation was so established. This system meant that you had to work your way up. Second flute in a third-level orchestra could lead to principal in a similar orchestra – from there to principal of a second-level orchestra, and so to a possible invitation to the big time. Later on, as musicians became more educated, and as orchestra committees became more powerful, strictly controlled, open auditions that actually favored the younger player right out of school became the norm.

So, if I were not going to go out of town to start at the bottom of this particular ladder, my options were somewhat limited. Vicky's father was encouraging me to go into publishing with the prospect of taking over at Crown some day. Maybe that was the way to go.

New York City Opera

1965

The year started with a typically quiet, January. Highlights of the ASO spring series were Shostakovitch Tenth, *Sacre du Printemps*, Mahler Second and, in April, the long-delayed world première of Charles Ives's Fourth Symphony. For this, Stokowski received funding for six extra rehearsals. His two assistants led sections where the orchestra was divided into three groups playing in different tempi. The final result was a most moving experience as well as a critical success that the orchestra later recorded.

Activity picked up in February, and I was merrily juggling concerts and rehearsals with teaching and quintet activity – a recital here, a guest appearance on an ASCAP concert there. In the middle of it all, I noticed a problem with the way my right hand was functioning. Because I was a lefty, and one who had injured his right pinky, that hand was naturally weaker, even though I was quite ambidextrous. This was something different – it seemed as if the middle finger wanted to rise off the key just as the ring finger seemed to be locking down.

Because I had started the flute when I was small, I had always played with my right arm reaching sideways out, with wrist twisted and fingers angled. I don't recall anyone commenting on this until Baker got to work on me, at the same time as I switched to an open-holed flute. His hands, with their short thick fingers, curled over the keys as if he had been born that way. My own right hand, with its longer, thinner digits and protruding middle finger, didn't enjoy that position at all. Baker also had been strict about my using correct fingerings. I was quite adept at using my left thumb for B♭, my middle finger for F♯. My right pinky was lax when fingering E, and I unconsciously kept fingers down in quick passages. None of this was acceptable to Baker, and he didn't let up on me. Years later I came to believe that my body knew better than he did about how it worked best; I have allowed some of my "faults" to reappear, and I am more tolerant in my own students. At this time however, I just assumed I had been playing too much and had strained something.

In April the quintet's horn player, Bill Brown, told me that New York City Opera's principal flute, Lois Schaefer, had taken the Boston Symphony piccolo job. In addition, the NYCO second flute Ken Schmidt had been fired some time earlier for his participation in organizing an orchestra committee. Auditions would be held for both positions.

I knew the contractor, Dino Proto, from the Brooklyn and Westchester jobs, so I phoned him to request an audition. At the same time, Bill was promoting me with Julius Rudel, the general director, with whom he was very close. The auditions were held in early May in the pit at City Center, with Lois and Julius and Dino sitting out in the audience. I don't know how many people applied. I was only conscious of the players just before and after me. The positions were not advertised nationally at that time, so probably not very many. I felt confident about my opera background, comfortable in the pit where I had played often with the ballet, and generally relaxed about the panel. I was not, however, comfortable with my hand and decided to play as my solo the "Sarabande" from the Bach *Partita*, rather than some flashy concerto movement. In fact they were more interested in hearing a good sound and something expressive, so I chose well.

Dino phoned later to say the final round would take place in two days. That would be impossible, I said. The quintet had a whole day of children's concerts in Dutchess County, courtesy of Claude Monteux, who had moved there to pursue his conducting career. The choice was mine, he said.

Reluctantly, I arranged a sub for the day and returned to City Center with my flute and piccolo. Bill had reported to me that Julius was not entirely happy with my vibrato. So I practiced long tones all day, and paid particular attention to the evenness of vibrato. Four finalists had been chosen. They wanted to hear us in all combinations. Julius would conduct from the podium. I didn't think much of my piccolo playing, but thought I handled the duets on flute well. With excerpts from *Carmen* and *Traviata*, I was able to keep my eye on the conductor – they love that!

Well, I did the best I could. I had had my chance at a proper job, and, if nothing came of it, perhaps it was time to move my life in a different direction. Vicky and I were joining her family at the latest great Chinese restaurant on the East Side. At the requested time, trembling, I went to the phone booth and called Dino to learn my fate. No, they had not been too impressed with my piccolo playing, but it didn't matter, because at that point they had been really considering me for the first position, which he could now offer me. Oh boy! That was a happy evening!

Vicky's life was also about to move in a different direction. She had reached the status of soloist with the company, and Balanchine had shown some real interest in her. She was a beautiful dancer, but she did not have the angular, prepubescent look that seemed to be becoming the Balanchine model. Balanchine did not fire dancers, but he was always creating new ballets. So, if he wasn't inspired to use you, your roles decreased as the ballets you were in passed out of the repertoire. Eventually, you found yourself only in the few old standards like *Swan Lake*, you got the message, and went on with your life. Vicky was far from this point, but she sensed that Balanchine was losing creative interest in her.

When she heard that Balanchine needed someone to stage *The Nutcracker* in Cologne that summer, she approached him about the job. Vicky has a photographic memory, particularly for the dance, and had always been someone who could be called on in an emergency to fill in anywhere. Once the steps were in her body they stayed there. She seemed to be able to remember them, even for roles that she only watched. Balanchine could not have known the depth of her ability in this area at the time, but he would himself be going to Cologne for the final rehearsals in the fall and may have felt he would be able to fix things then if necessary. In any event he agreed. Vicky, of course, was brilliant. Balanchine was pleased with what she had achieved when they both went back in the fall for the final rehearsals and opening.

She finished what would turn out to be her last season with the NYCB, and we made plans for a summer in Europe. We would follow her work period in Cologne with a visit to Keith and Jill Humble in Paris, and then Russell Meares, now furthering his psychiatric career in London.

Dino offered me two engagements prior to my entering the orchestra in the fall. The first was a revival of *South Pacific* later in May at City Center, the second was an outdoor Mozart season the company would have in Palo Alto, California, the first two weeks of August. I was determined to give my hand a rest, so I used the excuse that our trip was already arranged to decline the musical and said I would start in August. He explained to me that Lois would also do the tour and would play first for most of the performances. That was fine with me.

At the end of May we flew to Europe. I spent my days in Cologne acting the tourist or watching the new subway line being dug beneath our hotel window. Most evenings, while Vicky was still working, I was able to get passes to see the opera. In the European style, the ballet company was a junior wing of the opera company, participating in their performances and contributing a regular Ballet Evening. For someone about to become an opera musician it was a great experience, though strange to hear everything sung in German.

We had a good time in Paris, alone at first as the Humbles were on tour, and later catching up on Keith's latest adventures. At this time he was full of enthusiasm for a program where he was teaching kids how to write music. Using the insides of scrapped pianos and all sorts of beaters, as well as whatever instruments they might also play to create the ensemble, they "invented" a system of notation from scratch – starting with a single line to define high from low, then multiple lines for more definition. From this they went on to compose music for their group.

Back in New York in the middle of July, I had to admit that resting my hand had made no difference. I had a problem. I went to a doctor at my medical group. With supreme indifference, he somewhat testily asked, "What do you want, a prescription for drugs?" No, I did not, and I stormed out. I saw a specialist who asked me to touch my fingertips in front of my face, then did a few other rudimentary tests before pronouncing me well. This was long before anyone had even thought of performing arts medicine.

I began a year of sitting in front of a mirror, studying my hand, and basically redoing my technique. I spent a session with Sam Baron, who made some invaluable observations and suggestions. I built myself some "crutches" to help retrain my hand and to relieve the strain when I had to perform. I made a little splint out of a plastic collar-stay to support my pinky. I made a harness out of leather to keep my middle finger bent. I made a spacer by stuffing and sewing up two glove fingertips and attaching them to an elastic band. I wore this on my middle finger to keep my fingers spread without strain. Within the year I was able to discard all these and move my fingers around on the flute with none of my former exaggerated motions. Weaknesses remained, and under stress I always had some recurrence – indeed I still do. But basically I solved my problem. Curiously, as I stared at the mirror, I noticed that my left fingers also made large uneven movements. Well, it didn't seem to be a problem, so best leave it alone.

The New York City Opera season in Palo Alto in August was fantastic: *The Marriage of Figaro* with Norman Treigle, Joy Clements, Doris Jung, Frances Bible, and Walter Cassell; *Don Giovanni* with Treigle and Beverly Sills; and *Il Seraglio* with Sills, Ann Elgar, and, in the non-singing role of the Pasha, movie actor Albert Dekker. The latter had a moment of high drama when the set started to collapse around him. Standing in the palace entrance, his arms around the flanking pillars like some Samson, he cried, "Guards, guards!"

Rudel conducted everything, and played the harpsichord recitatives with great style. I really liked his Mozart, and I couldn't imagine anything I would rather be doing – except being warmer. We had charcoal braziers in the pit, but when the Countess in the third act of *Figaro* said, "The night is damp and chilly," it got a good laugh from the audience.

The trio of Rudel, Sills, and Treigle, usually joined by the tenor Michael Molese, was the backbone of the City Opera productions at this time. While Molese was a fine singer, no one thought about him as so many did about Sills and Treigle, that they were unfairly being kept from singing at the Metropolitan Opera. Sills was in her prime when I joined City Opera. Her voice was light in character, and I think that her decision to add heavier roles limited the length of her career. She was an amazing personality on the stage, and her voice had great flexibility and emotional quality. Her "*Marten aller Arten*" in *Seraglio*, an aria where the flute is one of the four *concertante* instruments, was spectacular; her emotional depth as Donna Anna in *Don Giovanni*, electrifying. Treigle was the greatest Figaro I ever played for. His fourth act aria, when he thinks Susanna has betrayed him, stands alone. He was a suave and elegant Don too. He was a modest man, and it was very sad that he fell out with Rudel and withdrew from our roster several years later, while still in his prime. He died alone in his apartment in New Orleans not long after.

I had a lot to do when I got back to New York from Palo Alto. The upcoming fall opera season consisted of seventeen operas, most of which I had never played. The operas that were new to the company would be reasonably well rehearsed – *Capriccio* of Richard Strauss, *The Flaming Angel* of Sergei Prokofiev, *Miss Julie* of Ned Rorem, *The Saint of Bleeker Street* of Gian-Carlo Menotti, and *Tales of Hoffmann* of Jaques Offenbach. But the rest would get one two-and-a-half hour rehearsal, regardless of the length of the opera. I spent the next weeks playing records borrowed from the public library and following along with my part. If I couldn't understand how I fit in, I played the section over until I could. I knew it would be easier having a conductor to follow, but I wanted to feel assured that I could manage without one.

At the same time, the quintet was rehearsing very hard in preparation for its first recording – Carl Nielsen and Anton Reicha. We scheduled two sessions in a very resonant chapel. The Reicha was a particularly difficult session. The writing is most virtuoso, and unusually so for the horn. The Nielsen allowed the group to shine at its expressive best and was filled with beautiful playing. It came as a great shock a few weeks later when Bill Brown phoned to say that the engineer had accidentally erased the entire Reicha session. After some discussion, we all agreed that we couldn't go through a repeat of that session, and Bill began to think of other options. What finally developed was a grant from the Scandinavian-American Foundation to record the rest of Nielsen's wind music to make a complete Nielsen LP.

We recorded these pieces at the end of the year, in a different hall, with a different engineer, producing what turned out to be an LP of historic significance. My own additional contribution was the incidental music from *The Mother* – three short pieces, one with harp, one with viola, and one alone. I also made my conducting debut, basically keeping the beat in order to save time in the charming *Serenata in Vano*. In that piece, Art Bloom's phrasing and exquisitely sustained lines in the clarinet solos were a wonder.

The opera season was both a great thrill and a nerve-wracking experience; by the time it ended I was thoroughly exhausted. I had such a pain in my groin that I felt I must have a hernia. I think that's what I thought supporting the airstream was – I certainly was giving my all. We played seven performances a week until everything had opened, then in the final weeks we played eight. Apart from our Mondays off, each day had two services. For example, we would rehearse *Carmen* on Thursday morning for Friday night; *Fledermaus* on Thursday afternoon for Saturday matinee; and *Butterfly* on Friday morning for Saturday night. Then we would play two different, previously rehearsed operas on Sunday.

The Italian repertoire was conducted by Franco Patanè – one of the greatest conductors I ever had the pleasure of working with. I could not have had a better teacher. The singers in general hated him because he knew the score from memory. He knew when he was supposed to follow them, and when they were supposed to follow him. When the latter was the case, he was not above beating his baton on the podium to insist on his tempo. In *Traviata*, though, the party scene had a solo for a castanets-playing dancer. She had impeccable rhythm, so after starting the dance, Patanè would put down his baton, lean back against the rail, unwrap a hard candy, and put it in his mouth. We had only to follow her.

He had a perfect baton technique and a total grasp of the unity of the opera. He was the only person I have known who could keep the third act of *Butterfly* moving. Normally, when one can't see the stage drama unfolding, this act can seem interminable. His pacing made *Traviata* a joy. In my mind, I still see the bass pizzicato in the third act prelude that he always indicated elegantly with the slightest gesture. He was a gentle man with twinkling eyes and totally without airs. But when a tenor asked him in rehearsal how he wanted a particular passage, he brusquely said, "*Com'è scritto*" (as it's written).

Franco Patanè

We never once saw him open a score until his last season with us, when he had fought for something different to conduct. They gave him an American opera, Lizzie Borden. When the orchestra teased him for using a score, he apologized that he had not received it in advance as promised. He spoke, or at least claimed to speak, no English, and Dino had to translate every question during rehearsal. When Bill Brown missed an entry in Bohème, he explained to Dino that he needed a cue. When this was translated, Patanè's mouth dropped open, and he said, in Italian, "For Bohème he needs a cue?" I once missed an entry in a Butterfly performance. The next time we played it, a week later, he turned to me at that moment, and gave me a cue.

Many things about Italian opera are confusing. One of them is that the score and parts often disagree, but that certain traditions are handed down as to which is really correct. When I pointed out to Patanè that my part in the overture to The Barber of Seville differed from the recently published "urtext" score, he just tapped the closed score and said it was rubbish – end of discussion.

Carmen was conducted by Antonio Coppola, somewhat affectionately known to us as "Tony the Butcher" for his fierce looks and slashing beat. Our principal cellist, Bob Gardiner, sat directly in front of the podium and seemed to feel he was the personal object of these bayonet attacks. In the middle of one performance he just got up and strode out of the pit. I was most impressed. I approached him next intermission wondering why he hadn't gone home. "I left my shoes in the pit," he explained.

My real boss was Julius Rudel. I had to please him to survive my year's probation. He conducted the Mozart again, the Prokofiev, the Strauss, and even took over Carmen after he became dissatisfied with Coppola. He conducted Faust and Hoffmann, both with Sills, Treigle, and Molese. Hoffmann, in a brilliant new production by Tito Copabianco, was a great success. Treigle played all the villains and ended the opera standing before the orchestra "conducting" – thin as a rake in a body stocking, emitting a maniacal laugh. Sills played the three females in Hoffmann's life with affecting contrast, and Molese sang the title role.

Vince LaSelva came in to conduct the Menotti, making it a most moving experience. Sherrill Milnes was a brilliant Barber of Seville, and the slightly awkward tenor debuting in one of the last Butterfly performances was Placido Domingo.

On the lighter side, I adored Fledermaus – the Orlovsky of David Rae Smith and the drunken jailer of Coley Worth. Coley was a vaudevillian from the old school, with amazing timing. I never tired of his punch lines. He'd pull a bottle from somewhere and call it "Beethoven's fifth;" a smaller bottle, "Schubert's tenth?" He'd throw a bottle off-stage, followed by delayed sound of glass breaking – "slow gin."

I suppose it is natural, but when a role is defined for you when you are young, that interpretation is rarely surpassed. I loved Jim Billings in so many roles but not in Fledermaus. And the great Sam Ramey could never replace Treigle for me as Mephistophele, or Figaro, or Reverend Olin Blitch.

The season ended in mid-November, and the NYCO bus and truck tour hit the road with Carmen, Barber, and Cav/Pag (Cavalleria Rusticana and Pagliacci) – four weeks of one-night stands around New York State and Ohio. It was quite a trip, and a real chance to get to know the rest of the company. The stars of the trip were Domingo, Milnes, and the wonderful soprano Pat Brooks, in Pagliacci. We had our bizarre nights on these tours, such as when the truck with the music got lost, and we had to play as best we could from whatever scores could be found, and assistants to turn our pages. Or the day it snowed continuously during what became a twelve-hour trip to Buffalo. We didn't arrive till curtain time. We finally got started at nine, and some judicious cuts, including the entr'actes, were made to avoid going past midnight with its dreaded overtime.

A part of my new job was to play seasons of Gilbert and Sullivan and musical revivals at City Center. So the day after our tour ended we began rehearsing Oklahoma, which would run through the holiday season (during which time the quintet was also recording Nielsen). In the following years I played *Carousel, The Sound of Music, Carnival, My Fair Lady, The King and I, Where's Charley, Brigadoon, Finian's Rainbow,* and *Most Happy Fella.* These were wonderful productions with superb casts, all under the supervision of Jean Dalrymple. After that series ended we did not play musicals until Beverly Sills took over the direction of NYCO and began to include musicals as part of the opera season. My repertoire then included *Naughty Marietta, The Student Prince, The Desert Song, The New Moon, South Pacific, Kismet, Pajama Game, Candide, The Music Man, A Little Night Music,* and *Sweeney Todd.* I got a crack at pretty much everything that used a flute.

This was NYCO's last season at City Center, although we would return between seasons for the musicals and ballets provided as extra work. The New York State Theater at Lincoln Center had been built for Balanchine and the NYCB. When both of the companies had been at City Center, many musicians played in both orchestras. When the ballet moved to Lincoln Center, the seasons conflicted, so those musicians had to choose their orchestra. Most chose the ballet, because the seasons were longer, the performances were shorter, it had fewer rehearsals, it was easier to put in a sub, and generally speaking was more prestigious. Now Julius and his associate John White had prevailed on Morton Baum, City Center's chairman, to transfer the opera to Lincoln Center also. Once again the companies would share the theater, with Richard Rogers occupying it during the summer for a musical revival. For years thereafter, we fought unsuccessfully to have the orchestras combined in some fashion, to provide something approaching full-time employment. But the artistic egos in each company demanded complete control over who would enter their orchestras. Eventually a few players did manage to belong to both orchestras, but a wonderful opportunity was missed.

The NYCO would open in its new home on February 22 with *Don Rodrigo*, a stunning opera by Alberto Ginastera, starring Placido Domingo. Another big event occurred the next morning – the debut of our first son, Russell Turner Wion.

1966

Right after recording the second side of the Nielsen album and finishing the *Oklahoma* run, I jumped right into the American Opera and the Mitropoulos Conducting Competition. At the same time, the quintet was preparing a Carnegie Recital Hall program for the end of the month, adding the Seiber, Dahl and Hindemith quintets to its repertoire. Once again we failed to get a *Times* review, this time because of a strike at the paper. As a result, we scheduled a second recital for May. We played the Nielsen for the third time, capitalizing on our recording, repeated Danzi B♭ and Dahl, and introduced Louis Moyse's beautiful *Quintet*. Finally we received an acknowledgment from the *Times*, and a favorable one to boot.

In the middle of this rather hectic January, an early morning phone call brought news that Vicky's father had died suddenly of a heart attack. He was fifty-eight. Bob had married for the third time a few years before and had settled into a lovely colonial home in Yorktown Heights, forty-five minutes north of the city. His wife was a forceful, youthful, English widow with three young children. After a quick cremation, she immediately began to plan her future.

In his last years Bob had come to understand that he was actually wealthy. His partner, Nat Wartels, being single, had never needed a large income, so the amount they had agreed to take as salary had always kept Bob rather frugal. Only with an accounting, done when they decided to sell a division of the company, did he get a sense of Crown's market value.

Our own future was to change, as the settlement of his estate would provide us with an additional income to bolster our limited financial possibilities in "the Arts." Bob sadly didn't live long enough to fully enjoy the success he had worked so hard for, but I know he would have been happy that his estate helped put his grandchildren through private schools and colleges. He was a soft-spoken, gentle man, and he would have smiled and mumbled something modest about being glad to help.

In February, rehearsals began for the opera's first season at Lincoln Center. I was familiar with the theater from attending ballet performances, but this was the first time I would be backstage and in the pit. Although things were in many ways better than at City Center in terms of facilities, the theater had been designed for ballet, not opera. Rehearsal space was inadequate, singers had trouble being heard from a stage that was geared towards minimizing sound, and the pit was strange at best. It was small and partly situated under the stage's overhang. That it was even as big as it was was due to an unplanned Balanchine visit when the theater was nearing completion. He was appalled to see that the pit would accommodate only half his orchestra. When he was told that construction had proceeded too far to make a change, he just shrugged that Balanchine shrug and wished them well – his company would not be dancing there. That brought the required jackhammers to remove the necessary rows of seats.

The best place to hear music was from the top ring of the house. At the orchestra level, individual instruments sounded as if they were coming from speakers to the sides of the proscenium – it was the strangest thing. Years later, when Beverly Sills took over the company, she arranged a renovation which improved the stage sound, enlarged the pit, and made the rehearsal room more bearable. Still a further renovation of the pit would be necessary before one side of the orchestra would be able to hear the other. And it took the placement of panels on the theater walls to remove the perception that the orchestra was being miked.

Despite all these limitations, NYCO's opening night on Washington's Birthday was thrilling. Ginastera's twelve-tone opera, *Don Rodrigo*, with Placido Domingo and Jeannine Crader in the leading roles and Julius Rudel conducting, captured the audience not the least with brilliant costumes and sets, and twelve French horns playing hunting calls from different places in the rings.

Two amusing occurrences are associated with later performances of this work. The first was when we introduced the piece to Los Angeles in our first season there. A pseudo-medieval quintet calls for a viola d'amore, in addition to an alto flute. The local player hired to play the viola, being less familiar with the score than the rest of us, had some problems in rehearsal. On opening night, just before this section was to start, we suddenly heard the sound of the viola d'amore. Julius waved frantically at the player to stop. He was in fact not playing but had started his tape recorder to memorialize the moment. He pressed "play" by accident and produced one of his practice sessions.

The second incident involved the first Julius Rudel Award winner, Christopher Keene. Christopher was young and brilliant, and decidedly awkward and inexperienced as a conductor. His reward for acting as Julius's backup was to conduct one performance. The score for *Don Rodrigo* calls for the most intricate off-the-beat ensemble entrances, but it is cleverly written so that the conductor has only the simplest of beat patterns to follow. Julius couldn't let that be, so he spent hours of rehearsal time indicating all the entries with some elbow, eyebrow, or finger, managing altogether the most amazing contortions. When Christopher took over, he just beat his enormous foursquare pattern, and the orchestra put its notes just where they were supposed to go. He got a rave review for handling this complex score with such aplomb.

The entire two-month season was glamorous and adventurous: Francis Poulenc's moving *Dialogue of the Carmelites* (a decade before the Met got to it); Gottfried Von Einem's *Danton's Death*; Douglas Moore's *Ballad of Baby Doe* with Sills, Frances Bible and Walter Cassel; Kurt Weill's *Street Scene*; Dmitri Shostakovitch's *Katerina Ismailova* (two decades before the Met); Igor Stravinsky's *Oedipus Rex* with Carl

Orff's *Carmina Burana*; Sergei Prokofiev's *Love of Three Oranges*; and Gian-Carlo Menotti's *The Consul* – an astonishing display in retrospect.

Our son Russell was astonishing too. Vicky's pregnancy survived the shock of her father's death, and right after the *Don Rodrigo* opening night performance we went to Mount Sinai Hospital, where Russell was born the next morning. As soon as we took him home, Vicky became uncharacteristically anxious and had trouble sleeping. This was resolved only when her mother arranged for a live-in nurse for a couple of weeks, to ease the strain.

With Russell Turner Wion at three weeks.

This new six-pound, three-ounce being in our life brought us joy from the first. He was precocious – walking and talking at eleven months, and developing a reasoning capacity at an early age. With a dancer's limbs and movement he figured out how to drop the needle on his toy phonograph before he was two, and marched around to his favorite "They're changing guard at Buckingham Palace."

Immediately after the season, the orchestra played for the Joffrey Ballet for its one-week season at City Center – the start of a new association. The conductor was Seymour Lipkin, and the ethereal star was Lisa Bradley. She was exquisite in Gerald Arpino's *Sea Shadow*. This ballet was set to the slow movement of Maurice Ravel's *G Major Piano Concerto*. When the publishers of that piece suddenly withdrew permission for its use, Mike Colgrass wrote a beautiful piece of the same meter and length overnight. And he scored it as a flute solo with string accompaniment no less!

I got to play the drum again, when a visiting German production of Georg Buchner's *Woyzeck* needed some incidental music. I got all dressed up like a clown with a pig's mask, and hit a base drum for a week. May was taken up with the musical revival at City Center. Following that, as a bonus, I began the Caramoor part of my job.

Dino Proto contracted the summer festival at this beautiful estate in Westchester County, and he used those members of the opera orchestra who were currently in favor. The Rosen family estate had two concert sites – the Venetian Theater, where Saturday night orchestral concerts took place, and the Spanish Courtyard for smaller events.

The former had been built around a set of pillars from a Venetian palazzo which framed the stage. Chairs were set out on the lawn for the audience, with a second set to the sides under awnings in case it should rain. The Rosen's home was a villa, four-sided around a cloistered, fountained square, purchased in Spain and reconstructed. One side contained the music room and art gallery, where winter concerts could take place, with the family listening from an overlooking indoor balcony. Outside, in the late summer afternoon, with birds chirping and fountain tinkling, we performed Benjamin Britten's church parable, *Curlew River*. This magical piece, based on a Japanese Noh play, is set in medieval England. The singers and musicians, all male (except for our harpist, Francesca Corsi) were dressed in hooded brown robes. The singers intoned a plainsong chant and carried candles as we proceeded through the cloister to the performing area. With the brilliant Andrea Velis acting the part of the madwoman who has lost her son, and City Opera regulars Ara Berberian, David Clatworthy, and William Metcalf playing the other leads, the moving drama with its culminating miracle unfolded. Julius led from the portable organ, and the other six musicians each had beautiful contributions to make. Strangely, I most remember the atmospheric ringing of Ray Desroche's finger cymbals as the sun set.

Among the Saturday night highlights of the Venetian Theater concerts was a program of Leos Janácek's music. I may have been Julius' new principal flutist, but he had hired Claude Monteux to play this concert, which included the sextet *Mladi* and the *Nursery Songs*, both of which would be recorded. However I was able to make my ocarina debut in the latter piece, imitating a cuckoo. With this recording in July, my first full year at the NYCO ended, and I had a son to introduce to his grandmother in Australia.

In May we had had a phone call from Bob Simon's widow, Oonagh. She was selling the house in Yorktown Heights and moving into Manhattan. When she undertook a project she always did it properly. In the midst of her search, she had come across the perfect apartment for us. It was just a few blocks away, and she suggested we look at it immediately. She would take it herself but for a problem of one bathroom serving two bedrooms, which would not suit the needs of her growing children.

We were skeptical, having spent the last several months looking to provide more space for our own growing family, and finding nothing in our price range. This apartment was in a co-operative building, something pretty new in Manhattan, and this was the way we should go, she said. With no idea of what we were getting into, we walked around to Riverside Drive and were sent up to the seventh floor by the doorman. The owners showed us around an enormous apartment and over to the window looking out across the Hudson. Below us in the park all the cherry trees were in blossom. Sold!

The price was an astronomical twenty-seven thousand dollars ($173,000 in 2007). I don't think we had enough to cover much more than the deposit. Oonagh said not to worry. She would speak to Nat Wartels and arrange for Crown to lend the money until Bob's estate was settled. Things were moving really fast. We met with the board of the co-op and with the building's lawyer. Vicky's stepfather handled all the legalities. At the end of June, amid Caramoor rehearsals, we moved.

What a day! We had a potential problem with the previous owners not quite moved out and might have to keep our stuff in the moving van overnight. No problem, said the mover. I came home from rehearsal to find no van. Vicky said they had filled it and had gone to 180 Riverside Drive, our new home. The van was *not* big enough for all our stuff and clearly we couldn't store our things there overnight. I ran the few blocks to try and deal with the fact that we couldn't yet move in. I finally arranged to unload the van into the building courtyard, praying we would not have a New York thunderstorm. The rest of the day, we shuttled back and forth between apartments, moving things upstairs as soon as a room was vacated. At five o'clock we were informed that the service elevator was shutting down. I negotiated a deal with the operator, but then the ex-owner got mad because the operator wouldn't take his stuff out – well, he was working for me! The light faded, and, after definitely doing more of the moving than any of the crew, we were finally in.

Two weeks later, after arranging for some major construction to be done (for about the cost of the plans I think, through an architect friend of Vicky's stepfather) and seeing the destruction but not the construction, the three of us left for Australia – Russell in his portable crib. After a stormy, scary night over the Pacific and a brief layover in Tahiti, we arrived in Melbourne.

We spent much of our time catching up with family and friends, meeting new spouses and new children. We stayed with my mother, which was always difficult for me. But with charm and tact Vicky always managed to make our visits as pleasant for everyone as possible.

Keith Humble and his wife Jill were there, he having once again taken a lecturer's position at the Conservatorium. He had hoped to arrange a concert but nothing eventuated. Les and Jessie Barklamb hosted a Sunday afternoon get-together of flutists. And my brother David introduced us to a former New Yorker, Sandy Feirson, who had recently lost his wife in a car crash.

Sandy, who became our dear friend, was one of those people who have an absolutely clear view of life, and who can make seemingly outrageous decisions based on the facts they see, as opposed to some sense of how they are *supposed* to act. We had rented the essential car for Australia's suburban culture, and commented to Sandy on the prohibitive expense of using it, based on the cost-per-mile charge. He raised an eyebrow and said, "You just disconnect the speedometer. In the States it's sealed, but here nobody would expect such behavior, so it isn't."

Sandy, working for IBM, had decided that he didn't want to work as hard as he would have to in New York to achieve his goals. He researched the world and settled on Rhodesia; when that became problematic he went to Australia. The style he would develop over the years would be to use his expertise to act as a broker in the sale of something large like a printing machine, then travel or otherwise enjoy himself until necessity required another sale. He lived simply, often in places that others would not consider, such as a former church or Salvation Army hall, and made a hobby of collecting fire engines, both real and toy, and Mickey Mouse toys (Mickey on a fire truck was a real find). Sandy could always tweak the system to his advantage and had no compunction about doing so.

On a trip around the world, in the days of weighed baggage, he packed all his heavy papers into his carry-on briefcase, then left it under his seat at the first point of debarkation on the way home. Ignoring pages, changing flights, and even airports, he managed to have it waiting for him in Melbourne when he landed weeks later.

Sandy Feirson with a part of his collection.

He became a master of the Round-the-World ticket. This would be issued by one airline with strict rules of use. However, Sandy discovered that other airlines were so greedy for a segment of the flights that they would always accept and rewrite the ticket, until it became totally unidentifiable. If his ticket called for him to fly direct from New York to Los Angeles, and he wanted to visit someone in Texas, he would find an airline that went to Los Angeles only via Texas. He would explain that he had a scheduling problem, and they would rewrite his ticket. Then he would get off in Texas and arrange a later flight to Los Angeles. Unless he now needed to go via Kansas.

We spent a week driving inland to Sydney, returning via the coast. Our major problem was that Russell always went to sleep in the car the moment I turned the engine on. That was OK, but it meant he didn't have a lot of need for sleep at night.

In Sydney I met Australia's other major flute teacher, Victor MacMahon, and had the opportunity to coach some of his students. He was one of those untraveled people who are curious about everything and he asked lots of questions. This was a breath of fresh air in a society that was generally too shy or polite to ask about anything. When Les and Jessie Barklamb had visited us in New York, we made it very clear that they would have to tell us what they wanted to do. Les explained that in fact he had just learned that lesson while staying with his former student Doug Whittaker in London. They had been sitting around Doug's house waiting to be invited to go somewhere or do something and finally realized that it wasn't going to work that way.

The last part of our vacation was a week on the Great Barrier Reef, off Australia's northeast coast – a first for the three of us. It was on the final leg of this flight that I truly lost my fear of flying. We were in a small six-seater plane en route to Brampton Island on the reef. The cockpit door was open, and I observed the pilot's nonchalance as the plane bumped around and rose and fell. It was quite obvious that this was what planes did, and he totally ignored the entire procedure – as have I ever since.

We were back in New York at the end of August for a four-week engagement the orchestra had with the Joffrey Ballet. During this time, negotiations were going on for a new contract with the NYCO management. An unheard-of strike was called during the rehearsal period, and the management was so shaken by this new militancy that they settled the same day. It would be something of a Pyrrhic victory, as the struggle between the two sides escalated at each confrontation. A series of strikes or lockouts took place every two or three years thereafter, until all the key personnel involved had gone on to other realms.

The pettiness and animosity can be summed up in one incident involving a dress rehearsal for Handel's *Julius Caesar*. The orchestra had won the position that a dress rehearsal was more like a performance than other rehearsals and should be compensated at a premium rate. So, at the *Julius Caesar* dress, with a full audience of patrons, and full costume and lighting, the management presented the three acts out of order. For a Baroque opera the sequence of events is not as important as the quality of the individual scenes and arias, and the set didn't change. The management felt that the audience's enjoyment would not be diminished, while their own needs would be met. They then insisted that this was no longer a dress rehearsal, and we would be paid at the lower regular rehearsal rate.

The fall season opened with the above-mentioned production of *Julius Caesar*, and what a triumph it was. Rudel conducted, with Treigle as Caesar and Sills as Cleopatra. Sills had been mounting a major publicity campaign to cement her claim as America's reigning prima donna, with her photo on the covers of *Time* and *Newsweek*. She was superb in this role, as was Treigle in his, and the whole production was later recorded for RCA.

Most of our continuing productions were given new sets and costumes, appropriate to our more glamorous surroundings and larger stage. After the splash of the previous spring, the only other new operas were *The Magic Flute* and *Tosca*. After the season ended, we went on to what would be the last of the truck and bus tours, taking *Tosca*, *Traviata* and *The Consul* as far north as Jamestown, New York, and as far west as Urbana, Illinois.

I was approached toward the end of the fall season by one of our violinists, John Palanchian, a tall, extremely handsome, and brilliantly articulate leftist: Would I like to join him in his car for the tour, instead of traveling on the bus? It would not have been a difficult choice in any event, but I was rather honored to have been approached, and quickly accepted.

So began a relationship that ended only with his death some twenty years later. John — JP as he was referred to — was a stunningly charismatic figure. The only son of a fine Armenian painter and a first-class Scottish sculptor, he was a child prodigy on the violin whose wide-ranging intelligence perhaps prevented him from fully developing that potential. After taking his masters degree at Manhattan and serving in the famous Seventh Army Symphony in Germany, he became a professional player in New York, finally joining the first violin section of the NYCO. From a position of being asked to become concertmaster, which he declined when his conditions were not met, his status was progressively downgraded, as he became more and more militant as the orchestra's

John and Gloria Palanchian

spokesperson. Finally he was placed near the back of the second violins, and eventually left to become vice president of Local 802.

In 1966 he was still a god. And for the first time since I had left Trinity, I had someone my intellectual equal with whom to argue away the night. Although I was an impassioned advocate, I eventually came to realize that John was more interested in the debate than the outcome, and it was always I who finally said it was time for bed. I adored him and couldn't wait to get back to New York to introduce him to Vicky. John and his wife Gloria became our closest friends. They introduced us to Martha's Vineyard, where we would spend many blissful summers together – until Beverly Sills abruptly advised us, through the pages of *The New York Times*, that we wouldn't be having any more summers off.

We played endless games of bridge, at which they were both more experienced and more brilliant than we were. Despite the Palanchians' perfectly mannered patience, it became obvious that Vicky and I either had to do some serious bridge homework or stop playing. We stopped playing.

The social evenings continued, and the tour debates continued, and the during-, between-, and after-performance beers at the bar continued. But as John's demagoguery became more pronounced, and he slurred more of his words, I began excusing myself earlier. I saw my possible future in him, and I decided I didn't like it. I withdrew.

Over the course of a number of years, it became clear that he was an alcoholic. We maintained our friendship to the end, but I was angry at what he had done with his life and disappointed in myself that I didn't try to help him change. His friends all talked about his diminishment, but it was easier to distance oneself from it and continue the status quo than to try to persuade him toward rehabilitation. We were certain he was in denial and would never change. A heavy smoker, he developed lung cancer, and, his magnificent body shrunken, his eyes a bloodshot yellow, he died of a stroke, an old man in his fifties.

1967

The previous fall had seen a lot of planning by the Larks. Bill Brown had left the quintet, and we scheduled an adventurous season of three recitals at Carnegie with his replacement, Jerry Warshaw. The first, in October, had added the Schönberg and Villa-Lobos quintets to our repertory. In January and April, we added the Elliott Carter, Michael Colgrass, Samuel Barber and Irving Fine quintets, along with the Janacek *Mladi* sextet and the Mozart *Quintet for Piano and Winds*. The *Times* had enjoyed the first concert and said the rest "should be well worth hearing," though it decided against finding that out for itself.

Our year at home got off to a bad start when Vicky, landing badly from a jump in class, broke an ankle. She ended up with a cast up to her knee, and we had to rent a wheelchair and crutches to get through the next weeks. As soon as she was mobile again, she accepted Balanchine's offer to stage another ballet, this time in Hamburg in the spring. She took Russell with her, and the three of us met afterward for a short vacation in Mallorca. This turned out to be a most pleasant time, with our precocious Russell running everywhere and pointing at all the horse drawn taxis and saying "hoy, hoy."

The spring opera season started with our first guaranteed rehearsal week. Prior to this, we just rehearsed whenever the management requested. That often meant turning down other engagements in the weeks prior to the season. This was the time when orchestras around the country were trying to gain year-round employment. Traditionally they had worked only the winter season, when the social set was in town. Now, with air-conditioned halls and wider audiences, that was changing.

Our orchestra would push this envelope over the next several years with some success, though, ironically, I myself would suffer for it. Under the old system, as principal flute I got all the extra work, which, particularly in the case of the musical revivals, often called for just one flute. When I started at NYCO I was working about forty weeks a year, but as we were able to increase the guaranteed weeks for the entire orchestra, some work was rotated, and my own share decreased.

The Lark Quintet, 1967.

In order to establish the concept of a rehearsal week at weekly salary, we had to agree to play enough hours that the new salary would approximate the old hourly rehearsal rate. This turned out to be thirty-six hours, or six hours a day for six days. It was horrendous. One hour in our rehearsal room, a barely orchestra-sized concrete box with harsh lighting and bad air, had always been a chore. Thirty-six, with the addition of singers belting at the tops of their voices, was impossible. We were squashed together, only too aware of every other instrument, half of which we would not hear clearly once in the pit. Our weeks eventually shrunk to a more wieldy five hours a day for four days, and in the fall when the ballet was not in season, we began to rehearse in the promenade of the theater.

Rehearsing was always problematic at the opera. Few rehearsals were held in the pit, because the theater was in use, either by the ballet if it was in season, or by the opera itself, doing staging or technical rehearsals. So we would waste endless hours in the rehearsal room, having conductors tell us we were playing too loud and that things were out of balance.

Because the company never had any money, rehearsals were always minimal, or nonexistent. Sometimes we could go from season to season without any rehearsals of standard repertoire. Later, Beverly Sills started raising money and decided it would be used for more rehearsals. Unfortunately, she hired some conductors who didn't know how to use the time. They would read through their opera, and then read through it again. All the things that were out of tune, or not together, stayed that way.

That was in the future. Julius's solution was always to have another opera on the stands. If he finished early whatever he was working on, we would spend the remaining time on *Butterfly* or *Figaro*, whatever — even if it meant a different conductor.

Orchestral players always think that, if they do their job really well, they might get out of the rehearsal early. Such things can't be planned accurately, and it is more likely that the end of the rehearsal is spent frantically trying to cover some impossible territory. But it does happen. At NYCO, without that incentive, other means would be used to lighten the load.

If you had to sit there for three hours regardless, the question became how little you could manage to play. The answer came in the form of the question. Just as a conductor was about to give a downbeat, someone would ask if this note was G or G♯. Long/short was good too; most recitative interjections are written as quarter notes, but sometimes they are long and sometimes they are short. Transposing instruments could get good time out of "is this horn in E♭ or F?" The best was deciding the string up- and down-bowing; it took a long time and the winds could totally tune out.

Our top questioner, without doubt, was our bass clarinetist, Aldo Simonelli, also at that time our fierce orchestra-committee chair. He could always be relied on for several time-consuming questions at each rehearsal. The most memorable occurred under the direction of the aged but absolutely charming Walter Susskind. He loved talking and spent a considerable amount of time in one rehearsal explaining one particular point. He finally finished and began his downbeat. Suddenly Aldo asked him a question on that very point; without batting an eyelid, Susskind explained it all over again. Something desperate was going on here!

Susskind had been the conductor in Melbourne when I was growing up. I loved his music making and adored all his talks to the audience. About to play the famous Henry Purcell *Trumpet Voluntary*, he gave a witty speech explaining that recent research had established that the piece was actually written by one Jeremiah Clarke. "And so now we would like to play for you *Purcell's Trumpet Voluntary* by Jeremiah Clarke."

He was quite a ladies' man. At the City Opera he conducted a later revival of *Coq d'Or*, with the voluptuous Carol Neblett as the Queen. In the middle of the dress rehearsal he just stopped conducting and said to her, "How can I look at you and conduct at the same time?"

The spring season introduced me to two exciting operas, *Der Rosenkavalier* and *Il Trittico*. Whereas *Capriccio* had had a relatively easy flute part, *Rosenkavalier* was a thrilling joyride from beginning to end, always pushing my technique to its limit. The score is so beautiful, and though it became harder for me later in my career, it was always a wonder to play.

I had quite an experience with this opera several years later, when Julius led it in a Los Angeles season. Vicky had brought the boys out over Thanksgiving break to take them to Disneyland in Anaheim, which we did the day before the holiday. That night was the opening of *Rosenkavalier*. I left Anaheim an hour earlier than I thought necessary to allow for pre-Thanksgiving traffic. As I pulled onto the freeway I knew I was in trouble – a sea of barely moving taillights. I also knew I had no alternatives. Driving the streets, even if you knew where you were going, took forever in the Los Angeles sprawl. So I sat and inched forward and looked at my watch and saw curtain time approach and pass.

Rosenkavalier costs so much in overtime, I think they would start without the conductor if they had to – they certainly wouldn't have waited for me! All of a sudden, all the traffic turned onto another freeway, out of town, and I was alone. I sped toward downtown, down the off-ramp, and along the deserted city streets toward the Music Center. A siren and flashing lights behind told me the saga wasn't over yet. Trembling now, I explained to the officer my predicament. Staring me right in the eye, he said, "That's no reason to speed."

I drove sedately to the parking lot, ran to the theater, and into the pit in my street clothes. About forty minutes into the first act of *Rosenkavalier* is a scene on stage where a flutist plays for the Marschallin's *levée*. He warms up with the most brilliant show-off display. I hurried to my vacant seat – my second had not moved over – sat, put my flute together, got it to my lips, and launched into the solo.

Next intermission, I went to Julius to apologize. "I didn't notice," he said, "until the bird calls at the opening of the act – then I just whistled them myself. We were just concerned that something had happened to you." Unfortunately, Julius and I had had to go through a lot of grief together before he could treat me with such affection.

Puccini's three-opera evening was also completely new to me, though I knew the famous aria from *Gianni Schicchi*, "O mio babbino caro." Patanè led the way to another exciting event; particularly memorable were Treigle's wily Schicchi, Sill's rendition of the above aria, and Domingo's Luigi in *Il Tabarro*. Domingo and Patanè were also involved in Frank Corsaro's new production of *Butterfly*.

After the season we played a week of *Coppelia* using the most dreadful manuscript parts, surely copied by someone's child, and then had runs of *The Sound of Music* and Burton Lane and Yip Harburg's *Finian's Rainbow*. What a beautiful show this was, with, for the time, an unusual honesty about race relations. Ironically, years later, Sills canceled plans for another revival because no less a person than Toni Morrison advised her that the book disparaged blacks.

In May we also recorded *Julius Caesar*, with Sills, Treigle and Maureen Forrester, and Rudel conducting. My own contribution was rather limited, apart from a pretty little solo for flute and strings. I recall that the session where the oboe was required was strangely scheduled on a day when Basil Reeve, our principal, was unavailable; Leonard Arner was hired as a replacement.

When Basil finally left, we had national auditions for principal oboe. We chose an excellent candidate at which point Julius said, "There is also Lennie Arner." Arner had not auditioned. I expressed particular reservations, given my history with Lennie in *Camelot*. Julius phoned me next morning, just because of these reservations, to personally tell me that he had decided to hire Arner. Lennie was particularly nice to me at first, but sadly the warm relationship didn't last, and silence fell between us once again.

The Wion-Arner feud came to an end many, many years later. I had been trying without success to initiate some contact, but whenever we passed in the corridor he would avoid my eye. One morning I was called for a jingle – a high-class commercial using a fragment of a Haydn symphony. Because the studio was small, the flute and oboe were set up in the booth normally used by the percussion. The oboist was Lennie Arner. As I walked in he looked me right in the eye, and said, "Pretty ironic isolation booth!" For the next hour or so, he barely stopped talking, as if we had been bosom buddies for a lifetime. My life at the opera then became a lot more pleasant.

In the summer I was called to play the Philharmonic parks concerts and thereafter became a regular sub. (A few years later they had auditions for second flute and made up a new sub list from the runners-up.) I almost lost the privilege when I repeated to one of the flutists in the orchestra something that Baker had said to me about Bernstein that I thought was very funny. My remark got back to Baker, who phoned me in great anger: He had never said such a thing. I never was very good at politics and was a slow learner at keeping my mouth shut. The caustic, solid as a rock, Paige Brook played principal that summer, and I enjoyed sitting next to him.

Bernstein left before I had the opportunity to work with him, and Pierre Boulez took over. I found him fascinating. One of his strengths was his ear – he could hear anything – and another was his rehearsal efficiency. The rowdy Philharmonic of that time didn't take kindly to either attribute. He would continually have to say, "I am not a policeman," as they chatted while he was trying to do business. He would listen to a complicated chord in Varèse and tune the brass, one instrument at a time. That same piece he read down from the top, then rehearsed from the end backwards. Why take time turning back to the beginning?

I enjoyed him, but one concert showed me an interesting side of his character. We were playing Harvey Sollberger's *Chamber Symphony* at one of Boulez's newly instituted, informal "rug concerts." The complexities of this kind of piece were right up his alley. In three sections, the middle one was a different tempo to the outer ones. At the performance, he made an uncharacteristic error and began beating the tempo change a bar too soon. Those who were playing at the time just kept going, but those of us who were resting thought we had miscounted and started in on the new section. He spent the next several minutes getting each of us, one at a time, back into the right bar, and the piece ended as it should have. Although the audience surely didn't suspect anything, he immediately turned to them, and said this was such a fine piece of music that we would like to play it again for them – which we did, flawlessly.

My other memories of these subbing times relate to a series of André Kostelanetz recordings. He always used players from the Philharmonic, though not its name. The more important members often chose not to do these sessions – hence the subs. In my first call I was asked to play third and piccolo in Maurice Ravel's *Bolero*. Never having played this, I got a score from the library. I found a duo for two piccolos, pianissimo, the first starting on high E – definitely not my strength by then. I practiced long tones and arrived early. To my delight, I found that, contrary to usual convention, the first piccolo part was assigned to the second flute. That player, also a sub, arrived nonchalantly, right at the last minute. Kostelanetz's practice in these sessions was to have his assistant, Leon Hyman, conduct all the rehearsals, while he listened from the booth. Then he would take the baton for the taping. When we came to the piccolo duet, my colleague's high E rang out at a safe *mezzo forte*, and Kostelanetz asked from the booth if we could play softer. We tried again, and he cracked the E. We tried a couple more times. Then we heard Kostelanetz asking the engineers if they could handle the dynamic level in the control room – no problem. "OK," he said, "just play it out." Later, I listened to the results – way in the background you heard the piccolos whistling away.

My other recollection was the recording of *Rhapsody in Blue* with pianist Peter Nero. I had actually worked my way up to first for that. (It must have been a really busy week for the regulars!) A lot of that piece is for unaccompanied piano. We just recorded the orchestral part leading into his solo. Then we cut to the end of that solo and recorded the next ensemble. I presume he recorded all the rest after we left; I never heard the recording.

The summer Caramoor season repeated *Curlew River* and added the American première of Britten's second parable, *The Burning Fiery Furnace*. (It would introduce *The Prodigal Son* two years later.) Again Julius conducted from the organ, and Andrea Velis sang the lead. After the Caramoor season, we took the two operas to Dearborn, Michigan.

By the fall I had been invited to run for the orchestra committee and was elected. I was desperately committed to improving the orchestra's lot, and now that I was tenured, felt an obligation to help. This was not a smart thing for a principal player to do. Over the next several years I believe I was an advocate for reason and logic and fairness, and I believe I was of some help at times. But at the same time, my committee activities became another factor in my worsening relationship with Julius.

In the early years Aldo Simonelli was the leader, until John Palanchian took over. Aldo was a tough fighter on the orchestra's behalf for more than twenty years, until he lost his personal fight with cancer. John was more charismatic, more articulate, and more intelligent. He led through manipulation. He would spend hours with his wife Gloria, or with some of us, planning how to get the particular result he wanted. He perceived Julius and his associate, John White, as evil.

Palanchian saw everyone and everything in black and white and had little patience for those who didn't. It always seemed so easy for him to cut through any shades of gray in a situation and define it in clear terms. After the committee's initial success, the opera board refused to allow John White to negotiate without a lawyer present. This person came to be Martin Oppenheimer. A lot of performers at the opera, including me, believe that Martie was instrumental in the company's failure to rise to its potential.

He was a brilliant strategist, skilled at labor negotiation in the commercial world. There, his responsibility was to minimize labor costs so as to maximize corporate profit. Regrettably, he brought these attitudes to the nonprofit area, where the equation is different. The lower your labor costs, the less money you have to raise. Conversely, the more money you raised, the greater your freedom to compensate your performers.

From our point of view, the problem at NYCO was always lack of money. The company received a considerable influx when it moved to Lincoln Center, to fit its productions to the site's glamour. But none was budgeted for salaries. The principal singers, whose fees were a pittance, used the NYCO and its New York reviews as a stepping-stone to careers elsewhere, including the Met. Our finest young singers followed Placido Domingo and Sherryl Milnes there – even José Carreras! However, if any singers tried to use a good review to get a salary raise at NYCO, they weren't rehired. The orchestra always earned less than any other at Lincoln Center – maybe half of what players at the Met earned – and the chorus and dancers were treated like dirt. Yet, at this time, NYCO was being hailed in the press as being the true vital force in opera in the city.

We felt it was our job to perform well, and the board's responsibility to raise money. The reality was that each contract negotiation would start with the orchestra's dreams of what it, rightly I believe, felt was its due. The management started with the position that it had raised no money. Probably this was quite true, but it is also easy enough in the arts to tell potential supporters not to contribute until contracts are settled.

The routine became familiar. Every two years we would have a lockout or strike, until the company had saved enough money on our salaries to pay for a small raise. At that point John White would say that the post-season tour would have to be canceled if we didn't settle by the end of the week, and the orchestra would settle. After everyone agreed that we deserved more, nothing was done towards achieving that goal till we faced off again for a rematch, each time with more animosity.

Despite this failure to meet its goals, the orchestra's militancy eventually led to salaries that were higher than the union's freelance scales. Bizarrely, this is what would finally disillusion me about our strikes. During one strike, a member of the orchestra asked me, "Why are we on strike? We're all out there freelancing, working harder for less money." The committee always supported the belief that the important thing was where you finished up in a contract, because that provided the base for the future. But I couldn't refute my colleague's argument.

The post-season tour became a big deal that fall, when the company was invited to a four-week residency at the new Dorothy Chandler Pavilion at the Los Angeles Music Center. This was a very glamorous season, as the local presenters were prepared to pay for the finest singers throughout, unlike in New York, where our casts deteriorated after each production's opening. (By season's end rumors circulated that certain singers paid for their opportunity to perform.)

The residency lasted over some twenty years, until Beverly Sills abruptly told them we wouldn't be coming back. Surely a factor in that decision was the music critic Martin Bernheimer, who wrote more and more critically of our efforts. Afterwards, he wrote a piece for his paper, saying how disgraceful it was that we no longer came.

The beach house at Hermosa Beach.

While it lasted, it was, for me and my pals, a vacation. Our only obligation was to play an opera (or two) each day. After one night downtown this first year, Palanchian got on the phone and found the SeaSprite motel on Hermosa Beach, forty-five minutes away. It and its surrounding properties would become our home away from home. We lived like kings right on the beach; our activities eventually centered around the beach house, where Palanchian and one or two others would stay, including our tuba player Lew Waldeck. Among a great many other talents, Lew was a master chef. We each had our chores preparing dinner, but Lew oversaw all. Thanksgiving was the main event, and Lew would create something like goose stuffed with prunes stuffed with foie gras. He was a voracious reader, and a devout fan of Nero Wolfe, Rex Stout's gourmet detective. He actually compiled a recipe book of the dishes described in those books and took it to Viking. They rejected the idea but later did indeed produce such a book.

Unfortunately, we would occasionally have a season that did not call for tuba and we had to improvise until oboist Livio Caroli joined our ranks and began producing Italian delights. Getting ingredients wasn't always easy in LA, and we would drive fifty miles to find some reputedly milk-fed veal or other vital need. Arborio rice seemed to be an insurmountable problem, and Livio tried the rice from the local health food store for his risotto. It was still inedible when we had to leave for work.

Livio also managed to come close to blowing us all up one year. We were cooking dinner around the oven, using all four gas burners. Suddenly a flame of gas shot up a vent at the rear of the range, we heard an explosion, and the front of the oven blew open. Those right in front were thrown back, with singed clothes and hair. The manager was called; the gas company was called. As we were describing the sequence of events, a question was asked of Livio, and we heard him reply, "What pilot light?"

Before we got to California, our fall season introduced *Coq d'Or*, again with Sills and Treigle at their very top and Julius conducting, and with Ricky Di Giuseppe as the astrologer, thrilling everyone with his high Ds. Also new for me was Jack Beeson's *Lizzie Borden*, which had been given to Patanè. The ballerina Vera Zorina directed a new production of *Cav/Pag*, with Domingo and Pat Brooks. The direction called for Brooks, herself also a dancer, to appear in a tutu. That was fine till some of the more typically built divas took over the role of Nedda.

By now the wind section was at its peak. Although it would not stay together very long, those who were there still remember it. Basil Reeve was the principal oboe, an exquisitely sensitive player with a free, open sound. He took umbrage at the fact that Julius gave him tenure only after saying he was not altogether happy about doing so. At the first opportunity, Basil left – first for Rotterdam, then Minnesota.

Clarinet was George Silfies, perhaps the greatest technician I ever came across. He could play anything, anytime, anywhere. We used to all go dining together between weekend shows, and George would drink two or three martinis and some wine, and go back and play the cadenzas in *Coq d'Or* as if they were child's play. The only way you could ever know he had been drinking was that he became less tolerant of less perfect people. If someone regularly played behind the beat, he would beat his foot audibly during that person's playing. George quickly saw no future at NYCO and took the position of principal in St. Louis.

Bassoon was Ryohei Nakagawa, another great artist. He was the last of our principal winds to leave, going to San Francisco at Seiji Ozawa's request, and then back to Japan.

Bill Brown was on horn, until he swung one too many punches at the contractor and got himself fired.

My second for the next twenty years was Florence Nelson, whose patience with my periodic moods was formidable. A wonderful colleague and long-time friend, she was always a part of our gang, though mostly in awed silence. The daughter of a highly respected cantor, she gradually grew from a rather inhibited follower to a tough-speaking leader. After a hand problem threatened her performing career, she followed Palanchian to Local 802, succeeded Waldeck as head of the American Federation of Musician's Symphony Department, and finally became the AFM's vice president.

By the end of the year, our family had grown to include my mother. At the end of September Vicky had bravely crossed the Pacific with Russell on her lap to stage a ballet for the Australian Ballet in Sydney. My mother had flown up to babysit, until she had to go back to Melbourne. At that point Vicky flew down with them for the weekend, and, with amazing confidence, left Russell with my mother for the week.

We had been trying to get my mother to pay us a visit. Finally she accepted our offer of fare money, and came with Vicky and Russell. She always insisted it was a loan, and indeed, when she died, the amount was specified in her will. She was a good houseguest and enjoyed Russell immensely, though her principal joy was in seeing me. (A few years later, after I had played a concerto with the Melbourne orchestra in front of a large, enthusiastic audience, my mother's only comment, as she gave me a hug, was how my hair just shone in the lights.)

She amazed us all when, in the new year, she decided to continue on around the world on her own. We arranged for her to be escorted at her chosen stopovers, yet it took some courage for a woman just turning seventy, who had never traveled alone before, to set out on this journey.

1968

After my mother left, Vicky and I took advantage of a lull before the opera season for a short vacation in Antigua. We left Russell with Bob Simon's widow, Oonagh, already remarried and living in Connecticut. Then the year began with a Pennsylvania Ballet season at City Center, coinciding with opera rehearsals during the daytime.

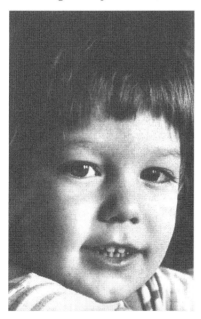

Russell Wion (Photograph by Craig Perkins).

The new operas for this spring season were *Bomarzo*, the second of the three Ginastera operas we would present, Robert Ward's *The Crucible*, Douglas Moore's *Carry Nation*, which we would record, and a new production of *Manon* for Beverly Sills. *Bomarzo* was noisy, *The Crucible* and *Carrie Nation* were forgettable, but *Manon* was a true hit. Sills was superb, Molese was an ardent Des Grieux, and Julius moved the score forward with great emotional sweep.

Julius always took it personally if one of his principals was not present when he conducted and showed his displeasure by ignoring the sub. I recall one performance of *Manon* when the clarinet sub was the truly wonderful Joe Rabbai, later principal at the Met. At the moment of Joe's big solo, Julius turned toward the second violins and gave them a cue.

When Patanè conducted the season's final *Cav/Pag*, we didn't know it would be the last time we would see him. During the spring musical Dino Proto told us that Patanè, who had a reputation as a reckless driver, had died in a car crash. We were all so sad that this man was gone from our lives. He knew just how every moment of his opera had to be played and sung, and exactly how to achieve it with his baton. He mostly saved words for editorial comment – (in Italian to the contractor) "Please tell the tuba player that Tosca is killing Scarpia with a stiletto, not an axe." His total lack of political know-how was all that kept him from the stellar career that his son Giuseppe would have. Although the City Opera still had many triumphs ahead, I think Patanè's loss was the start of its decline.

After the spring Gilbert & Sullivan season and revivals of *The King and I* and *My Fair Lady*, I was able to combine the Caramoor season with Ballet Theater, which was spending July at the Metropolitan Opera House. The principal conductor was the charming and brilliant Kenny Schermerhorn, and the experience was not unlike my first year at the opera, except that I had no time or music to prepare myself. We spent all day rehearsing, much of the repertoire new to me, then perform it that evening. This went on till everything had opened – meaning that the last week just had performances. This really was a month of sight-reading.

In August, we spent the first of many vacations on Martha's Vineyard at the prompting of the Palanchians. They put us in touch with a lovable but eccentric agent Catherine Allen, who found us an isolated saltbox at the western end of the island. We discovered a wonderful new way of life in this bleakly situated and unattractive house, apart from having to rush Russell to the hospital with a severe case of poison ivy. Mick and Libby Long came down from Boston, where Mick had a residency. They brought their three children including newborn American, Tom, now a movie actor. The one thing we had in that house was space.

Our biennial labor strife saved us from another thirty-six-hour rehearsal week, but the fall opera season, with hastily revised rehearsals, did open. The management seemingly had been prepared for a strike. The only new productions scheduled were Hugo Weisgall's *Nine Rivers to Jordan*, which was a huge flop, and *Faust*, which was brilliant. Rudel led an amazing cast, which included Treigle, Sills, Molese, and Bible.

During the season, Robert Kennedy and Martin Luther King Jr. were assassinated. When Julius's mentor Morton Baum had died earlier in the year, the orchestra had rehearsed and performed the funeral music from *Götterdämmerung* in his memory. Following Kennedy's death, the orchestra sight-read the flute solo from Gluck's *Orphée*; following King's death, we played the National Anthem.

The Los Angeles tour and the Christmas musical ended a routine year. However, expansion of both family and horizons lay just ahead.

Expanding Horizons

1969

This turned out to be an eventful year. It started right off with the birth of our son Anthony Robert on January 6. He was bigger boned and fairer than Russell. Where Russell was always moving and needing company, Anthony was calmer and content to be alone. They seemed to enjoy each other from the start; Russell liked the company of younger people, and his brother that of older people. We quickly decided that we would introduce Anthony to Australia that summer and began planning the trip.

I had been thinking to expand my solo career and wrote to several organizations in Australia to see what might be possible. I picked a bad year to start; Jean-Pierre Rampal was making his first tour there during the spring. The ABC offered me two broadcast recitals with pianist Margaret Schofield. The first would consist of Bach, Handel, and Schubert; the second, Henri Dutilleux's *Sonatine*, Edgard Varèse's *Density 21.5*, Mario Davidovsky's *Syncronisms* with tape, and Australian Don Bank's *Three Episodes*. My approaches to the universities were all officially declined, though I was eventually able to arrange some informal activity through the flute teachers.

The quintet began a bold project of two informal concerts in a recently opened space called Studio 58, where we had just recorded Ruth Crawford Seeger's *Suite* for the CRI label. Our January announcement offered "a variety of music accompanied by cognac and coffee." The first concert in February began with the Mozart *Clarinet Quintet* and ended with Janáček's *Mladi*. I contributed the Debussy *Sonata*, with Lanny's wife Libby playing harp and my friend from the opera, Larry Fader, playing viola. We also played our recording of Bill Sydeman's 1967 *Quintet* (which never was released), while projecting the complex score for the audience to follow. The concept was well received, and we got a great boost from a rave review by Byron Belt in the *Long Island Press*.

Recording with Powell 480 at Studio 58.

My contribution to the March concert, which occurred between two Sunday opera performances, was limited to the premiere of Stan Walden's song cycle, with mezzo Jan de Gaetani. I was to have a number of opportunities to work with this astonishing artist, including a mesmerizing *Pierrot Lunaire*, before her sad early death. The pianist in the Walden (as well as the Schönberg) was Gilbert Kalish, and thus began a relationship of a decade that would give me my most satisfying opportunities to make music. Walden himself would gain notoriety as a composer of the naughty revue, *Oh Calcutta!*

In April, we played Stan's piece again in a concert at the Center for Inter-American Relations. The program also included the premiere of Ruth Crawford Seeger's *Quintet* we had previously recorded. Mrs. Seeger was at that time known, if at all, as the mother of folk singer, Pete Seeger.

The spring opera season introduced Borodin's *Prince Igor* to the repertoire. Oddly the star turned out to be NYCB dancer Edward Villella in the famous "Polovetsian Dances." We also had a new production of *Rigoletto*, which introduced an exciting conductor, Gabor Ötvös.

My other spring activity was the preparation and recording of Max Reger's two charming serenades with violinist Stan Ritchie, whom I had known since music camp days in Australia, and violist Larry Fader. They were tough pieces to record, and the technical problems were complicated by the fact that Larry, a fine ensemble player, was not used to functioning as a bass. This led to problems of intonation, which were minimized by a lot of creative splicing by engineer Jerry Bruck. Studio 58 was a good place to record, and Jerry got a warm, natural sound. Peter Fritch at Lyrichord, which had released the Nielsen disc, agreed to add the recording to his catalog, and it was well reviewed on its release.

During all this activity I was shocked to read in February that one of my students had been arrested in an attempt to hijack a plane. Tammy had been one of my earliest students. Her mother brought her and her brother down from upstate New York for lessons each week. I think I was chosen because I lived in the same building as her brother's trumpet teacher. When I opened the door each week, this young teenager would stride past me without greeting, head down, to my living room. She would unpack, put her music on the stand, and start playing. Over the next few years, she would become a little more trusting and outgoing, and actually laughed at me one day when she saw me on the street. "I never thought of you as a real person," she explained.

She was a bright, artistic, and imaginative person, a sensitive musician, and a talented flutist. Her Christmas presents were always self-made – a tree decoration, a watercolor, a cutout paper design, a box of origami birds. A suicide attempt was an indication of her instability, but the thought that this delicate, sensitive young person could do anything violent was incomprehensible.

After using a spray can that they said was a bomb, she (flute case in hand) and her boyfriend had been easily apprehended. Although she was obviously mixed up, and a follower rather than a leader, it was absolutely the worst time to be caught in such an endeavor, and in May, eighteen-year-old Tammy was sent to federal penitentiary.

In the early summer I received my first letter from her, sent through her mother; she had been given permission to play her flute, and needed guidance and support. We exchanged letters until she was released on parole at the end of the following year. I was not the only person she wrote to, and her beautiful, intimate thoughts were published in book form in 1973, with her own artwork on the jacket.

Following her release, she was accepted by The Manhattan School as a flute major, received her degree, and began freelancing in New York. Although active in new music circles, she didn't quite have the necessary stability to be a successful professional performer and began looking for alternatives. She wrote a funny novel, which was never published. Later she was accepted into Harvard Law School. She is now a successful lawyer in Manhattan, and the joyful mother of twins.

The post-season revivals at City Center extended to the middle of June with an interesting series of zarzuelas. After the quintet made a flying visit to North Carolina for a concert at UNC Greensboro, the Wions went off to Australia.

Our enlarged family made staying with my mother impossible, so, after looking at various options, we rented a house. It was a large brick house, and it was freezing inside. We borrowed all the space heaters we could to try and make it comfortable – until we got our first electric bill. We would go outside into the winter morning and find it warmer than inside! We began socializing. We watched the moon landing on black and white TV. I recorded my two programs for the ABC and made trips to Sydney and Adelaide for informal sessions with flute students, arranged through their teachers, David Cubbin and Victor McMahon.

In Melbourne, Les Barklamb decided to take advantage of my presence and that of an even more established former student, Doug Whittaker (principal of the BBC Orchestra), to start a flute society. He invited former students from around Australia to participate, invited the MSO principal, Czech Arnost Bourek, and, to an enthusiastic and large audience, presented a long, unwieldy, but memorable concert. He was a truly proud father that Sunday afternoon.

Not one to ever say "enough," he organized another concert just before I left, asking me to play the Bach *Partita* and Varèse, and participate in the Anton Reicha *Quartet*, changing parts each movement. In addition, Keith Humble arranged two concerts for me. The first was an intimate recital in the Percy Grainger Museum at the University, but the second assumed more considerable proportions.

Keith's student from Paris, percussionist Jean-Charles François, had recently moved to Australia as the MSO's tympanist. Keith proposed that the three of us rent a hall and put on a concert of twentieth-century music. No one else in Melbourne would have presented such a venture. My contribution was Debussy, Varèse, and Davidovsky, and participation in a trio by Gilbert Amy. I did a newspaper interview, where I shamelessly derided Australia's lack of support for, or interest in new music and appeared on a TV talk show. For the concert we dressed all in black. We got a large and enthusiastic audience and terrific reviews in all the press. And, as Keith later wrote me, we didn't lose any money. On the other hand, the sum total of two active months didn't come close to covering the cost of one airfare. I wanted to do this on a regular basis, but I would have to try harder to make it pay for itself at least.

A high school friend came to the trio concert to renew our association. Jeremy Barrett, my best friend at "Grammar" and my reason for going to Trinity, resurfaced as a painter – talk about all us repressed artists coming out of the closet! His work was in abstract geometric design, largely acrylic on canvas. We visited his studio and came away owning one, which we still enjoy. On a later trip, my visit to his studio was for some reason rather coldly received. Perhaps he was just going through a bad period, but we have not seen each other since.

Strangely, at just such a concert in New York a couple of years later, another high school friend showed up out of the blue. Tony Archer, a bright, bubbly iconoclast, who had participated with me in some theatrical productions at school, had spent several years in India and was now in New York – yes, painting! He was honest about his work: "I paint snails, water color on paper, and, for the "up" market, tigers, oil on velvet. Most painters only have a couple of things that they re-hash continually. I admit it, that's all." We spent a couple of pleasant evenings together. Then he disappeared from our lives again.

The fall season brought tremendous excitement with Arrigo Boito's *Mephistofele* staged for Treigle, and Gaetano Donizetti's *Lucia Da Lammermoor* staged for Sills. Tito Copobianco's direction of the Boito was brilliantly original, Rudel was at his absolute best in making the most of this flawed score, and Treigle, rake-thin in his body stocking, leering through his heavy make-up, was a triumph. The opera started with a blacked-out theater, the downbeat for the orchestra being given via penlight baton. Heightened aural effects were obtained during the opera from the surround sound of brass choirs and choruses in the balconies to add to the visual effects on stage. Screaming whistles added cacophony to the overwhelming finale.

Sills was fantastic as Lucia. In her biography she was kind enough to comment on my contribution to her mad scene. "John memorized the entire mad scene, cadenzas included, and he played it while standing next to the conductor. He never took his eyes off me." When she was directing the company, and watching Lucia performances from the house this was true. However, at the time when she performed Lucia, the flutes sat behind the first violins, and I was unable to see her at all. I got crucial cues from the conductor, and for the rest relied on her absolute control and predictability. We had rehearsed together, of course, so I knew what she wanted to do. I didn't actually get to see her performance till she sang at the Met a few years later during the season I subbed there. I would play for many Lucias after her – Rita Shane, Pat Wise, June Anderson, Ruth Welting, and Gianna Rolandi come immediately to mind – but none inhabited the role as totally as she did.

Once again, Los Angeles and musicals ended the year.

1970

The spring opera season introduced me to Britten's *Turn of the Screw*. Its chamber orchestra scoring demanded considerable virtuosity from everyone, in my case on flute, piccolo, and alto. Quite the opposite was a new production of Debussy's *Pelléas et Mélisande*, with Julius conducting and Pat Brooks as Melisande. While this is a work of great beauty and was well received by the audience, the flutes had very little to play. Also new this season was Rossini's *Cenerentola*. Of particular interest was Frances Bible's singing of the aria on which Chopin based his flute variations. Although I enjoyed the Lucias and Seraglios and the return of Shostakovich's *Katerina Ismailovna*, I was more involved in events away from the theater.

Bill Brown, founder of the Lark Quintet, had decided to form a new ensemble of winds and strings. Drawing on his experience with the Nielsen recording, he was able to obtain the patronage of the Netherlands Consul by agreeing to play at least one Dutch work on each program. The group was called The New Amsterdam Ensemble. The membership came basically from the opera orchestra. Gilbert Kalish would be the pianist, and Rudel would conduct where appropriate.

My solo contribution this first season at Carnegie Recital Hall was Schubert's *Introduction and Variations on "Ihr Blümlein alle"* from *Die Schöne Müllerin* with Gil. Although we received a nice review for it, my real memory is that this was the moment in my career when I decided that excessive body movements would make a better impression. Fortunately, our newly arrived au pair, young Sydney flutist Suzy Powell, came to the concert and set me straight.

Less glamorous, but equally rewarding, were the concerts given during these years at the Bloomingdale House of Music on Manhattan's Upper West Side. One program this spring included a memorable performance of Ravel's *Chansons Madécasses* with Jan de Gaetani. The pianist was the highly respected lawyer Bob Miller.

With the demise of City Center's light-opera wing, large blocks of time were now available at the old house on Fifty-fifth Street, and the orchestra faced a potential drop in income. Over the next years, the void was filled by a number of visiting dance companies, as well as local ones like the Joffrey, Paul Taylor, and Alvin Ailey companies. During one of the latter's seasons I had the thrill of sitting beside the legendary jazz flutist, Frank "Magic" Wess.

After Ballet Theater's glamorous season at the State Theater, with Erik Bruhn and Carla Fracci in La Sylphide, and an exciting Petrouchka under Schermerhorn's pulsing direction, I left for a two-week trip to Australia. I fitted this in before the month of August, which Vicky and I had set aside for Martha's Vineyard. I had envisioned such a trip during the previous year's visit, and had worked towards it from my return to New York. I was trying to create a situation where I could spend a large part of my northern hemisphere summer in Australia, in some combination of performing/teaching residency. Ultimately I dreamed of a position in a conservatory that would accept as valuable the concept of a four-month residency. It was a fantasy. My immediate goal was to find enough "gigs" to cover the cost of my fare. I wrote to all the universities, the music clubs, the TV stations, the flute societies, colleagues, friends, and, of course, the ABC. I actually achieved my goal but only by working every day.

Getting off the plane at ten in the morning after twenty-four hours of travel, I met the director of the Melbourne Conservatorium for lunch and spent the afternoon teaching a class at his institution. This residency provided the basis for my trip. In the early evening, I had a rehearsal for the following night's ISCM concert, where I was to perform Lou Harrison's Concerto for flute and percussion. This did not present a problem until the director Keith Humble pointed out that the notations ♯ and ♭, requested by the composer as indications that the following note should be sharpened or flattened, meant not that F sharp, for example, should be sharpened, but that F natural should be sharpened. My training was so automatically to finger F♯ when I saw F♯ that I just couldn't adjust. I finally had to excuse myself as jet lag took over; I went to my mother's home to sleep. Instead I lay awake wondering how I was going to survive the next day, and its now terrifying concert. Eventually I did sleep and awoke to find that the problem was not insurmountable; I went on to teach and participate in a well-received and enjoyable concert. (Many years later one of my students contacted Harrison who said this was in fact an incorrect interpretation of his notation.)

Another day of teaching, then a quick trip up to Sydney to play an evening concert arranged by the local flute society. Back to Melbourne for a lunch hour concert with Humble and François at another university, and back to Sydney to rehearse the Carl Reinecke Concerto and Kent Kennan Night Soliloquy with the Sydney Symphony the following morning. An unaccompanied lecture recital at the University of New South Wales was followed by an afternoon tutorial with the ABC's training orchestra. Next morning I taped the concertos for later broadcast, and flew to Melbourne for an afternoon class at the conservatorium

The next day I taught some more, rehearsed with pianist Margaret Schofield for a broadcast of the Reinecke Sonata, and flew to Adelaide. In Adelaide, David Cubbin and I rehearsed and taped a program of baroque duos and trios for the ABC, and I gave an evening class for his students. The second week began with a rehearsal for a concert of baroque music, which we performed that evening. The next afternoon was a concert sponsored by Lufthansa in the art gallery. Immediately I flew back to Melbourne where I spent the evening recording the Reinecke, along with the Bach Partita and Arcade 3, which Humble had written for me. I had done the premiere at our ISCM concert; this was a version with tape accompaniment – the tape consisting of a synthesizing of my earlier performance. Apart from my need to coordinate with the tape, it didn't present any new problems.

The following day I played a lunch hour recital at the conservatorium, and spent the evening with family. In the morning I flew to Sydney for a rehearsal and an evening recital. I was also supposed to play a lunch hour concert at the University of Sydney, but I withdrew. In my negotiations throughout the year I had finally agreed to a minimum fee of $50 for any engagement. (The ABC paid $75 for their broadcasts.) When I phoned the university to make final arrangements, I was informed that the fee would be $40. Reluctant to cancel, I offered to play an unaccompanied recital, which would at least save me a trip to the campus to rehearse. I actually thought I heard the professor sniff as he said that didn't sound too interesting. On that down note I flew to New York. In two weeks I had played eight concerts, taped music for three broadcasts, and taught six classes. I felt I deserved my month on the Vineyard.

After struggling to find a replacement for Patanè, the opera introduced Giuseppe Morelli in the fall. He was a lovely, elderly gentleman from the same school as Patanè, but if he had once had the fire to go with his elegance, it had gone. As one golfing wit in the orchestra put it, "you feel like asking him if he minds if you play through." He was quite a ladies' man, and occasionally, if things went just a little more briskly, you felt he might have a date ahead.

The most emotion I ever saw on his face came during a particularly sleepy matinee of *Butterfly* in Washington one spring. Both the second and third acts of this opera start in similar fashion – four-four time with the first three beats silent. The fourth beat in Act 2 is for unaccompanied flutes; in Act 3 it is a loud entrance for the entire orchestra. On this occasion, maestro Morelli somehow thought we had already played Act 2 and gave the grand gesture of commencement for an orchestral tutti. When the plaintive two flutes were the only response, his calm repose gave way to a split second of sheer panic.

This season introduced the Donizetti "Queen" operas to our repertoire with *Roberto Devereux*. By the time we had gotten to the third of them a few seasons later, some mutterings could be heard in the orchestra that maybe someone was writing these things as we played. In truth, they were not too much fun for the orchestra, but they provided a wonderful vehicle for Sills. If *Julius Caesar* had put her on the map, these made her mark permanent. We didn't see much of her heavy Queen Elizabeth makeup except at curtain calls, but the fury of her stage presence was plain to the ear. However, it was also the heavy drama of these roles, substituting for her lovely lyrical elegance, that I felt started to make her vocal mannerisms and problems more evident. Although she was to give us many more superb evenings, I felt she would not have an extended career. In his final season with us, Domingo was the ardent Devereux.

Our most recent contract provided a penalty rate for playing more than thirteen performances in two weeks. For the first time, therefore, I was able to get a regular break, which I tried to take on a Saturday or Sunday. (Our weekends usually consisted of a Friday afternoon dress rehearsal and five performances.) Recently a pirated tape of one of this season's *Devereux* performances was released on CD, to capitalize on Domingo's later fame. (I find that though I feel used when we receive no payment for these thefts, the historian in me is glad that the moment has been preserved.) I purchased a copy to discover that this performance was on a Saturday night I had chosen to take off.

The other hit of the season was Janácek's *Makropoulos Affair* (twenty-five years before it appeared at the Met). The orchestra played the awkward score with great skill and Maralin Niska had a personal triumph as the "everlasting" diva Emilia Marty. The production by Frank Corsaro with its film projections was the talk of New York. City Opera seemingly could do no wrong. Niska and the elegant Johanna Meier were a great asset over the next years, until Sills removed them from the roster when she took over.

The Lark Quintet, apart from its school concerts, participated in a concert of Swiss music in November at the Recital Hall, spending many hours struggling to tame Heinz Holliger's fiercely difficult quintet H.

In Los Angeles for our annual opera season, The New Amsterdam Ensemble took advantage of a free evening to make its local debut, and I got a very nice review for our Mozart D Major Quartet.

The year ended with a dance season and Menotti's *Amahl and the Night Visitors* instead of Rodgers and Hammerstein.

1971

Vicky and I had been thinking for some time about buying a weekend place. Knowing nothing, we thought a hundred acres an hour from the city seemed about right. Quickly, that became ten acres within two hours of the city. We began looking at ads in The New York Times the previous fall and bought the first place we looked at. Eighty miles north of the city, the house was a small, one-bedroom box built in the fifties, with nothing particular to recommend it until the owner took us for a walk over the property.

The land was a nine-acre strip about a hundred yards wide, running up from the road at the bottom of a little valley. Next to the road were a creek and a swampy meadow. The dirt drive went steeply up a hundred yards to another meadow where the cottage was situated. Behind that, the property went up another three hundred yards to the crest of a ridge, from which we had a sweeping southern view down towards the city. You could see no fences up there, and no neighbors. The sun was shining as we walked back down and looked at the brilliant fall foliage on the opposite slope across the valley. It was spectacular. The cottage, which would be sold fully furnished, consisted of a kitchen, a tiny bathroom, a bedroom, and a living room with fireplace. An unfinished cellar was accessed by a trapdoor and a steep little stairway led to low-ceilinged attic, also unfinished. It was all we needed for the moment, and the price was right. We were really buying the land. If it didn't work out we would sell; if we liked it we would build an addition. We closed in January and took possession. Everything was bare, and three feet of snow covered the driveway as we parked on the road and trudged up to the house. The fuel-oil tank was almost empty, and we had no prospect of delivery. We certainly had a lot to learn.

Our snowed-in cottage.

Thirty-five years later we were still learning. Over the years we sealed the driveway, we built our addition, we turned the swamp into a pond. It was a great place for the kids growing up and income from renting it later on helped put them through college.

The spring opera season introduced me to Gustav Charpentier's *Louise*, Verdi's *Ballo in Maschera*, with Gilda Cruz-Romo before she became a Met staple, and Menotti's latest, *The Most Important Man* — not, as it turned out, the most important opera.

Again, my interests were more in chamber music and trying to create more solo work. Both the Lark Quintet and the New Amsterdam Ensemble were active. The latter's Carnegie series included the Stravinsky *Octet*, the Mozart *D Major Quartet*, and Pierre Boulez's *Sonatine*.

The Boulez was something I was determined to conquer. I had bought the music some years before and tried unsuccessfully to follow along with Severino Gazzelloni's recording. I would learn much later that this was at least in part because he and his pianist had a casual approach to ensemble. Each would go like crazy through a section, re-grouping before heading off into the next.

With our performance scheduled for April, Gil Kalish and I had a lot of preparation to do. Hour after hour I worked at my part, and week after week I strode up West End Avenue to his apartment to try and fit our parts together. We made slow progress on all but one horrendous piano interlude, which we always skipped. One day, I arrived to a broadly smiling Gil. "I finally decided I had to learn that solo section and set aside a block of time yesterday. But the more I looked at it, the more I said, 'I know this music.' Then I realized that George Rochberg had quoted it in one of his piano pieces that I'd had to learn years ago!"

On the solo front, I had been in contact for some time with the director of the Martha Baird Rockefeller Fund about the possibility of a grant to do some recording. I believed that I had finally won approval and that a quickly scheduled audition was just a formality. I was in the middle of the opera season and my other activities and didn't give it much attention. I played with the pianist they provided and, not surprisingly, did not make much of an impression on the judging panel.

I had been also writing to my Australian contacts and believed that Keith Humble was making a grant proposal to the arts council on my behalf. To my great disappointment he never got around to it, and I was back to scrounging around for a workable package. I decided to try to add New Zealand to my itinerary, and by the end of April had worked out a little tour and a radio broadcast there.

The Australian part was tougher, and not until just before I left for Auckland at the end of May was the repertoire settled. In mid-March the ABC had offered broadcasts with the Brisbane and Melbourne orchestras, as well as one with piano. Not until two months later, however, did they write again asking me to learn some Australian concertos, which they still hadn't sent me. They also sent a list of more standard concertos for which they had orchestral parts, should I not have time to learn more than one new concerto! Music arrived, and I agreed to learn the *Concerto* by William Lovelock, an Englishman residing in Australia. For the rest, I proposed the Reinecke *Ballade*, the Saint-Saëns *Romance*, and the Hofmann *Konzertstück*, pieces for which I either had or could borrow parts. They agreed and promised me a solo part to the Lovelock (they had sent me a piano score) on my arrival in Australia.

New Zealand, at this time, was very isolated and, perhaps for that reason, I was made to feel most welcome. I played at four of the universities and taped two radio broadcasts. The latter provided me an interesting learning experience. I was recording Debussy's *Syrinx* in a small fiber-glassed room and hating it. The engineer explained that when they added reverb it would sound just fine. I had not come across this process before, so I reluctantly made a "take" and went to listen to it. He was right – the sound was beautiful, but I wasn't *playing* beautifully. I went back and played again with that other sound in mind, and everything turned out fine.

The other surprise came with playing Mario Davidovsky's *Synchronisms* with tape. At the first run-through at one of the universities, I thought I must be suffering jet lag or something. Not only was I sharp to the tape, but I kept getting ahead of it. The engineer explained that New Zealand's current was 50 cycles instead of 60, so the tape actually was turning slower than 7.5 inches per second. I pulled out the head-joint and took a nice leisurely tempo.

The Saint-Saëns/Hofmann session in Melbourne went very well considering the circumstances. At ten o'clock in the morning, the studio was cold. We read through each piece, then we taped a performance. The Saint-Saëns was simple enough; but the Hofmann had some very sloppy tuttis and some messy ensemble moments, and I ended the slow movement below pitch. However the conductor seemed happy to leave it at that and dismissed the orchestra. As the policy was to not splice tape (they would record right over the previous performance), I suppose he thought a second performance might not be any better.

The Lovelock/Reinecke session in Brisbane produced similarly sloppy orchestral sections, but at least it was warm. Mr. Lovelock came to the taping and seemed delighted. Brisbane was very provincial at that time, and I couldn't wait to leave. However, the four-week tour had opened up some interesting possibilities. I was already thinking about the following year.

The remainder of the summer passed quickly between Caramoor and Martha's Vineyard, and I was back in rehearsal for the fall season. Three operas were new for me: *Cosi Fan Tutte*, Carlyle Floyd's *Susannah*, with an amazing Norman Treigle as Rev. Olin Blitch, and Britten's chamber opera, *Albert Herring*.

This latter was to create my most serious problem at the opera to date. The combined flute/piccolo/alto flute part was even more challenging than *Turn of the Screw*, and the weight of the alto was proving to be particularly troublesome to my right hand. During the first rehearsal I was easily swayed by an assertion by our horn player, Bill Brown, that we should be paid a premium for such work. I went to John White, Rudel's associate, where I was summarily rebuffed. If nothing else was possible, I asked that I be relieved of the alto part. In fact both the oboe and clarinet players were already having second players to cover the English horn and bass clarinet parts. Instead of a discussion, I got a phone call from the contractor saying I had been rotated out of the production entirely, and my second, Florence Nelson, would play that opera. To say I was angry would be an understatement, but contractually, I actually had no argument. The union became more and more involved, and things started getting out of hand. As I simmered down, I met with Julius and smoothed things over. But I had missed my chance to play this great score.

My big excitement that fall was the opportunity to play the Bernhard Molique *Concerto* with a local amateur orchestra conducted by the Lark's clarinetist, Art Bloom. I had previously decided that, if I was to make any dent in the solo field, it would be through playing and recording unfamiliar repertoire. Specifically I felt the nineteenth century was worth exploring – even the Reinecke *Undine* was largely unknown at this time.

In looking for concerto repertoire, I had spent a reading session with Dobbs Franks, an irrepressible conductor from Arkansas who had gone to Australia to conduct for the Australian Ballet, and who had conducted my Reinecke *Concerto* in Sydney the previous year. I had been discussing with him my hope to record some concertos in Sydney, using the grant I was sure I would get from Martha Baird Rockefeller. On a visit to New York, he came to my apartment, and we read through a whole bunch of nineteenth century works I had gathered. The surprise was the Molique. I had read through it as a student and played its beautiful *Andante* in lots of concerts. I remembered the *Rondo* as being somewhat charming and the first movement as a bore. Now we discovered that the first movement was actually strong. I needed only to find a set of parts.

Les Barklamb had told me he had played Molique with the orchestra when he was young, and that he had used his own parts. Now, however, he claimed that he didn't recall where the parts had come from. I was sure they must be buried in his garage or attic, but I could hardly argue. Neither the Library of Congress nor the Fleisher Collection listed it, and neither the original publisher in Germany nor the reprint publisher in the States could help. I tried the British Museum and other libraries in Europe to no avail.

I was talking on the phone to the music librarian at the Library of Congress about something else, and asked his advice about Molique. As if by magic, he pulled out an old catalogue from Mapleson's – originally librarians to the Metropolitan Opera – and said that it had been listed for rental. I phoned Mapleson, and was told by the person on the phone that he had never heard of Molique. I explained the circumstances and was asked to hold. When he came back he said they did have some parts, but not a complete set, and no score. They had parts for one flute and two each of oboes, bassoons, horns, and trumpets, plus timpani and strings. Presumably, at least one flute and two clarinet parts were missing.

A bit later I was talking to the librarian at the great Fleisher Collection in Philadelphia (which had provided the Hofmann parts). "I know you don't have it listed, but do you know anything about the Molique *Concerto*?" "Well, actually, we do have some parts, but never catalogued it because the set is incomplete." What parts did they have? Exactly the same as Mapleson's. Excited now, I asked if he would send me one of each part, as I thought this must be the complete instrumentation. He did. I made up a full score and compared it to the published piano reduction – nothing was missing! So, in December, I finally got my chance to hear this wonderful piece. None of us gave a terrific performance, but it made me eager to perform it again and to record it.

To end the year on a perfect note, the following week, the Larks, minus oboe, recorded the beautiful Ludwig Spohr *Quintet* for the Vox label. The pianist was Mary Louis Boehm, who had made a specialty of playing music from this period. Though Rutgers church was cold at midnight when it made most sense to record in New York, the session went well. *Stereo Review* featured the recording as "Best of the Month" when it was released. "How a group of New York musicians of the Seventies could be so sensitive to the Biedermeier sensibilities of Central Europe in the 1820's is beyond me, but there it is."

I had missed the opera season in Los Angeles for these two events, but they were well worth it.

1972

My travails at the opera mounted during the spring season, which held little excitement apart from Beverly Sills's performance as Maria Stuarda, and the debut of a young Spanish tenor, José Carreras, as Pinkerton in *Madama Butterfly*.

Those travails came to a head during the post-season residence at Washington's Kennedy Center, one Saturday between shows. I was scheduled off from the evening performance, and Julius requested a meeting, at which he gave me a working over. He said that everything wrong with the wind section was my fault; that I had a bad attitude. He went on and on, as I sat stunned. He ended by saying I should give serious thought to leaving. In turmoil, I slowly managed over the next days to ask my colleagues what was going on. Relieved to talk, they all explained that our oboist had been trying to gather support for getting rid of me.

I thought about how to handle the situation, and finally asked for a meeting with Julius back in New York, where I repeated everything I had been told by my colleagues. From that moment our relationship improved, and he eventually invited me to play a concerto with the orchestra at a Caramoor Festival concert. I played the Hofmann and he gave me a wonderful accompaniment. It was the best performance I did of that piece, but unfortunately one that was neither reviewed nor taped.

Other interesting things were going on in my life. Two of the more unusual events around this time involved jazz greats old, Benny Goodman, and new, Ornette Coleman. Goodman was considering doing a concert or perhaps a recording of classical wind quintets. Lenny Hindell, the Lark's current bassoonist, became involved, and arranged for me to be invited into the group. It was a strange situation, working with this legend in his lovely apartment on the Upper East Side. He was inexperienced with the repertoire, and somewhat defensive about his shortcomings. We had a few sessions, then the project fizzled out.

The Coleman connection was Art Bloom, the Lark's clarinetist. Ornette had written a wind quintet, and we were hired to play it in Carnegie Hall – not the recital hall, the big hall. We assembled in his Soho loft and got to work. All five parts were totally different – bars, meters, tempi, overall length. It didn't matter he said. We slowly sorted out what he had in mind, and in due course presented ourselves backstage at Carnegie.

Art began by walking out on stage alone, sitting down, and starting the piece. A minute later Howard Howard on horn joined him. Eventually we were all on stage, wailing, and Ornette was behind a screen listening intently. The audience grew restive; we heard groans and whistles. One by one we each finished our music, and at last, mercifully, it was all over and the lights went up for intermission. Eventually the penny dropped, and we realized that we were the warm-up act. After the intermission the "real" quintet would be on.

We would some time later participate in one of Ornette's recordings – another bizarre experience. While a scat singer sang and Ornette's group wailed, we sat in a corner of the studio playing stuff he had written that seemed totally unrelated to anything else. In the playback I heard it didn't seem to matter too much.

During the spring, I also played a nice performance of Henry Brant's *Angels and Devils*, with my opera colleague Gerardo Levy conducting, and participated in a terrific performance of the Stravinsky *Octet*. This was part of a New Amsterdam Stravinsky concert that Robert Craft conducted at Alice Tully Hall. The concert was in honor of the opera's bassoonist, Ryohei Nakagawa, who was leaving to join the San Francisco Symphony, much to my sorrow. On the same concert our clarinetist, George Silfies, gave a spectacular reading of the *Three Pieces*.

Deciding that our boys at six and three were old enough to appreciate Europe, we invited Vicky's brother Steve along as baby-sitter and set out for London. With our Australian friends Tony and Janneke Casson as guides, we visited Hampton Court. Then we took the hovercraft to France. Not surprisingly, it turned out that the most memorable treat Paris could offer our boys was the amusement park in the Bois de Boulogne.

En route to visit Vicky's family in the south of France, we stopped near Lyon for our first "three star" dinner, at Fernand Point's legendary Restaurant de la Pyramide. This was our first experience with a full French menu. Foie gras in brioche was followed by a mousse of trout in a truffle sauce. Salmon with champagne sauce was followed by duck with green-peppered cream sauce. Cheese was followed by not one but four desserts, including the celebrated marjolaine cake of cream, chocolate, and nuts. By the time the meal was over, we could only waddle and giggle. The kids enjoyed their own meal in our hotel that night. For years after, Russell's birthday request was for turbot with hollandaise sauce.

Russell

The biggest event of the year was being invited to participate in the Newport Music Festival. The other members of the quintet had played the previous year, and they had lobbied successfully on my behalf. Now in its fourth year, the festival had grown out of a summer season of the Metropolitan Opera at Newport and was the brainchild of one of the opera's administrators, Glen Sauls. He had taken one look at the mansions and saw chamber music, nineteenth century, in their ballrooms. Glen settled in Newport and planned and organized each festival. His partner John Stranack acted as music director. The concept was brilliant and the festivals were brilliant, except for two minor problems. Glen drank a lot, and John didn't read music.

The two-week event in July consisted of concerts in the mornings, afternoons and evenings. The daytime concerts tended to be shorter and lighter, to attract the tourists who had come to Newport to visit the mansions. The evening concerts were more glamorous, and attracted the local society. The performers, drawn originally from Met instrumentalists and singers, consisted of mixed strings and winds, pianists, and at least a vocal quartet. Sometimes a dance program or chamber opera was scheduled.

Anthony

John Stranack planned the programs by sifting through old concert programs, encyclopedias, biographies, and histories to find forgotten composers who had been celebrated in their time. Then he scoured the world's libraries to track down their long out-of-print music. His basic theory once a piece arrived was: if it has lots of black notes, go with it. Some forty programs were put together, each with a catchy title, many with a theme. Then the performers arrived to see what they had to deal with; usually, a piece would not get its first reading until a day or two before its scheduled performance.

Once the elegant, glossy festival program book was printed, we were under great pressure to perform these scheduled works. Usually we did – at least in part. Many composers capable of writing pretty tunes were unable to develop their material, so we might cut right from exposition to coda. Our resident violist, Emanuel Vardi, was called Dr. Vardi for his skill in reducing the proportions of some of these pieces. Every now and then we found a real winner, and we were responsible for a return to the repertoire for many composers. Every now and then we hit on a loser that even Dr. Vardi's considerable talents couldn't save. En masse we would descend on Glen and insist that we substitute an encore performance of one of the hits.

The ballroom of the Breakers, the Vanderbilt summer cottage, was the spectacular site for the evening concerts. A stage was set up at the foot of the grand staircase; the open French doors on one side looked across the portico and sweeping lawn to the ocean. My less than glamorous debut consisted of an evening of ballet. I played Arthur Foote's *Night Piece* and some wind quintets, but we were off-stage and generally ignored.

Over the next days, I participated in concerts at the Breakers, Rosecliff, and Marble House, on the cruise boats, and in a quintet concert outdoors at Fox Hill Farm. I was introduced to the *Theme and Variations* of Mrs. H.H.A. Beach, the August Klughardt Quintet, Amilcare Ponchielli's riotous Quartet (a takeoff of an operatic scene for flute, oboe, clarinet, and Eb clarinet with piano accompaniment), and played Cecile Chaminade's *Concertino* with a quasi chamber orchestra made up of whoever was available.

The highlight came in a Breakers concert of hits from previous festivals, where my assignment was Giulio Briccialdi's *Ballabile di Concerto*, a bravura concertino of three connected movements, for which Peter Basquin played the piano reduction. This was not the only reduction. I had so many notes to play, and so few rests, that I had to reduce the music, so as to fit several pages on the stand.

I was a nervous wreck the whole day of the concert, and it took me a while to settle into the piece, but the storm of applause at the end was a new high for me – it was like the reception to a great aria at the opera. Press coverage of the festival was extensive, but the Briccialdi was singled out for praise. One reviewer wrote, "The *Ballabile* had John Wion sending out the pearliest of sounds from his flute and a brilliant, coloratura display to boot. Wion had the fair sized audience mesmerized by a virtuosity which seemed to encompass 85 notes to the bar." It was hard not to be flattered. I couldn't wait for next summer.

The fall opera season was memorable for a strange new production of *Don Giovanni*. No one seemed to approve of the musical interpretation of Italian composer Bruno Maderna. He took a Boulez-like approach to the score. He insisted on whatever marks were written in the score and none of those that weren't – not a very satisfying approach to Mozart. The performance was clean and neat and metronomic and quick, but it didn't work.

Outside the opera, I played the Bach *B Minor Suite*, again with Gerardo Levy, and gave a recital at the New York Flute Club with Gil Kalish. To give variety to this program I added the Molique *Quintet* with violin, two violas, and cello. I had recently found a copy of it in the British Museum and had read it through with some colleagues from the orchestra. They now joined me for this first of many performances of this delightful music.

Of final interest was a chamber music concert in New Hampshire organized by oboist Phil West. What most intrigued me was meeting pianist Robert Levin. (Bob, who would go on to become a recognized musicologist, had among other qualities an astonishing grasp of the U.S. highway system stored away in his memory.) Our program included the Beethoven *Trio* for flute, bassoon, and piano. Every pianist with whom I have played this piece has commented on the awkwardness of the piano part – surprising given the keyboard skill of the composer, even if he was young. Bob was no exception but soon solved the mystery. "This must have been written for a two manual keyboard," he decided.

The year ended as usual in Los Angeles and in New York at "the old house" on Fifty-fifth Street. I was already well into planning a Pacific trip with Gil Kalish for the following summer.

1973

I celebrated my birthday by playing a Carnegie recital with my harpist friend, Susan Jolles. It was a lovely event, which included transcriptions of Bach and Enesco, but the highlight was the Debussy *Sonata* with Larry Fader joining us on viola.

The interesting new opera for the spring season was Henze's *Der Junge Lord*, which introduced the former director of the Met, Rudolf Bing, in an important non-singing role. Carreras was singing a lot of the Italian repertoire, and a young Sam Ramey made his debut. I was more interested in my summer activities, New Zealand, Australia, Newport.

When in November 1971 I received a letter from the Chamber Music Federation of New Zealand regretting that they would not be able to offer concerts in 1973, I was not surprised. Such rejections were the rule. The surprise was a letter a month later offering a tour of at least eight recitals. I spent much of the next year defining and refining this tour and writing to every prospect to build around it. When it came time to actually sign a contract, Gil Kalish's hesitation gave me a bad moment, but he finally agreed, as long as I guaranteed his expenses. He then decided to take his two young sons along and make this into something of an adventure. Eventually everything fell into place, and at the end of May we headed off to the University of California at San Diego where Keith Humble, now a professor there, had arranged for us to play our opening recital. Nothing old for this avant-garde La Jolla crowd, we began with Olivier Messaien and ended with Pierre Boulez, and included Mario Davidovsky, Chou Wen-chung, Luciano Berio, Henry Cowell, Edgard Varèse, and, naturally, Humble. Then Gil took his boys to Hawaii for a quick look, and I caught up with Keith and Jill in their new life.

After the long overnight flight, I arrived in Auckland to find that the Kalish party had not arrived as planned. A couple of scary hours later they were found, safe in bed at their hotel, and the tour began.

We were offering two programs: Bach E Minor, Davidovsky piano *Synchronisms*, Schubert *Variations*, Boulez, and Reinecke in the first, and Bach B Minor, *Syrinx*, *Density 21.5*, Milhaud, Messaien, Berio, and Prokofiev in the second. After my initial surprise at the sea of faces welcoming us to the first concert in Auckland, we settled into a most invigorating schedule, interspersed with humorous moments when our cultures didn't quite mesh.

Our major problem was lack of heat. None of the halls were centrally heated, most having some form of electric space heat, which was used to take the chill off the room until the audience generated enough warmth of its own. For rehearsals we were lucky if we got a single radiator on stage to tease us.

Food was another problem. New Zealand had few restaurants at that time, fewer still that were open after our concerts. So we were fed at the post-concert reception. As the guests hovered around with glasses of wine, we were seated and fed at a table. But everyone was most hospitable, and the audiences were large and enthusiastic. We were continually surprised that these towns of forty thousand would produce audiences of four hundred. The whole country had a population of only about four million. One saw more sheep than people, and to see another car on the road in some parts was an event.

Our strangest evening was spent with Americans, some sixties hippie types who had escaped to Paradise. Being graciously invited to join them for dinner, we planned how we could escape if things got awkward. The homemade beer was unusual, but the real problem was a special break in their vegetarian routine – a friend had provided fresh venison. This they pan-fried, and after joining hands for a ritual chant we began trying to cut and eat it. The former was a challenge, the latter an impossibility. They offered no dessert – they had taught their children that such things were not "goodies" but "baddies." Things were looking grim as Gil and I eyed each other after our merciful release from the table. However, before we could swing into our escape routine, our host stretched out his hand and said, "Well, I'm sure you two must have a lot of things to take care of."

With Gil Kalish.

I had arranged to record the newly written Walter Piston *Concerto* with the broadcasting orchestra in Wellington, under its resident English conductor. Doriot Dwyer had just premiered it in Boston; I was aware of it because Art Bloom had copied the parts. I was waiting in my hotel to be picked up when the orchestra's manager phoned to say that the conductor was running behind schedule on the morning's recording and wouldn't get to the Piston till the afternoon. This did not bode well for a piece that none of us had yet heard.

By lunchtime he had still not finished, but I was taken to the studio to be ready. After an hour the maestro came in and apologized. He was looking forward to the Piston, which he said he had played through with someone in London. Knowing this could not possibly be true, I became suspicious. After the orchestra's mid-rehearsal break, we finally got to work, with about an hour left. No sooner had we started, however, than the conductor suddenly said, "Where are the trumpets?" Well, they had no parts, so they had left. The manager went in one direction to find the players, the conductor in another to look for the music.

After about fifteen minutes, both were successful and we tried again, with less than half an hour left. We read through the opening, rhapsodic section, but when we came to the quicker, alternating meter music, things fell apart. The conductor proposed recording the first section. By then time was up. He raised a fainthearted question about whether overtime was allowed, apologized once again, and said he was going right to the management to complain about their scheduling so much material on one day. He shook my hand and left – both the studio, and New Zealand, on the evening flight to England.

Slowly I put it all together and realized that he had engineered the entire day to avoid dealing with that score. I met him again several years later when he conducted a Caramoor concert. I reminded him of our day together. With a wicked twinkle in his eye he said, "I was naughty wasn't I."

On my next free day of the tour, I was flown back to Wellington for another crack, this time with the concertmaster conducting. He did a perfectly professional job, but unfortunately, as with all my New Zealand performances, I was unable to get a copy of the tape.

In Melbourne I did all I could to see that Gil and his boys had an interesting time during their four day visit. Our recital, drawn from the two New Zealand programs, was a huge success. Headlined "Recital of the Year," a glowing review ended, "It is this sort of artistry that turns critics into PR men."

Before Gil left, we were also able to record two half-hour programs for ABC broadcast. We had been asked to play two Australian works along with the Prokofiev and Boulez. The sessions went very well, apart from Gil breaking a string in the Boulez.

My attention turned to Molique. The ABC had proposed my playing Georg Philipp Telemann's *A Minor Suite* with the Melbourne orchestra, when I had been suggesting Piston. They regretted that Piston was not conservative enough for their concert programming needs, but I could make a studio recording for broadcast. I declined Telemann and proposed Molique. They counter-proposed Mozart and eventually accepted Molique. Then the Piston recording was dropped because of conflicting schedules.

I was pleased by the way the Molique went, as well as by the reception it received at all three concerts. The critics didn't have much praise for Molique, however. One headline read, "Wion injects life into insipid music." The conductor was a young Israeli, Yuval Zaliouk, and he provided an excellent accompaniment, as well as excellent company. When I got back to New York, I made a private LP from the broadcast performance, along with the Hofmann and Reinecke *Ballade* from my earlier trip. After paying all the expenses for the tour I lost about $750, but it was absolutely worth it.

Then it was back to Newport. Accommodations for the festival were in the dormitories of Salve Regina, a Catholic college. The rooms were Spartan, two single beds and a chest of drawers, and the bathrooms were down the hall. Rehearsals took place downstairs in the common rooms, where breakfast was also offered.

In this my second year, I started to have a better feel for the society that supported this endeavor. One of my favorite people came to be Kittymouse Cook – Mrs. Benjamin Cook – born Vanderbilt. White-haired, she was in her vital eighties, and would chuckle over how she used to play ping-pong in the gold room of Marble House, where she spent summers as a kid. A most beautiful life-size oil painting of her as a child adorned a wall of her present house, where she made us all feel welcome.

The Lark Quintet performing in 1972.

Longtime artists would stay there as her guests; newer ones used it as a place to change before swimming off her beach – something she did every day. She had an irrepressible humor, a perpetual twinkle in her eye, and a great ability to reduce any social pomposity to its base reality.

My first formal dinner was at Lydia Foote's, and Kittymouse gave me suitable preparation. Even so, the ritual amazed me. Everything was strictly timed and structured. What I really loved was that the hostess started the dinner by talking to the gentleman on her right, whereat every other gentleman began conversing with the lady on his left. Seemingly without cue, in the middle of the event, she turned to the gentleman on her left to converse, and the other guests followed suit. Finally a bell tinkled, and she led the ladies into one salon, while the gentlemen moved into another for "cigars and brandy."

The power behind the festival was Anne Brown, wife of John Nicholas Brown, President Truman's Assistant Secretary of the Navy for Air. Although quite detached and patrician, she had a great ability to move through a reception speaking warmly to everyone and then disappear without anyone being aware. Much more approachable was Bill Crimmins, who was always lending a hand with something or offering someone a lobster roll. The more distant figures were the Auchinclosses, the von Bulows, the Firestones, the Wood-Princes, and of course the Countess Szapary, current Vanderbilt resident at The Breakers.

This year, I also had some input into what I performed, choosing the Molique *Quintet* and the Schubert *Variations*. However, the real thrill was the concert at The Breakers where we played the Hofmann Octet and the Rheinberger Nonet, two fabulous pieces, virtually unknown before Newport. The strings included the great violinist Guy Lumia, Emmanuel Vardi on viola, and the legendary George Ricci on cello. We brought down the house.

After the regular family August on Martha's Vineyard, I had, as a member of the orchestra's negotiating committee, to deal with the biennial skirmish at the opera. This time we had hired the renowned lawyer Victor Rabinowitz to represent us, but the result was no better. Right after opening night we went on strike, collapsing into a settlement a month later, when cancellation of the rest of the year was threatened. For our pains we got a three-year contract.

The highlights of our shortened season were Delius' evocative *A Village Romeo and Juliet*, and my first *Ariadne auf Naxos*, with a sparkly Pat Wise as Zerbinetta. Our Donizetti "three queens" cycle ended with Sills at her most dramatic as Anna Bolena. Placido Domingo returned, but as a conductor, in *Traviata*.

1974

Kalish and I had booked Carnegie Recital Hall for our New York "debut" recital, February 5, and I had asked my friend Marjorie Kaplan to manage the event. Marjorie and her husband Dr. David Kaplan had been among our earliest friends at 180 Riverside Drive, living two floors above us. She had lived many lives – as interior decorator, nurse, art dealer – and was a free spirit who was always on the verge of something original and outrageous. A collector of people, she gave frequent parties which never failed to be interesting. You might meet an Algerian UN diplomat, a *New York Times* correspondent, a writer, a painter, or an actor. You never knew just whom she might have charmed. Once, when Peggy van Pragh, director of the Australian Ballet, was staying with us Marjorie arranged, at Peggy's request, to have the playwright Marc Connelly join us for dinner. (Among Marjorie's idiosyncrasies was an aversion to central heating, so she had all her radiators removed. After she sold the apartment, when the first icy wind blew across the Hudson, the bewildered new owners phoned the building manager to ask how to turn on the heat.)

She did a perfect job as a neophyte manager, and the concert was successful. Donal Henahan wrote a pleasant review in the *Times*. Everything was favorably received, and the word "splendid" was even used once, but I sensed a certain coolness that was disappointing after the enthusiasm of our recent tour reception.

The highlights of the spring opera season were Cherubini's *Medea*, which starred a brilliant Maralyn Niska, and in which I was delighted to find a lovely extended flute obligato, and Sills's latest triumph, Bellini's *I Puritani*. I also met an Australian debutante, soprano Glennys Fowles. Although she would go on to play a leading role at City Opera until she was swept out along with Niska and Johanna Meier when Sills took over, she began, modestly, in a new production of *The Mikado*.

This production was used as a backdrop for the movie *Foul Play* with Goldie Hawn and Chevy Chase. We spent over six arduous hours recording the overture and several selections. I was amused to hear Julius, listening to an early playback, say, "But nothing is together." That was always a problem with his conducting, but he had to hear it through two speakers to become aware of it. His skill was in the drama and vitality of his presentation, not necessarily its neatness. The cast later filmed their parts during our L.A. tour, lip-synching to the recording.

When I finally saw the movie I had to laugh. The overture, which we had spent so much time on, started the movie when the owner of the recording put his new purchase on the turntable. After a few seconds, however, he is killed and falls over the phonograph, stopping the music. The *Mikado* performance, which purported to be taking place at the San Francisco Opera, used our performers and sound for brief snippets, but filmed, I presume, the local orchestra pretending to play.

I played a lot during these years with the Orchestra Da Camera, a Long Island based ensemble that mostly played school concerts. However, this spring they had a fund-raising concert at Lincoln Center's Alice Tully Hall and asked me to play the Mozart *D Major Concerto*. I had not performed this piece since I was in high school and I thoroughly enjoyed the experience. I decided to offer it for the next Pacific tour, already a subject of correspondence.

That spring I declined my final offer of an Australian job. At different times I had been under consideration for principal positions in different orchestras. These offers had finally ended when I refused to audition for the Melbourne orchestra. I was known to the members of the orchestra from my youth onward, and I had played concertos with them. The union insisted, however, that I audition like all other applicants.

Now I was approached again, to teach at a new national conservatory in Canberra, the country's capital. The wonderful Doug Whittaker, another Barklamb student, who had spent his career as principal with the BBC orchestra in London, had no sooner returned home with his family to take up the position of head of woodwinds, than he succumbed to a heart attack

The offer from director Ernest Llewellyn was persuasive, and Vicky and I seriously considered it. I felt that my job at the opera was limiting my growth and after ten years becoming something of a routine; and I felt that chances of another orchestral position were minimal. A teaching position in the New York area seemed unlikely, and the thought of a position that would encourage my solo ambitions was tempting. Vicky and I sent off a list of questions, the answers to which would help us make our decision. We waited and waited for a reply; finally, having to make decisions about the immediate future in New York – everything from remodelling a kitchen, to schools, to employment commitments – I wrote to decline. As it turned out, a prompt and satisfactory reply had been sent surface mail by mistake and arrived a couple of months later.

After the Caramoor season, I went to Newport for my third festival, where I had been given a concert of my own, a morning concert in the gold room at Marble House. I began the program with my two latest finds, the Bernhard Romberg *Quintet* and the Heinrich Hofmann *Serenade*.

The former I had found in the British Museum. It was one of a set of three works for flute, violin, two violas, and cello, published as the work of Andreas and Bernhard Romberg. An examination of the music showed that two were by Andreas and the third, which was superior, by Bernhard. While I personally preferred the Molique, it was nevertheless a fine piece and was well received.

The Hofmann had come from the Fleisher Collection in Philadelphia and turned out to be absolutely charming. Scored for flute and string quintet, it is one of only a handful written for such a combination. I would learn later that the commission was from a German flutist, Eugene Weiner, who had settled in New York, where he played concerts with a string quintet in lieu of an orchestra. Following the success of this *Serenade*, Hofmann had re-scored some others of his works so they could be played by these performers. These manuscripts are now in the collection of the New York Public Library. I ended the program with Franz Doppler's *Hungarian Pastoral Fantasy* and an abbreviated Giulio Briccialdi *Carnival of Venice*. The overflowing audience was enthusiastic, as were the critics, not only about my playing, but about the "shamefully neglected" composers Romberg and Hofmann.

I could hardly expect the rest of the festival to match this high point, but I was sufficiently disappointed by my remaining assignments that I later wrote a letter to program planner John Stranack to that effect, making some suggestions for future festivals. I must have had my head in the clouds.

The biggest joy was hanging out with that year's subbing oboist, my dear friend and colleague from NYCO past Basil Reeve – at least until our dinner when I bit down on a fragment of lobster shell and sheared off half a molar.

Earlier in the year, I had seen a notice for a convention of flutists that would take place in Pittsburgh in August. With considerable trepidation I flew off to see what this was all about. I discovered it was the second meeting of the National Flute Association, which had come into being the previous year in Anaheim, California. The experience was overwhelming. Not only did I meet and hear such orchestral legends as Donald Peck of the Chicago Symphony, Bernard Goldberg of Pittsburgh, and Michel Debost of Paris, but I heard Albert Cooper speak about his improved flute scale and was introduced to other new ideas in flute making. I had arrived feeling very alone, not knowing any of the non-New Yorkers; I came home inspired, with many new friends, feeling now a real part of the flute world. Still, little could I imagine that in ten years I would become the president of this organization.

The greatest pleasure of the fall opera season was being introduced to Puccini's beautiful *Manon Lescaut*, which Maralyn Niska sang with great fervor. However, my thoughts at the end of the year, while playing opera in Los Angeles and the American Ballet Theater season in New York, were much more on a curious stroke of good luck. I had gotten to know Kazuko Hillyer, manager of the Tokyo Quartet, through our children being in the same class at The Ethical Culture School, and had mentioned the idea of playing a concert with string quartet. Naturally, the Tokyo was impossibly booked. Then a cruise it had been hired for in January 1975 was canceled, and Kazuko phoned early in the year to see if I was still interested. I had reserved Alice Tully Hall for my birthday and began planning.

1975

I was so lucky with the Tully Hall date. Very few were open in the period when the quartet and I were available. Naturally, January 22 popped out at me when offered. Someone had a hold on the date until the middle of April. When pressed at that point for a commitment the person declined and I grabbed it. No sooner had I done that than he phoned Tully back to reclaim the date, but was told it was too late. I had chosen a program of Newport pieces, Molique, Beech, Foote, and Romberg, along with the Mozart D Major Quartet. The fact that both Molique and Romberg called for two violas was a potential problem, but Kikuei Ikeda, the second violinist, assured me that he was equally adept on viola.

(Photograph by Craig Perkins).

Our first rehearsal was scheduled for early January in the basement of a house in the suburbs that the quartet used for this purpose. After reading through the pieces they seemed surprised that I had little to say. But their reading was of a higher level than any of my previous performances. What could I say? I was thrilled.

Marjorie Kaplan again handled the publicity and managed to create a fair amount of interest. We got a good-sized, appreciative audience, played a lovely concert, and had a great party at Bert Lucarelli's afterwards. Mr. Henahan was warmer in his praise, concluding that we "played the entire program with the utmost polish and homogeneity." Altogether, it was a nice birthday celebration. I had hopes that I might be able to record some of these pieces with the Tokyo, but Deutsche Grammophon, to whom they were contracted, politely declined. However, I do have a tape of the concert to remind me of this special event in my life.

I was able to squeeze in two more concerts before the spring opera season claimed my time. In a program that Gerardo Levy organized at the Greenwich House Music School in the Village, I asked to play Doppler's *L'oiseau des Bois*, in addition to my other assignments. The flute is the bird in this piece, twittering and trilling at a great rate, to the evocative background of a quartet of horns, placed, in this performance, off-stage. That was a lot of fun. More seriously, I played the Molique *Concerto* again with an orchestra in Brooklyn, conducted very capably by Martin Canellakis.

Things were going better for me at the opera, in terms of my relationship with the management, and the year gave me much enjoyment. In the spring I was introduced to *Turandot*, in a splendid new production, the somewhat worn sets for which had come from Venice. In a potentially disastrous accident, a rather large Turandot fell through the set's high platform during a dress rehearsal in Los Angeles later in the year. Catherine Malfitano was the touching Liu. *Salome*, with Niska in the lead, was also both challenging and satisfying. I sometimes think that no one is really listening to the orchestra, so I took it as a compliment when a friend in the audience overheard a comment from behind, "Wait till you hear what this guy does with the flute solo."

In all, however, the biggest thrill, challenge, and surprise was Erich Korngold's *Die Tote Stadt*. The production by Frank Corsaro, with its imaginative projections and scrims (none of which I saw of course), was a tremendous success. The leads, John Alexander and Carol Neblett, sang with great fervor and beauty, and the famous "Marietta's Lied" brought down the house. The post-Straussian score was a challenge to the orchestra – I have never seen a flute part with more notes.

In the fall, the company had a big success with Sills's stage-filling *Daughter of the Regiment*, but my personal joy, I think my best opera experience ever, was *Die Meistersinger*. This was lovingly conducted by Julius, and nobly sung, in English, by the great Norman Bailey as Sachs. John Alexander was Walther, and Johanna Meier was Eva. The flutes have little to play, but I was so overwhelmed by the musical experience that I actually took a performance off and went out front to enjoy its entirety.

When I found I had no chance of recording Molique/Romberg with the Tokyo Quartet, I was able to interest the excellent Manhattan Quartet. I approached Dr. Naida, the head of the Musical Heritage Society. He accepted, agreeing to pay the production costs and a $360 advance in royalties – 18 cents for each of the two thousand copies they would press. The players accepted this as their fee, so I was in business.

The sessions took place in April at the CBS studio, under the direction of Naida's assistant, Dan Nimitz. I found it a very strange experience. The idea was to record in quadraphonic sound so that each player (the two violas were treated as one) would have an individual microphone and track. The results could later be manipulated and mixed as desired. At the time I didn't understand what this meant; I only knew that we were being asked to make intimate chamber music seated in a big circle, about eight feet apart from each other, with the directional microphones in the center pointing out. I suppose it was a measure of our professionalism that anything came of it at all.

Alice Tully Hall Flyer, 1975.

After the never easy process of making the editing decisions, I went back to the studio with Nimitz in December, between the Los Angeles opera season and the American Ballet Theater season, to prepare the master tape. This we took to the CBS engineers for the mixing session.

The first question I was asked was what (or who) did I want each player to sound like? It was just a question of listening to each track and boosting certain frequencies to change the quality of the player's tone. I was given several examples of such modifications and only recall that I asked them not to change my flute sound, please. Then the four channels had to be mixed down to two and the instruments placed and balanced. Did I want the flute to appear to be in the middle or on the left? If on the left, here or six inches more toward the center? Each option was demonstrated. I found it all very weird.

Eventually the recording, for which I wrote the liner notes, was released, and I eagerly took a copy home to play. I hated it. Apart from anything else, something had gone wrong in the pressing, and the two channels were not equally balanced. MHS promised that they would correct it for the second pressing – right! But I couldn't complain too much – they had been sufficiently impressed by the music and my playing that they had agreed to record the same two composers' concertos.

After signing my contract for Newport and agreeing, additionally, to act as librarian and general organizer of rehearsals, I took off with Vicky and the boys in May for a Rome-to-Paris trip. After a few days in Rome, where I got sick just thinking about driving in that madness, we rented a car, and with the help of a very kind gentleman who led us to the correct exit ramp, headed north. One of our goals was to visit Bussetto, Verdi's birthplace, where we stayed at the inn that the tenor Carlo Bergonzi had opened so that pilgrims could visit in comfort. We visited the theater which the townsfolk of Bussetto had built for Verdi. This theater is a one-fifth-size copy of La Scala. Verdi's operas were performed there, though I don't believe he ever attended.

At magical Lake Como, I received the news that Glen Sauls had been fired from Newport and wondered how that might affect me. From Como we drove straight across France, suffering a nightmare Friday afternoon rush hour traversal of Paris to return our car. With no money and no hotel, we left our bags and took a metro to American Express. While Vicky stood on one line to deal with money, I stood on another for a hotel. When I got to the front the young lady, obviously already thinking of her weekend, said, "I am sorry monsieur, Paris is full." We returned to collect our bags and consider whether we would have to spend the night in the airport. Nearby was a new high-rise hotel, and we decided to give it a try. The reception area was mobbed, but we worked our way forward. Do you have two rooms? Yes. Do you take credit cards? Yes. We didn't ask the rate, just started crying with relief.

Back in New York, I found a message to phone Ann Brown in Newport. Yes, Glen had been fired. Apart from his drinking problem, some questions had arisen relating to the endowment fund. The board had hired a businessman, Mark Malkovich, to direct the festival and would like me to serve as his music director. Unbelievably flattered, I flew to Newport to meet with Malkovich, was charmed by him, and signed on. In every way, this ended up a big mistake. I eventually realized that I was the necessary body who could offer continuity, who could make possible the musical running of this year's festival, the programs for which were largely in place. Mark signed my program book, "Music Director extraordinaire!" But I heard that he was angry that I had been listed as such. He made it very clear the following fall that he had his own ideas for future programming and had no further need for my services. I felt truly used.

I spent the month before the festival running myself silly, gathering together the strands of programs, renting music, hiring extra musicians, scheduling rehearsals, and incurring the wrath of Sauls and Stranack who believed I was somehow the cause of their problem. They had planned for the festival to present a two-year celebration of the country's bicentennial, with all

American music. But the festival's nineteenth-century focus didn't offer much of true importance to draw on, and the 1975 part was something of a critical and financial flop.

My solo performing contributions consisted of some Sydney Lanier, and the Hanson and Persichetti *Serenades*. In addition, with the entire Lark Quintet back in residence, a full program of American quintets had been scheduled. (The quintet repeated this program in the fall in Scranton, Pennsylvania. We played a terrific concert. It took the presenters an hour to rustle up music stands, expecting we would have our own. By that time we just *had* to make it worthwhile for the audience.) To fill out a rather weak and incomplete Saturday evening concert at The Breakers, I proposed an un-conducted Stravinsky *Dumbarton Oaks*, which calls for fifteen players. I got some grumbling and grandstanding from some of the string players, but we pulled it off.

In August, my mother came from Australia for a quick trip, and my cousin Eleanor came from Pennsylvania to participate in the event. On her return to Australia, my mother wrote that my brother David and his wife had separated. Following her earlier visit my brother Richard and his wife had also separated, so the therapeutic value of her visits was rather diminished.

My extracurricular activity as the bicentennial approached was to compile and publish a family history. I had been collecting material ever since I had arrived in New York and felt this was the right time to collate it. Using library phone books for addresses, I wrote to cousins all over the country, amassing their current history and tying it into my research. In these pre-computer times, I had to hire someone to retype my Smith Corona version. Then I sent the pages off to a printer.

It turned out to be quite a slim volume. Apart from some suggestions of the early eighteenth-century migrants to Pennsylvania, I outlined the history of the descendants of my great-great-great grandfather John and his wife Catherine, who had arrived in Central Pennsylvania from somewhere further east just before 1800, tenant farmed, and raised thirteen children. Of their six sons I was able to find descendants of only four – Solomon, John, and the twins, James and my own ancestor Benjamin. James's line disappeared in the Civil War with two sons dying as prisoners in the South and the third having a single daughter. So my book traced the remaining three lines to the present, mostly in Ohio and further west, and in our case, Australia. In the New Year I proudly sent my first publication to the many cousins who had ordered it.

1976

My bicentennial year began with American Ballet Theater, now playing in the new Uris Theater on Broadway. This had a dreadful pit, completely unsealed from strong, frigid winds that swept in from the back. The most memorable event was the premiere of *Push Comes to Shove*, Twyla Tharp's ballet for Mikhael Baryshnikov.

I was more involved with the Bernhard Romberg *Concerto*. I had been made aware of Romberg by my friend and neighbor, Piero Weiss. Piero, a most cultivated pianist of Italian descent, had ceased concertizing and become a musicologist. He and his wife Carol became as good friends as our children had become, through living in the same building. After dinner one night, I had mentioned I was looking for nineteenth-century concertos and asked him to look through the alphabetical listing in Franz Vester's catalogue of flute repertoire.

The two names that struck him were Mercadante and Romberg. I had no success with the former, but I did track down the latter concerto in the famous Musikfreunde Library in Vienna. It sent me a microfilm of the set of parts – no score or piano version existed – which turned out to be slightly out of focus and barely readable. I did however impose on some colleagues to try and read it through one afternoon. From that I felt confident that this was a solid enough piece for me to write back to the library and ask for real photocopies.

Following my success with the Romberg *Quintet* at Newport, the violist in that performance, Emanuel Vardi, was enthusiastic when I proposed playing the *Concerto* with his community orchestra in New Jersey. I made up a full score, as I had done for the Molique, and got down to learning the piece, now scheduled for performance in February, before the opera claimed me. I was delighted with the results and the enthusiasm from both audience and orchestra. I now had a piece worthy of recording with the Molique and set a date in June to do so.

The spring season at NYCO introduced Beverly Sills as Lucrezia Borgia. For once I was not blown away; I still had my Caballé memories. Of particular interest was *Ashmedai*, a contemporary Israeli opera by Josef Tal that was particularly badly received. However, the money that made it happen also paid for its conductor, Gary Bertini.

This was the kind of first-rate conductor that we normally couldn't or wouldn't afford, even if our seasons were planned far enough in advance to make such things possible. He turned out to be a first-class leader and a perfect gentleman. Hoping to draw us into this rather thorny work, he told us the story in some depth. As he did so, with considerable eloquence, it occurred to me that sitting as we do we rarely know what even our most popular operas are about. With a twinkle I asked, "Maestro, could you tell us the story of *Traviata*?"

Also this season we made our first live telecast, *Baby Doe*, with Ruth Welting in the role that Sills had made famous. And not the least of the season's activities was preparing for contract negotiations.

The New York Flute Club got into the celebratory spirit of '76 with a March concert and subsequent recording featuring American composers. My contribution was the charming *Danse des Moucherons* by Sydney Lanier, the Civil War poet and flutist. The same month I also managed to squeeze in a Telemann *Suite* for Gerardo Levy's Caecilian Orchestra concert and Fukushima's *Mei* for a Japan Society concert.

As my June concerto recording date approached, I became concerned about my ability to master some very awkward passages in the first movement of the Molique. I met with Lark clarinetist Art Bloom, who would conduct, to play through the concertos and I made my familiar stumbles. "John, you're not cutting it," he said. I went into my spiel about Molique being a violinist and not writing very thoughtfully for the flute: "We'll just have to do it in sections and splice it together. Do you have a better idea?" He looked me right in the eye and said, "If the recording was tomorrow I'd say to cancel it, but you have a week. Why don't you practice?"

So began perhaps the first time I had ever really practiced. Confronted so forcefully, I finally faced the matter head on. I said to myself something that has since become familiar to all my students: "If I can't play this passage at 132 to the quarter (my preferred tempo), then what speed can I *really* play it at?"

The answer was a sobering 96. So I built on that. Not allowing myself to move through the moment of "beginning discomfort," when normally I would have shrugged the feeling off and plowed ahead, I moved the metronome forward only when the previous speed was effortless and totally reliable – "a piece of cake," I now describe the feeling. On the day of the recording the only splices made were because of orchestral errors.

Musical Heritage Society had hired the CBS studio for four hours in the afternoon, from two to six. The orchestra was mostly made up of my friends, so I felt well supported. I decided to record the outer movements of each concerto, assuming they would take the most time. Time, of course, was the problem. With the twenty-minute contractual break per hour for the orchestra, I actually had two hours and forty minutes. Some of the tuttis were difficult, particularly in the first movements, and the orchestra was seeing the music for the first time.

While the orchestra practiced the opening of the Molique, the engineers arranged the microphone balances – no more mixing for me! We started recording. I was using a meditative technique at this time of my life, and I feel it was instrumental in getting me through this long, stressful afternoon. On the orchestra breaks, I was able to sit in the control room and completely relax. Even so, time disappeared in a way that always happens at recording sessions. One is allowed fifteen or twenty minutes of finished product per hour of session, depending on the situation, but it is rarely achieved. I have spoken to engineers who figure one minute per hour in certain repertoire.

The Molique took too long to get down, so the tuttis in the Romberg were less successful. When we got to the two slow movements I only had fifteen minutes left. Everyone was tired – only I was running on sheer adrenaline and willpower. With no time to rehearse, we started the beautiful Molique slow movement. I knew I wouldn't get a second chance and focused myself accordingly. Suddenly the bassoon made a false entry – no point in continuing. We went back to the closest point where a splice might be made. But Art, who had done such a terrific job all afternoon, was also tired. He didn't check his tempo and began slower. I tried to move him but couldn't. The orchestra lumbered on to the end. Five minutes left to sight-read the Romberg slow movement straight through and it was all over.

Every time I hear the moment in the Molique where it gets slower, I wish I had paid for another half hour. But it was a very expensive afternoon, and I don't know if people could have stayed longer anyway. The next morning, Vicky and I took the kids to Bermuda for a few days of well-earned R&R.

On July 4, we had a party so our friends could watch the historic parade of tall ships sailing up the Hudson. The trees in Riverside Park were smaller then, and we had a splendid view. To honor the day, I made omelets topped with red caviar, sour cream, and a blueberry.

Parade of tall ships on the Hudson, July 4, 1976.

Caramoor was then the first stop in a busy summer. This was the year that Julius had invited me to play a solo. He had proposed the Mozart *Flute and Harp Concerto*, but I asked him to consider the Hofmann. After listening to my tape, he agreed and scheduled it for a Saturday evening in July. The night before, we would be playing Britten's *Curlew River* again, so it would be a heavy weekend.

Julius and I met at the State Theater to run through the piece, with him playing a very musical version of the orchestral score on the piano. I had always enjoyed working with him at Caramoor, where he seemed like a different person dressed in a T-shirt, shorts, and sandals, always charming and witty, totally disarming. Now my appreciation for his skills reached a new level. He gave me such a lovely, delicate accompaniment, always supportive, always right there. I suppose I was the Beverly Sills for those few moments. Years later I reminded him of this experience, which had been one of the high points in my solo career, and he couldn't remember it at all.

<blockquote>
Julius Rudel, *conductor*
John Wion, *flute*
Charles Haupt, *violin*
Caramoor Festival Orchestra

PROGRAM

Symphony No. 5 in E flat Major, Op. 82 — Sibelius
 Tempo molto Moderato — Allegro Moderato — Andante mosso, quasi allegretto — Allegro Molto

Concertstuck for flute & orchestra, Op. 98 — Heinrich Hoffman

Intermission

Concerto in D Major for violin & orchestra — Paganini-Wilhelmj
 Allegro Maestoso

Symphonic Poem, No. 3 "Les Preludes" — Liszt
 (after Lamartine's "Meditations Poetiques")

Many in our audience have requested there be no smoking during performances. May we, therefore, respectfully suggest that you take note of your neighbor's comfort.
</blockquote>

Caramoor Festival program, July 10, 1976.

In Newport, I felt like a bit of an appendage. Mark Malkovich was starting to show the direction the festival would go. The stars were Régine Crespin and Andrei Gavrilov in his US debut. Mark also brought in some foreign performers who had names but not necessarily chamber music skills. Mercifully the American theme had been modified by considering the melting pot of cultures that made up the country. That meant we could play just about anything as long as the program had an appropriate title. The quintet played Nielsen and Barber, but my lone solo assignment was Quinto Maganini's *Night Piece* in a program dedicated to Newport's own composers. I was definitely on the way out.

At the National Flute Association I was on the way in. Don Peck, principal flute of the Chicago Symphony, was in charge of planning a two-concert traversal of the Bach sonatas for the upcoming convention. He asked me to play the *E Minor Sonata* to close the second concert on Sunday afternoon following Bernie Goldberg's *Partita*. This seemed a good way to get my feet wet, and I felt honored to be invited. Then I got a call from Bill Montgomery, who was the chair of the program committee. Tom Nyfenger had pulled out of the convention, and would I consider replacing him on the final concert? My assignment (this was before the NFA could afford orchestras) would be the Mozart *D Major Quartet* and the Arthur Foote *Night Piece* and, to go with the latter, an unpublished *Scherzo* by Foote that Montgomery had located in the Library of Congress. Considering that I had played Mozart and Foote with the Tokyo Quartet the previous year, I felt pretty confident in accepting.

I flew down to Atlanta with my Martha's Vineyard all-over tan to conquer the world. The convention had its strange moments. The most memorable non-musical moment was finding that not only had the hotel accepted another convention, but it had set up its Saturday night banquet in the foyer outside the ballroom where our concert was to take place – a concert that closed with a dashing Godard *Suite* played by William Bennett. Equally upsetting was the loud Muzak that suddenly burst into the middle of a Bach sonata being performed by a very pregnant Ellie Lawrence.

Of my own Bach I remember nothing in particular. The string quartet, while understandably a comedown from the Tokyo, were good musicians, and the rehearsal went well – the Foote *Scherzo* turned out to be a Mendelssohnian delight. But the closer I got to the evening concert, the more I clutched at the thought of performing for all these famous flutists. When it was over, I felt very disappointed at not having shown my fullest capabilities.

I had been trying for some time to find a tertiary institution to teach at, feeling frustrated that I was not able to work with serious students of college age. The opportunity came that fall when I was asked to teach at Kean College in New Jersey. I would just have a few students, and only one was really serious, but it was a start.

Of more direct concern as summer ended was the expected strike at the opera. Both sides would jostle to take the best advantage of the situation, but nobody doubted a work stoppage would occur at some time. I was heavily involved in the negotiations again when suddenly my life took an unexpected turn.

I had long felt that the only reasonable hope I had of moving up the orchestral ladder was the Metropolitan Opera; I had certainly done my apprenticeship. When Harold Bennett retired from the Met, his place had been taken by Victor Just, a respected player who had been with the ABC orchestra. Every now and then I would bump into Jimmy Politis, the other principal at the Met, who would tell me vaguely that Victor didn't seem to be working out. My Met colleagues at Newport made similar comments, but nothing ever seemed to come to a head. Suddenly James Levine asked Victor to retire, and then insisted that he stay home until the matter was finally arbitrated.

I was a very convenient stopgap for this interim period, though I was much too flattered and elated to think of it that way. With Julius's and the Union's approval I was given a temporary leave of absence to immediately change houses three weeks into the NYCO fall season, when the Met's rehearsal season began. With impeccable timing, our orchestra went on strike the following week.

What a thrill this was! I had played in the Met pit for Ballet Theater, but this was a whole other thing. In our rarefied field, I was about to see how the other half lived. The difference was remarkable, and I couldn't get enough of it. My first assignment would be *Die Meistersinger* with Sixten Erhling conducting, and "our own" Norman Bailey as Sachs – in German this time.

Politis asked me if I would play the whole thing. *The whole thing? Is he crazy?* He went on to explain that at the Met, one principal played the first two acts, and the other came in to play the two-hour-long third act. The flute part wasn't that demanding, he continued, and since his health was not the best, this would help him out. Of course I agreed.

Next was *Figaro* - no surprises there. Then we rehearsed *Aida*, which I had played only once, years before in Brooklyn. The orchestra's rehearsal room at the Met is enormous – a beautiful wood-paneled, high-ceilinged space that accommodates orchestra, chorus, and soloists, with enough expanse to not threaten eardrums. The front wall is mirrored, and risers for the singers have been built in the rear. We started rehearsing and I heard this incredibly warm, enormous sound from behind. I glanced in the mirror and saw, seated and appearing to be exerting no effort whatsoever, the Russian mezzo Elena Obratsova. This was going to be fun! An elderly Carlo Bergonzi had been summoned as Radames for the season's October opening.

As the weeks went on I got a clearer idea of how the system worked. In the first place, everything was serious – every rehearsal, every performance. If the other principal was scheduled for a particular opera, you were invited to all the rehearsals and paid accordingly if you showed up. You would also play the pre-dress rehearsal, so you were ready to step in if needed. The principals split the week, so you played three or four performances only. Normally you were assigned operas for the season, though standards like *Bohème* would be shared to even out the weekly load.

After the *Aida* opening, my next thrill was *Meistersinger*. Although I had loved my exposure at NYCO, this was another experience altogether. The orchestra was bigger and better (and sounded better in this pit), and when the final scene arrived with its brilliant lighting and trumpet fanfares, I could only feel blessed to be a part of it.

No sooner was the season underway than Jimmy Politis was taken to the hospital. He had an inoperable cancer and would not be returning. I was shaken. I had known and admired him since my earliest dates in New York at the Bear Mountain Festival. He was a brilliant man and fabulous flutist. My final visit to his hospital bed ended when his emotional daughter rushed in. I left and he died shortly after.

I had a meeting with the contractor Abe Marcus, and we agreed that I would become the "senior" principal (mostly meaning that I would play Levine's operas), and Trudy Kane would move up in the section to act as the other principal. Assuming I could get my leave extended, I would play through the spring tour that followed the New York season. Naturally they would have to have auditions, for both positions if the arbitration went as expected.

So I moved into an even more exalted realm. One of my first assignments was to take over Politis's *Il Trovatore*. This was a big production, with Pavarotti and Scotto; the conductor was the elderly, white haired, aristocratic Gianandrea Gavazzeni. As its run had already started, I was coming in a bit raw. One of the soprano arias contains a slightly extended passage with the flute, not something one would worry about. In the intermission prior to my first performance of the aria, I was asked to rehearse with Madame Scotto. I was met at the pit door by Marcus. We collected the conductor and went to Scotto's dressing room. In this large suite with dressers bustling around, I was introduced. Then a rehearsal pianist played, Gavazzeni conducted, and we went through the passage. I was thanked and returned to the pit – and I was paid extra to do this!

At City Opera, if we had a new Lucia who had not been given a rehearsal with me, I would be *told* to go to her room during the break. When I finally found it, I would be kept waiting while she dressed, then the two of us would muddle through the mad scene – no stand, no piano, no conductor, no money, no thanks.

My next wonder was *Lohengrin*, which I had last played in Melbourne in 1958. Levine conducted, and I found him magical. For this opera I sat next to the great oboist Al Genovese, who left for Boston shortly after. To hear his phrasing was a lifetime experience in itself. As usual for Wagner, the flutes have very little to play, but after one long rising passage, Al reached over and shook my arm, telling me how Levine had radiated joy (I think drooled is probably closer to what he said) as I played (I had my head down, struggling to get through in one breath). Maybe I had a future here.

The Magic Flute presented no problems. I only covered Massenet's *Esclarmonde*, revived for Joan Sutherland and conducted by her husband, Richard Bonynge. He could treat her, and did, as no other conductor could: "If you would just watch me luv, we would be together."

Then came *Lucia* with Beverly Sills, finally accepted at the Met. I thought it was neat that we two "second class" performers would be united again like this. I arrived for our rehearsal — yes, our own rehearsal, in the theater. I set up in the pit, next to the podium as instructed. She came onto the stage. Barely a smile, no recognition, a token "How's it going?" in a flat voice. Maybe her distance vision wasn't so good. Maybe, but I was really brought down.

The performances went well, and I finally got to see her. At one performance she threw me a curve in the middle of the cadenza by turning her back to the audience for one entry, meaning I couldn't know when she would start. Normally she was impeccable in such things, giving just the slightest movement of a hand to indicate the moment she started or planned to move off a long note. If one has to wait to hear the sound, it is too late to coordinate these passages.

Tosca, *Bohème* were a breeze, as was Poulenc's *Dialogue of the Carmelites* that the Met was getting to ten years after NYCO. I was only covering *Salome* and *Le Prophète*. Then, putting all else in the shade, came my first *Die Walküre* with Erich Leinsdorf conducting. Again, I had nothing to play, sometimes literally for half an hour, but to be a part of this! I loved Leinsdorf, who knew the score backwards and really rode the orchestra. The resulting performances were truly sensational, at least from my seat.

During all of this, I was putting together my Pacific tour for the following summer and rehearsing with Gil Kalish. As part of our preparation we played a recital for the New York Flute Club in October, performing for the first time the fine Ignaz Moscheles *Sonata*, which I had found at the Library of Congress. I had found it listed in their catalog, but when the volume was brought to my desk, it contained his piano sonatas. I went through it carefully anyway, and found the piano part for the flute sonata bound in. As was the publishing custom of Moscheles's time, the flute line was not included. I consulted with the librarian who had a sudden flash of inspiration. He sent down for the folder that contained the orchestral parts for Moscheles's piano concertos. Tucked inside was the flute part to the sonata.

An interesting extra-Met event happened when I was called in December to play in a concert at the UN. This was, quite coincidentally, a UNICEF benefit presented by Australia, and the soprano June Bronhill was to sing Adam's *"Ah vous dirais-je Maman"* variations with flute obbligato. The lovely evening was directed by Robert Helpmann. As Vicky had worked with him in Australia, I felt comfortable introducing myself. Dame Joan and her husband participated, along with Zoe Caldwell, Marjorie Lawrence, Cyril Ritchard, and other well-known Australian performers.

The year ended in unusual fashion as I spent the evening of Vicky's birthday playing *Lucia*. The next morning I flew to Los Angeles, where an audition for principal flute with the Philharmonic had been announced. In the midst of all this ongoing happiness, I had applied for the position and had been accepted into the final. Why was I doing this? I think I hoped the possibility of my being offered that position would lead the Met to drop its own audition plans and offer me the job. Well it didn't, so I had to follow through. Now, if I got the job there....

Crisis Looms

1977

The year of my fortieth birthday marked a major turn in my life story. The youthful sense of increasing expansion was coming to an end, and I would have to plan a new life course. Symbolically, the turning point might have been when the smaller apartment next to ours was put up for sale and we considered adding it to our own. The price was ridiculously low, though we were concerned about the additional maintenance charges. Realizing that in truth we only wanted one extra room, we began looking at larger apartments in the neighborhood. The search showed us just how lucky we were to have what we had, and we gave up thoughts of moving. Less symbolically, the first cracks were appearing in my playing ability, and my career aspirations were about to be brought down to earth.

The year began in Los Angeles. I stayed with our actor friends Bonnie and Bill Daniels while acclimatizing myself for the Philharmonic audition. The Daniels had recently moved west from our building, where our son Russell and their son Robert had become best friends. After a life basically in the theater, Bill wanted to move more into TV and movies, something he felt he could not achieve from New York. He moved first to test the waters, then the family followed. Enjoying their warm hospitality, I could not have been in a more relaxed situation for the audition, except that I was having technical problems in my left hand.

Probably the first indication was at the editing session of the quintet recording in 1975. Dan Nimitz, the producer, happened to mention how often I seemed to approach high G uncleanly from an ascending scale. Then, while playing at the Met the following fall, I began to notice a certain stiffness when I had a trill from G to G♯ or A. In preparing for Los Angeles, I was shocked to find in what poor shape the required excerpts were. Presumably, this was because these pieces were no longer in my repertoire, and, well, maybe I just hadn't practiced enough in recent years. I tried to force them into shape, but the Saint-Saëns *"Volière,"* always so easy for me, just refused to cooperate.

Having read something about the Alexander Technique of body awareness, I began lessons with a teacher near Lincoln Center. I learned a lot about basic body use and thoroughly enjoyed the sessions. I didn't see how to apply it to my flute playing, however. During one lesson, I asked if I could play for my teacher and launched into *"Volière."* A horrified look crossed her face: "you're like a wild man when you attack that." Well, I knew I put a lot of intensity into my playing, and I knew I could get awfully sore in the process, but surely I wasn't a savage. In any event, she didn't seem to have any suggestions, or maybe I still wasn't listening, and we didn't continue with this experiment. Years later, in different circumstances, I would achieve far more productive results.

The audition was on the stage of the Dorothy Chandler Pavilion, where I had so often played in the pit. (In fact, I was probably playing in the same pit raised to stage level.) Zubin Mehta and the committee were out in the hall. I felt I knew Mehta from his New York debut years before, and I knew the orchestra's new pianist, the astonishing Zita Carno from New York. Apart from her encyclopedic knowledge of everything about *Star Trek*, Zita had identified printing errors in the piano part of the Boulez *Sonatine* when she was learning it. The two of us now played through the Chopin *Cenerentola Variations*, and I moved into the excerpt phase, eventually to *"Volière"*.

My playing was messy, as I had somehow hoped it wouldn't be. The committee asked if I would like to try again. I thought for a moment and declined. They all had a nice laugh with me, and we went on to the ensemble phase. Seated with other wind players of the orchestra, I realized that this was what I really did – now I was making music! Not surprisingly, though, I didn't get the job. I wasn't too disappointed – I didn't really want this job – and flew back to New York, concerned more by how this would affect my standing at the Met, and vowing to get my technical act together.

I was playing on a new flute. After my eye-opening experiences at the Pittsburgh flute convention, I began to think of changing from my old Powell 480. For the last few years, I had been playing this with one of the new wing lip-plates introduced by Sankyo. As so often seemed to happen, I had not enjoyed a certain edgy quality in the sound that I heard in editing the recent recordings. I tried a new Powell, now being made to Cooper's specifications; then, while at the Met, I had acquired a gold Muramatsu, which I thought was a big improvement. The final touch was a Cooper headjoint that I bought from Baker.

I now was certain that I would have to audition for the Met job. The most recent player hired had managed to avoid the process and this had created resentment in the orchestra. A date was set for early March, and hundreds of applications came in. As Victor Just's retirement had been confirmed, two principal openings had been announced.

The orchestra's policy was that everyone would be heard, behind screens, in the preliminary round, including me. The exact material to be played was photocopied and sent to everyone, along with metronome markings, just in case people didn't know how the music was supposed to sound. The chairman of the orchestral committee told me that, because of my experience, I actually had an unfair advantage. I had fun with some of my colleagues. The excerpt from *The Barber of Seville*, a passage in triplets, is written in groups of two slurred and one tongued, and was written that way in the audition material. I knew that it was always slurred in threes because of its speed. So I asked the principal clarinet (the clarinets also play this passage) how I should play it. He replied seriously that I should play it the way it is written, because that's what all the inexperienced auditioners will do.

As the day approached, I became more and more uptight. I knew how these auditions worked. For the first few auditioners the panel could make comparisons, but after that discrimination was hopeless. The first thing the panel did was eliminate anyone who made a finger slip, which was human nature. So here I was playing in this great orchestra, making my share of mistakes along with the others, but having them say what a great job I'm doing, and how sorry they are that an audition is required. And then I would become an anonymous one-in-a-hundred, and they would be on the other side of a screen passing judgment. The statistical chances of making the final were close to zero, but I had to accept that my chances otherwise were truly zero.

The day arrived. Vicky, who was now expanding her new career staging Balanchine, was away. I barely slept the night before, and felt very much alone as I went to my locker at the Met. Colleagues wished me luck as they went off to their positions, and one member of the committee quietly wished he could know when I played. "No way," I said. "You people created this situation – you deal with it." I was scared and also mad. I played OK, but tensely, and was hurt to hear my good friend oboist Bill Arrowsmith ask to hear something again. As expected, I was eliminated. I found out by going to see one of the secretaries, who didn't know me and just went down a list.

I was devastated by the reality. I couldn't just show up that night, sit down, and make music with these "judges," and so I quit. For the next week I was an absolute basket case. The contractor phoned and said I had a contract for the season, that what I was doing was unprofessional. He certainly understood my emotional reaction and would give me the week off as sick pay. I could start back the following week.

I learned that one position was given to Trudy Kane. When the committee discovered that they had eliminated me, they declared no other winner. So, was I being offered the job? No, they would have to hold another audition. "And you will eliminate me again," I said. "No thanks!" One after another the committee members phoned me, pleading with me to come back. I learned that Trudy Kane had been recognized from a non-flute sound she had made – I don't imply it was planned. I was just too confused and angry and distraught to do much more than shout and quiver. Later, in more rational mind, I described my feeling about the whole process to Vicky's stepfather. It's as if I've been living very happily with someone who now says she has decided to get married, but thinks it makes sense to see what else is out there before settling for me. In the meantime, of course, there's no reason for me to move out.

I was very angry about the whole audition process. At the beginning of my career, if an opening occurred in a major orchestra, two or three principal players around the country might be invited to play for the conductor, who would choose one. When Baker went into the Philharmonic, I don't believe anyone else was considered, and I am sure he didn't audition. In a chain reaction people would move up the ladder and, possibly, some kind of open audition might be held at the entry level. Now I felt that, having reached the point in my career when I might have benefitted from this system, the rules had been changed.

The open audition favors the young performer who has all the excerpts polished, is in the routine of auditioning, and has nothing to lose. The older, busier player only prepares each particular passage for an upcoming performance. If you were about to be operated on, would you prefer the whiz kid just out of med school, or someone who has been around the block a few times? Oh, I was really mad.

So, suddenly, I was unemployed. I had been asked to cover a couple of things at NYCO in my free time and now was able to do a bit more subbing, but I could not resume my position until the Washington tour in May. I had, however, two concerts to prepare, one with Kalish, and one with the quintet. The former was a benefit concert in the Fifth Avenue penthouse of United Artist mogul, Steve Ross. We played material we were preparing for New Zealand – a Handel sonata, the Beethoven *Serenade*, the Aaron Copland *Duo*, and the César Franck *Violin Sonata*.

The latter concert resulted from an invitation to participate in a Westchester County series as a replacement for a cancellation. At this point, the quintet was nearly defunct, and I had to fudge the fact that we had no publicity photos or press kit to provide. We couldn't even get our clothing coordinated, but we played a first-rate concert of our standard pieces. I felt uncomfortable in that Howard Howard, our horn player, as well as the Met's, had been my principal promoter at the Met. I had a sneaking feeling that his politicking on my behalf had backfired in some way. I was determined to play a great concert and did so. His rueful comment after was, "If only they all could have heard you tonight."

In late March, when Vicky was working in Australia and I was feeling down, my student David Barg said, "Why don't you come with me on the QE2?" And so I did. David is a wonderfully outgoing, entrepreneurial type, who can make the kind of social gaffe that makes me cringe, and smile right through as if totally unaware. He regularly made this trip, usually with a pianist, as a way to get back and forth between continents, when studying or performing situations arose. For a couple of short concerts, a cabin and full board was provided.

The trip was interesting. The passengers were older and less glamorous than I had expected; this was the final leg of a round-the-world cruise, and the average passenger was well over seventy. Still we ate well, played lots of table tennis, walked the deck, and watched the shows at night. The highlight was finally arriving in Paris around 2 a.m. and going to eat at Au Pied du Cochon, a brasserie near Les Halles, that has since become my ritual for a first night in Paris. Fish soup with garlic mayonnaise and croutons, then off to sleep on the floor of one of David's friends for a few hours before flying back to New York.

I had been doing some serious thinking about my Met experience and how it related to NYCO. I knew now that this would be my playing job for the remainder of my career, and I wanted to try to avoid slipping back into a negative attitude. I decided that a big part of the problem was the schedule. Playing twice a day for six days a week, whether rehearsal or performance, was too much. I got too tired and felt I was just churning out stuff. Playing only three or four performances a week at the Met made each one seem like a special event, which of course it was. So, during the Washington tour in May, I approached Julius with a proposal. Let me trade my 25 percent over-scale for a four show a week contract, instead of the regular six. I presented my arithmetic, showing that it wouldn't cost the company anything and might even save them something. After some thought, he agreed.

The second Wion/Kalish trip to the South Pacific had been in planning since 1974. We had agreed on August 1976, but Gil suddenly informed me that he was unable to get away from his annual commitment to Tanglewood, particularly in that bicentennial year. We finally settled for the month of June 1977 – fourteen recitals that would begin in Suva, Fiji. In addition, I would play the Molique *Concerto* with Dobbs Franks and the Canterbury Orchestra and record the Mozart D Major *Concerto* and the Griffes *Poem* with the NZBC Orchestra for later broadcast.

We had chosen three programs. The first had Bach E Major, Luciano Berio *Sequenza 1*, Charles Ives "Alcotts" movement from the *Concord Sonata*, Copland Duo, Mozart K13 *Sonata*, and Franck. The second had Handel G Major, Olivier Messaien *Le Merle Noir*, Ignaz Moscheles, a New Zealand piece for flute and tape, George Crumb excerpts from *Makrakosmos* and the opening to *Vox Balenae*, and Nepomuk Hummel D Major. The third had J. Joachim Quantz, Schumann *Romances*, Beethoven *Serenade*, Berio again, John Cage *Amores*, and Prokofiev.

With Gil Kalish.

We presented this last program in downtown Suva to start our tour. The evening was tropical hot, and the theater's open sides let in not only breezes but also Saturday night's roistering. Prokofiev probably won out, but I doubt the more delicate parts of Berio were heard at all. We spent Sunday driving leisurely across the island back to the airport.

Gil was accompanied this time by his wife Dianne and twelve-year-old daughter Judith, to make up for their missing the previous trip. Where last time we had to make do with buses to get around New Zealand, we now either flew or used a rental car. This made for a much more relaxing trip and gave us more freedom.

The concerts went well, and we accumulated a slew of excellent reviews with headlines like "Flautist Triumphs," "Old and New Exhilarating," "Superb Concert," "Musical Revelation," "Wion's Artistry Is Impeccable." We did radio interviews, and our photographs appeared in the papers. Altogether the return tour was successful and hopes were expressed about us coming yet again. A new experience had been playing a quasi-baroque flute whenever a harpsichord was available. The wooden instrument was a conical bore Boehm system design, developed by a new name in flutes, Brannen Brothers.

I enjoyed catching up with Ruth and Dobbs Franks in their new home in New Zealand's south island. The former was concert-mistress of the Canterbury orchestra, and the latter provided a lovely accompaniment for the Molique. I was feeling much happier than I appeared in the rather severe and distant photo that ran on the March cover (back; Beethoven got the front) of the *Musical Heritage Magazine* when the concerto recording was released.

Musical Heritage Review Magazine, March 21, 1977.

At the end of the month, the Kalishes returned to New York, as I had been unsuccessful in arranging any July concerts in Australia. I did my recordings with Michi Inoue and the NZBC orchestra and, now joined by my family, flew on to Melbourne.

My dealings with the Australian Broadcasting Commission had been tortuous, as always. I had a good relationship with the New York office, but even they were frustrated by their inability to get answers from Sydney. Over two years of sporadic communication, three concerts with the Sydney orchestra in Sydney became two in Sydney and one in the country, then two in Sydney and a different engagement in Adelaide. Broadcasts with Kalish turned into concerts, but long after the period when Kalish was available.

Miffed that I was unable to play with Gil, I insisted that I would not prepare and play a duo recital with an unknown pianist. I would play a program of flute solos with and without piano accompaniment. They expressed surprise at my reaction; they had never considered Kalish because I had told them he was unavailable for the period in which they were planning these concerts.

Trio concerts with clarinet became trio concerts with cello, when the paucity of repertoire was explained. Sessions with the training orchestra were not in Melbourne as advised but in Sydney. A recording of the Amy Beach *Variations* in Melbourne was proposed. I offered to send the parts from New York but couldn't get a clear commitment. I finally packed them just in case. Then a letter arrived while I was in New Zealand, saying that they had just discovered from the original publisher in New York that the music was out of print. Unless I had the music with me, they would have to cancel the session, given they knew of no other repertoire for this combination! Advised that I indeed had the parts, they sent a telegram urging me to forward them "prontoissimo" [sic]. The project was finally canceled because the Xeroxed parts were not clear enough – the same parts the Tokyo had sight-read so brilliantly two years before.

I also had a problem with the fees. With the Australian dollar declining, my long accepted fees were eroding. Finally, they agreed to a formula to protect me. (In April the following year I received payment for two studio broadcasts, with a note regretting lack of earlier settlement "due to some confusion as to whether the recitals did take place.")

After the round of family reunions in Melbourne and an unaccompanied studio broadcast in lieu of the Beach session, I flew with Vicky and the boys to Adelaide for my performance of the Doppler *Hungarian Pastoral Fantasy*. The conductor was Henry Kripps, whom I reminded of our encounters twenty years earlier. He gave me a very stylistic accompaniment. I rather enjoyed the experience and was sorry that I left town too soon to get a tape.

With some bravado, as seen in retrospect, I interrupted my tour to take the family on vacation to central Australia. Australia is a big country and travel was, maybe still is, expensive. So I had never managed this wondrous trip in my youth. As I told my friends that we were going, they all said we would love it. Had they ever gone? Actually, no.

We flew to Alice Springs, made famous by Nevil Shute's *A Town Like Alice*, and then to Ayers Rock (now Uluru), an enormous monolith in the middle of nowhere. Nowhere may be relative, but one could travel a thousand miles in any direction from Ayers Rock and not see a single person. The oxide in this quarter-mile-high rock (like an iceberg, its main bulk is below ground) makes it change color from blue gray to bright red as the light changes; it is spectacular at sunset. At first daylight, we assembled with the other tourists to climb it.

We were unceremoniously dropped at the foot, along with some breakfast rations and instructions to be sure to return by the set departure hour – no guide, no advice. As the head of my family, I led up the rock face, which at its steeper inclines had a steel holding-chain anchored to its surface. As I climbed, I began having pains in my left arm. I started telling myself that I was forty years old and didn't have to prove anything to anyone by actually reaching the top of this monster. I finally stopped and waited for Vicky to catch up. Telling her to take care of the boys, I went down to wait.

Massaging my arm and walking around contemplating my incipient heart attack, I saw around a corner some metal plaques on the rock. "In memory of.... Fell off the rock...." Oh boy, not only was I dying down here in the middle of nowhere, but my family was in danger above. This rock had no trees. If you started falling, it would be all the way.

Seeming ages later, a tiny speck appeared on the horizon and eventually became Vicky, inching her way down on her butt. "Where are the kids?" "They went on." One by one people from the group straggled back down. Then two more specks and lots of childish laughter. The boys were scampering down Ayers Rock, even jumping back and forth over the intermittent chains. We all survived to go on to our next adventure, Palm Valley.

This was an all day trip; the bus would pick us up at our hotel in Alice early in the morning. Instead, a taxi arrived to take us to the bus. One look at the bus and you could see why. This prewar Bedford was literally held together with string; it was foolhardy to make it go any further than necessary. We set off on the nicely surfaced road. The bus had no speedometer. The driver would accelerate until the vibration was too much to control, then he would ease back before another assault. Eventually, we stopped to move into four-wheel drive, and continued into the outback along dry riverbeds. An occasional tree here, a dingo on the skyline there.

We stopped for lunch at a picnic area, and I noticed the men gathering around our bus. Yes, we had broken an axle. No jack, no tools, certainly no spare axle – oh, and no radio either. So a jack was borrowed from a passing car, and some stones put under the bus to support it. A rusty chain was found to strap the axle to the chassis, and a nut-and-bolt was found to secure it. Onward! Actually that was the only possibility – the chain arrangement precluded reversing. Finally we got close enough to Palm Valley to walk, which we did while the driver dealt with turning the bus around. The whole trip had been amazing, but this last leg was unique.

Here we were, walking in the sand in the middle of the Australian desert, when all of a sudden, around a bend, was an oasis with palm trees that exist nowhere else in the world. As we splashed in the icy, sparkling spring water, we would not have been surprised to see a dinosaur raise its head over the trees.

The trip back was uneventful, except for dinner served in a dry riverbed. The sky was black velvet and filled with brilliant stars so close you could reach them. A roaring fire was built, a slab of iron sheeting thrown on it, and steaks thrown on that, with jugs of Australian red to wash them down. What a tired family crawled into bed late that night – such a day could never have been planned!

I had chosen to play a pretty insubstantial program with my new accompanist, Stephen McIntyre – apart from my unaccompanied stuff, Handel, Chopin, Enesco, and Doppler. Stephen is one of Australia's finest pianists. Later, after we became friends, I learned just how distressed he was. We recorded some of the pieces for the ABC, then, leaving my family behind in a flat that Mick Long had lent us, I set out with Stephen and Philip Green, the MSO's principal cellist, for our little country tour around New South Wales.

For the first time, I was actually a "visiting artist" and given the corresponding treatment. We had an ABC retainer to carry our bags and take care of hotels, tickets, and transportation – not bad! One of the concerts was our recital program. The other three with Philip gave me a chance to play the Heitor Villa-Lobos *Jet Whistle* and the Carl Maria von Weber *Trio*.

It was a fun tour, but I lost my composure playing Schumann one night after intermission, when a family began eating the traditional chocolates in the front row, as if they were at a movie. (I suppose now it would be popcorn.) The *Romances* had very little romance that night! My family joined me in Sydney. I taught a class and played the recital program at the Sydney Conservatorium, then geared up for Mozart at the Sydney Opera House.

This world famous building has the strangest history. Its designer was fired before ever revealing what was supposed to go under those soaring sails. Many adjustments were made. First the engineers discovered that the proposed curve of the sails was irregular – each ceramic tile would have to be individually made. So the curve was changed to a regular one, giving the roof a slightly more box-like and less elegant shape. The ever-increasing cost was met by proceeds from a state lottery, until the government finally said, "That's it!" The Australian Opera was still a fledgling organization, so the ABC stepped in and took over the opera theater for its orchestra, the opera being assigned a smaller one. Stage machinery like that at the Metropolitan Opera in New York, no longer being necessary for the big hall, and not fitting the small one, was sold as scrap. The opera company would have its own trials caused by this change, but that is someone else's story.

Thirty-First Season — 1977

THE AUSTRALIAN BROADCASTING COMMISSION presents the

SYDNEY SYMPHONY ORCHESTRA

in the Fifth of the 1977 Youth Concerts

Conductor:
WILLEM VAN OTTERLOO

Soloist:
JOHN WION

In the CONCERT HALL
of the SYDNEY OPERA HOUSE

Tuesday, August 9, 1977 at 6.30 p.m.
Wednesday, August 10, 1977 at 6.30 p.m.

These concerts are arranged by the Australian Broadcasting Commission in conjunction with the New South Wales Government and the Council of the City of Sydney.

My conductor was the highly respected Willem van Otterloo, and the Mozart was straightforward. I thought the first concert went well, but for the second I was a bit frazzled. I had been doing business downtown and then couldn't get a taxi. By the time I got to the opera house for the early evening concert, I was flying and no longer relaxed. I was given a tape of the concert that was broadcast, but don't know which of the two it was.

My other assignment in Sydney was to talk to the young hopefuls of the Australian Training Orchestra, and record with them the Telemann *Suite* and the Griffes *Poem*. After the students struggled a bit with the former, the conductor suggested we do only the Griffes.

We caught up with our former au pair, Suzy Powell, and her husband Richard Miller, tympanist of the SSO, for a fun social evening at the senior Miller's dinner theater, and then flew back to Melbourne for a recital for the Flute Guild, and a week of final farewells. Then it was back to Sydney to pick up our Qantas flight to San Francisco. Vicky and the boys continued on to New York and I attended the NFA convention, where I had been nominated to the board of directors and was about to be not elected. I don't remember much about this convention, but suspect I was both exhausted and jet-lagged. Without a break, I went right into opera rehearsals in New York. I had been away almost three months.

Apart from enjoying my newly won four-show schedule, I was determined to use the new space in my life to practice basic technique more seriously and regularly, and repair those cracks of which I had become aware. That plan fell through after two phone calls.

The first was an invitation to teach at Mannes College. That would be an honor and not a problem. Mannes was a small school, and I might have three or four students who would come to my place for lessons.

The second was more problematic. The call was from Bert Lucarelli, the quintet's oboist, who was chair of the wind department at Hartt College in Hartford, Connecticut, a couple of hours from New York. They had been having trouble contacting their flute teacher, John Wummer, and had just learned that he had died on the West Coast. Would I be interested in the job?

For days I stalled. I didn't have a car; I didn't want to be away overnight; I didn't want to give up my one free day in the week; I wanted to practice; I was committed to the opera's Los Angeles tour in November. Bert was very patient and met my every request – I could even go to Los Angeles. I finally agreed, telling myself that if I didn't like it I would back out. So, I was back in the rat race, teaching at three schools including Kean and playing the opera.

The Wion and Miller families at the Music Hall, 1977.

Mannes was indeed a pleasure. The kids were bright and New York savvy. They were getting their real education by sneaking into all of New York's concert halls. This came to include NYCO, and for the next few years I felt I was playing for someone in particular, and usually I was. In my first class was Linda Toote, one of the most talented students I would ever have; she would go on to become principal of the Milwaukee Orchestra before pausing to have twins.

Hartt College, about to become the Hartt School of Music (and now The Hartt School), was a founding department of the private University of Hartford. It was the creation of Moishe Paranov and his father-in-law, Julius Hartt. Paranov, recently retired at this time, had made Hartt, by sheer force of personality, into a major music conservatory. Now, with a new dean, it was in a period of adjustment. This would actually prove to be a period of long decline, as the university sapped Hartt's autonomy.

The original faculty was made up of many members of the Hartford Symphony, including its two flutists, Carl Bergner and Stanley Aronoff. When the local teachers could not attract a national student body, Paranov began to import recognized professionals from New York and Boston (and even beyond in the case of cellist Raya Garbousova who flew in from Indiana). Thus Wummer had joined the faculty, and I now inherited his class of nine.

I was somewhat overwhelmed by the whole experience. The students were technically highly proficient, particularly in Joachim Andersen's opus 15 *Etudes*, which I had never studied. I somehow felt that I ought to be able to play everything they presented to me, and actually spent the month at Martha's Vineyard the following summer learning these etudes. I was also intimidated by Carl Bergner. He had set ideas about everything related to the flute and was quick to state them. Two of my freshmen who went on to professional careers were Ali Ryerson in the field of jazz and Janet Arms, who became my colleague at both the opera and Hartt.

And so, hitching rides with car-owning faculty to Hartt, taking the train to Kean, teaching into the holiday season, I juggled everything through to the end of this tumultuous year. The reduced schedule at the opera was a big help, and I enjoyed the season, which introduced me to Puccini's *Fanciulla del West*, with Niska as Minnie and Sergiu Commissiona making a wonderful debut as conductor. Many years would pass before I would get over my Met experience, but already I was regrouping and ready to charge ahead, albeit in a slightly different direction. So why was my stomach so upset?

1978

1978 was my year of gastritis. It had started as a more than usually upset stomach, stress related for sure. Refusing to go away, the difficult-to-break cycle had begun. At first I worried about cancer and ulcers. When those fears were allayed, I just worried. Vicky's stepfather said, "Oh, you're going through that one." That was reassuring. After months of eating bland food and trying to relax, I saw Bert Lucarelli's internist, who assured me he could find nothing wrong and that I could eat anything. Eventually the gastritis passed, to be replaced by something even more problematic the following year.

In January, I turned down what would be my final Australian offer, to join the newly founded contemporary music ensemble, ACME. I felt Vicky and I were committed to New York, and both kids were in the middle of growing up as New Yorkers, so my decision wasn't difficult. My mentor in ACME, Keith Humble, quickly found that the ensemble was not developing as he hoped, and the stress led in June to his first heart attack.

The spring, juggling the opera and three colleges, finally passed, and with Russell graduating from the Ethical Culture School, we arranged a celebratory three-day cruise up the Hudson on a schooner. I was enjoying a relaxing, friendly trip – just what I needed – until my stressed stomach seemed unusually troubled after one lunch. No one had ever told the cook about separating the stuffing from the turkey. The weakest, or unluckiest, of us found ourselves in full retch, then speeding by ambulance to the closest hospital, where we spent a miserable few hours, until the poison worked itself through our bodies and the glucose drip restored us to some sense of normality. The trip down river the next day was a quiet one.

In the summer, I played again at Caramoor and Newport. At Newport another flutist was now in place but, in celebration of the tenth anniversary, the Lark Quintet was invited to play a recital in Marble House's beautiful gold room, and I did a rerun of the Briccialdi *Ballabile di Concerto* in a Breaker's concert of festival hits. The local paper reported that groupies who came from Boston just for my performance were not disappointed by "a show of virtuosity that overcame the music's lack of substance."

Martha's Vineyard was again a respite, apart from learning Andersen opus 15 studies each morning while my family was

Bluefish catch at Martha's Vineyard, summer 1978.

at the beach. Palanchian and I did some successful bluefishing, and my stomach didn't start burning until the drive home to New York.

In the fall season of the opera, I enjoyed a new production of *Andrea Chenier*, and June Anderson's debut as the Queen of the Night in *The Magic Flute*, but my attention was more focused on what would be my final Carnegie recital with Gil Kalish in October.

We performed a Handel sonata, the Beethoven *Serenade*, the Copland *Duo*, and the Franck *Sonata*. We got no review due to a *Times* strike, but a tape of our run-through at Hartt shows that we were in good form. I had dropped Kean College from my schedule and was teaching two full days at Hartt. To accommodate the fuller role that teaching was playing in my life, I flew back for a week in the middle of the opera's Los Angeles season to keep everyone on track.

Throughout this year, I corresponded with the Australian Broadcasting Commission, and by mid-year received an offer of 18 concerts plus airfare for seven weeks in 1980. I immediately ran into problems with Kalish, who had been offered fewer concerts at lower fees, including his solo appearances. When I complained, the ABC abruptly withdrew their offer to him. I wrote on his behalf to explain that we were a duo, that Kalish was a respected soloist here and had to be treated equally. Eventually they agreed to pay equal fees but couldn't, because of prior commitments, offer more engagements; nor could they fit his offered engagements into a shorter time. As the contract was between the ABC and Gil, I could do nothing further. By year's end he had declined the tour, and I had agreed to play duo recitals with my Australian accompanist of 1977, Stephen McIntyre.

1979

The year got off to an exciting start with a televised Lincoln Center concert by Pavarotti and Sutherland on my birthday. The contractor for the orchestra was Loren Glickman, the NYCO's bassoonist. One of the most influential contractors of freelance orchestras, and a longtime colleague with whom I had a cordial relationship, Loren had never before hired me for his jobs. Was it my union activity, my relationship with our oboist whom he did use regularly, or didn't he really care for my playing?

He had played in my orchestra for the concerto recording, and I decided he must have changed his mind about my ability. That made me feel good. Neither he nor our oboist played the concert as they were busy elsewhere. Apart from having a great time, I thought I did a good job. Loren never used me for another concert. Years later the "penny dropped." I had hired him once, and he had returned the favor, taking advantage of a situation that avoided the personality conflict between me and the oboist – end of story.

The day before the concert, I slipped on some ice outside our country cottage, landing on my left wrist. An x-ray showed no break despite the pain. I played the concert with a bandage for support and had to ask my second to remove the head-joint from my flute at the end. The twisting movement hurt too much. I will never know if this was the trigger for my later problems. At the time I gave it no thought – a few days later I was back at tennis.

The whole concert was a thrill, with the two superstars in top form and an electric, adulating audience. But for me, the highlight was the mad scene from Ambroise Thomas's *Hamlet*, which I hadn't come across before, in which Dame Joan was spectacular. The aria has a tricky flute part, which I negotiated with success. I was flattered when Julie Baker appeared on-stage after one rehearsal. He had heard it over the PA system while down in the Philharmonic's locker room and had come up to see who was playing.

An era came to an end at the opera that spring. Julius Rudel, in conflict with the chairman of the board, was asked to step down, to be replaced by Beverly Sills. Apart from this personality conflict, it seemed that the board as a whole was unhappy with Rudel's repertoire choices and that he seemed to be more interested in his developing international conducting career. Things were not going smoothly, in fact. Julius made so many of the company decisions that in his frequent absences certain things went undone. At the time, I don't think that any of us were sorry to see him go. He had a difficult personality that often got in his way. He was a second-rank conductor in the best sense of the word and a wonderfully intuitive man of the theater. Only in the dreary array of conductors who followed in the next decade did I come to fully appreciate his strengths.

Apart from all the drama surrounding Rudel's departure, the highlight of the spring season was actually ballet. As part of a double bill, Balanchine choreographed Strauss's *Bourgeois Gentilhomme* for Rudolf Nureyev.

This season I found myself back in the freelancing world, when I was asked to play with Richard Westenburg's Musica Sacra and David Katz's Queens Symphony. Over the next several years, both would give me opportunities to play repertoire not otherwise available to me. With the former, I played principally Bach's music via his Basically Bach festivals, though his regular series also presented choral works of other eras. The soloists were always first class, as was the orchestra. Apart from the thrill of the *Matthew Passion* and the *B Minor Mass*, I played numerous Bach cantatas with flute obbligato, *Brandenburg Concertos*, and an ill-fated *B Minor Suite*. I was performing in front of two thousand people at Lincoln Center. I missed a repeat. I was so thrown that I couldn't get back in again and spent eight bars improvising. I was kindly received at the end, but I felt so awful that I ended up in my dressing room banging my fists against the wall – of all the places to mess up!

David Katz, who had been one of Stowkowski's assistants, created his own orchestra in the borough of Queens and put on pairs of weekend concerts for many years until his death. He had a good orchestra of freelancers and presented selections of the entire repertory from Beethoven's Ninth to Bartok's *Concerto for Orchestra* and was able to attract some fine soloists. Although I was now starting at his request, I would similarly stop years later, when, fighting cancer, he fired me before his final season.

Around that same time I was also not rehired for Musica Sacra. While I didn't have that much respect for David Katz, and probably showed it too easily, I loved working for Westenburg, had a good relationship with him, and always believed he admired my work. I wrote to ask what the problem was but got no answer. A few years later, he showed up at a concert where I was playing (his wife was singing) and warmly reminisced about our collaborations. He said we should talk, but we never did.

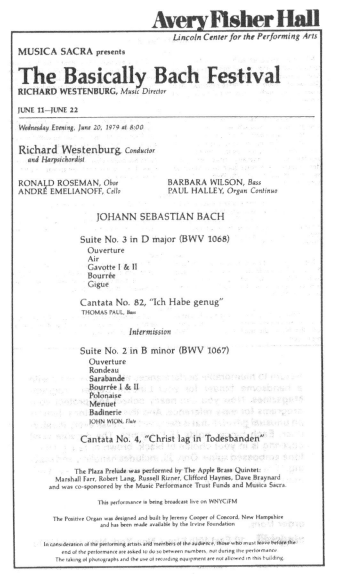

I eventually learned to be more philosophical about these things. I realized that whenever I started a freelance job, I was replacing some fine player who had not been rehired. And the reason probably had nothing to do with ability. I was never interested in or good at playing politics, so I should not have been surprised when my own turn came.

In 1979, another of my freelancing activities came to an end, when the Caramoor Festival hired a new orchestra for the following year. The St. Luke's Ensemble was organized in such a way that the festival would not have to pay certain taxes on behalf of the orchestra's members, thus saving substantially on its budget. Caramoor had been a wonderful experience for me over many years. I'm not a fan of playing outdoors, but Caramoor's environment made it an enchanting experience. Rudel was always at his most charming, and we had many fine soloists (Claudio Arrau, Jorge Bolet, Rudof Firkusny, Garrick Ohlsson come to mind), guest conductors, and interesting repertoire. As a bonus, I could commute from our cottage, so I could combine the festival with summer family weekends.

In June before this final Caramoor season, Vicky and I took the boys to Kenya for a look at the wildlife. For the three males it was a fantastic experience. I'm not sure Vicky quite shared our enthusiasm. We had an excellent guide, Peter, who drove our minivan. Our group also included two single visitors, a male doctor and a female librarian. Leaving Nairobi we traveled around pretty much the entire country, visiting the different game reserves, from open plains to mountains.

Our first experiences were a bit disappointing. Peter would stop and point out giraffes in the distance, which we almost took on faith. But as the days passed and we saw our rhinos and hippos and prides of lions hunting and eating, and crocodiles, and finally the great animal migration across the Serengeti, we got more and more into the experience. Even in our lodges at night we had a feeling of vulnerability, heightened by machete carrying guards walking the grounds, or a trumpeting elephant that had decided to cut through the compound. Peter had to keep reminding us that the lion ignoring us a few yards away did so only because we were in the car. If we put any body part outside it would be in his world, and the reaction would be quite different.

Just how different we didn't learn till the last night. Peter had always declined our invitation to join us at dinner but that night he accepted. Such stories he told – about having his van bogged down and nearly crushed by an elephant separated from her calf; about the tourists who ran out of gas, and the men who went for help and were never seen again. By the end of the meal we had all become quite silent. The morning after, our two companions called in sick for the final drive. The drivers use no roads on these sorties – they just head off cross-country where experience or reports suggest something to view. Due to the general unrest in the country, they were allowed neither radios nor weapons. We felt very insecure that morning, and each time Peter would turn into a damp-looking depression seeking a way through some trees, Vicky would state with firm determination, "No way!"

The trip was not a total vacation for me. I had agreed to play two solos at what would be my final Newport Festival, and I felt I had to keep in shape. My fellow tourists and family accepted the sounds that floated from our room before dinner, but I was a little miffed when one manager asked me to stop as I was disturbing the animals.

After Caramoor, where Alexander Gibson led a complete Berlioz *Romeo and Juliet*, we took the boys to their summer camp for two weeks and headed up to Newport. My assignment was to play François Borne's *Carmen Fantasy* at an afternoon concert at The Elms, and the entire Briccialdi *Carnival of Venice* the same evening at The Breakers. I thought I played the *Carmen* quite well, until a woman approached me afterwards to ask if I had ever seen the opera. I laughingly said no, meaning that I had played it a few times but didn't actually see much. She plowed straight on, saying that if I had seen it I wouldn't have played it the way I did. Oh well.

The evening concert was much more of an event, the entire concert being videotaped. My Briccialdi preceded Dmitry Sitkovetsky playing Paganini's *La Campanella*. I don't think I embarrassed myself. According to the paper next day, "the fireworks began with a virtuoso performance by Wion...a veteran of the festival absent in recent years. His performance last night was breathtaking." The Providence paper was even sillier: "Move over Rampal and Galway." We picked up the boys and headed for the Vineyard.

At the Dallas convention of the NFA in August, I was elected to the Board of Directors and sat in on the final Sunday meeting, where I was deeply impressed by President Robert Cole's professional manner and warm efficiency. I didn't know what was expected of the board. I found it did nothing during the year but quite a lot during the convention, which was a whole year away.

The fall opera season was Sills's first as director, but she was also singing those commitments that couldn't be canceled. A couple of years would pass before we would see her plans for the company's new direction. We had our traditional strike, midseason this time, and some memorable evenings, including Sarah Caldwell's production of *Falstaff*, which she also conducted. The legendary Victoria de los Angeles made a brief appearance, but she proved to be no longer in her prime and quickly withdrew.

My principal worry now was my left hand, which was causing me more and more concern. As this was coinciding with the signing of my contract for 1980 in Australia and the development of that repertoire, I worried that my problem was psychological. On the advice of my longtime Australian friend Brian Coogan, I began therapy in the fall. While this would go on for some years and prove to be enormously beneficial in developing a greater understanding of myself, I learned that my hand problem was basically physical. It was surely compounded by stress and other factors; but as my mental understanding improved, my playing continued to spiral down, and I was developing serious tendinitis.

Not satisfied with preparing for Australia I had also undertaken to make a solo recording during some free time the following January. Ever since I started teaching at Hartt, I had become aware just how popular the French repertoire had become, as a result of Rampal's influence. I had studied very little of this in Australia, where the repertoire was much more Germanic, and only a few pieces in my New York studies. I decided that the only way to come to grips with the problem was to make a record – then I would *have* to learn it! Musical Heritage was under new management and no longer producing any records itself. However, I thought I had a general expression of interest in releasing such a record, should I produce it myself.

I decided to record a mixture of *concours* pieces (music written for the annual exams at the Paris Conservatoire) along with some shorter, more lyrical ones. The pieces that I decided to learn for the project were Philippe Gaubert's *Nocturne and Allegro Scherzando*, Louis Ganne's *Andante and Scherzo*, Paul Taffanel's *Andante Pastorale and Scherzettino* and Benjamin Godard's *Suite*. Two little pieces would also be new for me, sight-reading tests composed by Jules Massenet and Gabriel Fauré. Fauré's *Fantaisie*, George Enesco's *Cantabile and Presto*, Emile Pessard's *Andalouse*, and Georges Brun's *Romance*, pieces I already knew, would fill out the album.

The only time I had for learning the repertoire was during the opera's Los Angeles season. This had always seemed like a vacation anyway, with the only obligation being an opera in the evening. So I spent the daytime practicing. By tour's end I had learned the material, but the muscles and tendons of my forearms were a mess, and my fingers responded only to the most powerful signals, as they violently slapped the keys. Back in New York, I rehearsed with my colleague from Newport, pianist Tom Hrynkiw, who had agreed to participate in the recording. Tom was an absolute pleasure, playing everything perfectly at sight and with the greatest sensitivity. The engineer would be Jerry Bruck, who had done my Reger recording. He had discovered the newly opened Merkin Hall near Lincoln Center and booked two afternoons, the second and third of January. I would make this happen somehow.

Crisis

1980

Jerry Bruck was a very slow and methodical worker with terrific ears. Having chosen a good space to work in, he spent a lot of time setting up the microphones till we were all satisfied with the placement. Linda Toote, my former Mannes student, had agreed to act as my ears, and was a great asset in noting errors in the takes. With two afternoons scheduled, I divided the repertoire into two parts; I would have time for two complete takes of everything, plus a few bits and pieces.

Considering the state of my tendinitis, the only enjoyment was the triumph of actually pulling off the recording. Of all the nasty licks, the most problematic was an unaccompanied cadenza passage in the Godard *Waltz*. No matter how much I practiced, it was hit or miss – mostly miss. I knew that if I didn't get it on the first try it wouldn't happen, so I steeled myself, focused, and went for it – safe landing!

In bed at night after the first session, the adrenaline was still pumping, and my fingers pounded on the mattress the technical routines of the afternoon. After the second session, I was even worse. Assuming no shocks at editing time, I thought I had a good record.

In fact, I found many fine moments and much to be proud of. I also found moments that didn't quite make it – a smear here, questionable intonation there. Confident that Musical Heritage would be happy, I was disappointed to discover that in the intervening months they had committed to Carol Wincenc's first recording. A part of her prize for winning the Naumburg Competition, her recording duplicated too much of my material.

Resorting to plan two, I licensed the tape to Lyrichord in exchange for a set number of free records and an understanding that the master would be returned if the record went out of print. That is indeed what eventually happened, when they moved out of the classical music area. I was able to re-master the tape, add some new material, and release it as a CD.

After a few days of needed rest in the Caribbean, I was swept into the seven-day-a-week routine of the spring semester's teaching at Hartt and Mannes, the opera season (including a recording of Weill's *Silverlake*), Queens Symphony, and Musica Sacra, along with other freelance jobs. I was also preparing for Australia and worrying about my hand.

During a therapy session, I mentioned how much my hand hurt trying to negotiate the top octave passage-work in Prokofiev's *Love of Three Oranges*. The therapist suggested I take off the next performance. Well, I had never done anything like that. When I started at the opera, we had no sick leave, and even after it was introduced, you had to be close to death before you would think of using it. And then the contractor would often have someone phone you, under the pretense of well-wishing, just to make sure you were really home. Over my years at NYCO, I accumulated hundreds of days of sick leave, while the younger members of the orchestra routinely took their days on the slightest pretext. With much trepidation, I did call in sick, and somehow the performance went on without me.

In the spring I acquired a new flute, Brannen Brothers number 55. Bick and Bob Brannen, workmen at the Powell factory in Boston, had decided to start their own company in collaboration with the English flute maker, Albert Cooper, who had been largely responsible for the specifications relating to improved intonation of flutes. The company's original offering was for gold flutes. Subscribers would pay in advance for the necessary gold, paying the balance when work started on the ordered instrument. I had been tardy placing my order, and my flute was one of the last to be made.

As the time for construction approached, I had a long conversation with Bick about possible modifications, confiding in him my history of hand problems. After some considerable discussion he said, "Why don't you change to covered-hole?" I gasped. That was for beginners only; all professionals played the French model, open-hole system. "Not true," he said. "Many Europeans play covered-hole – indeed the famed Marcel Moyse himself did so." Well, I knew that, but was still reluctant. Finally, after further prodding, including the comment that Cooper believed that covered-hole flutes were acoustically superior, I agreed.

I couldn't wait for my flute to arrive. Finally, fearful that it had become lost in the mail, I phoned. Bick was most apologetic and explained one of the reasons they had gone out on their own to make flutes. He believed that a reason for some flutes playing better than others related to the evenness of the tubing. All tubing for flutes is produced commercially, and although it is ordered for a specific thickness, certain spots are slightly thinner.

Bick felt that if such a spot was situated at a nodal area, that particular note would not resonate at the same fullness as other notes. His plan was to carefully inspect each piece of tubing and design the flute in such a way that weak spots would be situated where tone holes would be cut. In the case of my flute, they had almost completed it, when they discovered a weak spot they had missed. They had scrapped the flute and started again. I was impressed.

The flute that finally arrived was beautiful, though I was not happy with the head-joint and went on using my Cooper head until I had the new one modified. I only played it for a short time, however, deciding that a silver flute with its lighter weight and more brilliant tone was preferable.

I immediately appreciated the comfort of the covered-hole system and noticed how much easier it was to play certain low note combinations, such as in the slow movement of the Prokofiev *Sonata*. However, my left hand was the focus of my life now. Bick Brannen made me a beautiful thumb crutch to see if that would help, then a number of angled attachment screws to see if I could find a position that would be comfortable. None was.

My hand problem was making me more and more concerned about the advisability of the Australian tour. I had worked so hard to make it happen, and if I canceled and my hand "strain" eased, I would feel terrible. If I canceled, I felt it highly unlikely that the offer would be made again. On the other hand, if I went ahead and played badly, my reputation could be damaged. I decided I would keep quiet about my problem and proceed as if all were well. I had made my hand work for the recording and would do so for the tour.

In April, I played a contracted recital at Kean College with Tom Hrynkiw, and in May went to Mexico with the opera for performances of *Barber of Seville* in Guanajuato and Mexico City. The highlight was a televised performance with Sills singing Rosina. In the lesson scene, she sang the *"Ah vous dirais-je maman"* variations. Up until now, an actor had mimed this on stage while I played from the pit. But for this performance, I was wigged (gray) and costumed, and doddered onto the stage to play.

Back in New York, I was rehearsing the Schubert *Variations* with pianist Abba Bogin when he mentioned that he had recently had carpal tunnel surgery. I was immediately interested and finally mentioned my own problem. He gave me the name of his surgeon, and I arranged an appointment for the end of May.

The lesson scene from The Barber of Seville with Beverly Sills, Mexico 1980.

Dr. Robert Beasley was wonderfully supportive but explained that my problem was not carpal tunnel. Still, he made it clear that this was not something I was imagining. He explained that this dysfunction was absolutely real, but that they didn't yet have instruments fine enough to measure it. Performing arts medicine was yet to come. He said that the ridge running down my palm from middle finger to wrist was the swollen tendon, and that a slight click when I moved that finger was caused by it popping in and out of its sheath. He could, and did, give me a shot of cortisone which might offer some relief, but which was not a solution. In this state, after a week of Hartt's annual chamber music workshop, I left for Australia on June 6.

The whole of the previous year and much of the current one had been spent in correspondence, establishing fees and dates and repertoire, and modifying same. I also had to resolve questions of masterclasses in the different states, each of which had to be cleared with the ABC. I would be playing Ibert, Romberg, Lovelock, Griffes, Hofmann and Kennan with the orchestras and a single recital program of Bach, Humble, Franck, Poulenc, Fauré *Morceau*, piano solos, and Borne with Stephen McIntyre. This program would be played in five country centers that were not usually visited by the orchestras.

On arrival in Melbourne, I stayed a couple of days with my mother before flying to Adelaide for three concerts with the orchestra. The first engagement was for a young people's concert, the Griffes *Poem*, listed as a first Australian performance, and the Lovelock. Then came two subscription concerts with the Kennan (also a local première) and the Hofmann. I was angered by the Hofmann program notes, which belittled the piece – hardly encouragement for the audience, and certainly grist for the critics. I achieved some lovely moments, but I could no longer play some of the technical passage-work. No matter how hard I forced, my fingers just didn't move together and arpeggios became scales or just a sloppy mess. I listened to the tape of the first Hofmann to see if it was as bad as it had felt, It was. Not only did fast material suffer; certain slow passages also lost any sense of legato.

Curiously, despite my unhappiness, I accumulated lovely reviews throughout the tour, specifically commenting favorably on these same aspects that were frustrating me. I must have been successful at least in selling the quality of the music and presumably looking as if I were having a good time.

With my cousin Buzzy and her husband Wesley.

On the brighter side, I was feted by my grandmother's Adelaide relatives. Her sister had married well into one of the large "station" families, and the son, the current "lord," invited me for the Queen's Birthday hunt. One of my cousins, "Buzzy," who was particularly close to my mother, made sure that I had a most relaxing day, following along in a station wagon, and providing a picnic on the tailboard.

Back in Melbourne, Vicky and the boys arrived from New York, and we moved into a house in the suburbs for our two-month stay. My first engagement was three performances of the Lovelock. Because of a power strike, the concert was transferred to a hall that had its own generator, but at which the ABC was unable to record. Given my state that was a blessing.

The first recital was in Geelong, some fifty miles from Melbourne. In the local paper I got the first and still only bad review of my career. The headline read, "Why bother with Bach?" The critic commented on the basically French program content, noting the silliness of the *Carmen Fantasy* among other jabs. I found it ironic that this was not the kind of program that I would ever have played with Kalish, and that I was in fact trying to cater to what I perceived as the popularity of French music – well, apparently not in Geelong.

After two Rombergs in Tasmania with horn player Barry Tuckwell as conductor, I returned to Melbourne for a masterclass. The ABC showed a certain reluctance to allow these classes and in my naiveté I didn't understand why. Someone finally explained to me that these classes were usually situations where the "master" listened a bit to the student, then proceeded to play the music as it should be played, to the great delight of an enthusiastic audience. Enjoying the more informal atmosphere and opportunity to actually hear the master speak as well as play, audiences were tending to prefer these evenings to the formal concerts which were the reason the ABC had brought the master all this way.

My own experiences would be more truly called workshops, I came to realize. I found myself in a hall full of people, and in my condition I was not about to play. So I tried to make my teaching interesting to the lay audience and to keep things light and humorous. I can't imagine what they thought. I did play a few notes on one student's flute, just to prove that it worked and she would have to practice a bit harder.

We took the weekend off and Mick Long, my Trinity roommate, flew the four of us to his sheep farm north of Melbourne. The boys had a great time with the four Long kids, particularly in the heated pool, and I gave Russell his first driving lesson, using the low gears of a four-wheel drive on the station's tarmac. Although I was trying to rest my arms, I couldn't leave the flute alone and spent some time doing really slow work on the Ibert *Concerto*, the piece for my upcoming, most important concerts in Sydney. I had added this piece to my repertoire, never having performed it before, because I had found playing it easy. Now it was proving to be a nightmare, particularly the opening.

Before Sydney, however, I had a recital and a Romberg in the sunny north, leaving my family in Melbourne. The conductor for the Romberg was the fine German, Thomas Mayer. The local critic wrote that it gave me "every opportunity to display brilliant technique and a stream of tone of unbroken purity – a magnificent exposition of flute playing in excelsis." I enjoyed hanging out with the orchestra's flute section and was able to give a nicely pressure-free workshop for the local flute students on my last day. I flew to Sydney for a similar event the same evening, and my family flew up from Melbourne for my Ibert at the Sydney Opera House.

When I played Mozart there, I had used a makeshift area off-stage as a dressing room. This time I got the full treatment. The dressing rooms are so far from the stage in this complex that it requires a full-time employee to take visiting artists back and forth – up stairs, along passages, through doors. You couldn't to do it unaided. Before the first performance, the ABC's manager came by to wish me well, then I was led off to my fate. I didn't have too much fun, I'm afraid, and I felt any one of the orchestra's flutists could have done better.

So how to explain the headline, "Shades of the arch-flautist"? "James Galway is a hard act to follow, and it's a brave flautist who will appear on the same stage in the same season…. Without any fuss or razzamatazz, he played the flute well enough to make the memory of….[oh boy!] Wion seemed to have no trouble breezing through [the outer two movements] while the nostalgic slow movement revealed that he can make the instrument sing with poignant beauty. It was the kind of performance where you just sit back and enjoy a master musician at work." Another critic wrote, "as if he were juggling bubbles, a complete master of its light-hearted difficulties." Seriously folks, I heard the tape! However, at the second performance next night, I did my only decent playing of the tour.

Our friend Sandy Feirson, now a Sydney resident, had become a fire engine enthusiast and collected not only toys but the real thing. At noon he arrived at our hotel in fashionable King's Cross driving a large red fire truck, making Russell and Anthony's day. He drove us across town out to the Heads of Sydney Harbor, where Vicky and I had a luncheon date with my longtime friend Russell Meares and his wife, the painter Sandra Leveson.

The four of us ate outside in Sydney's brilliant sunshine, looking across the sparkling water at the city skyline from Doyle's seafood restaurant at Watson's Bay (a visit that is de rigeur ever since). With Sydney rock oysters and superbly fried John Dory went a large amount of chilled Australian white wine. Later, quite a bit later, we went to look at one of Sandra's paintings currently on display at the state gallery, then back to our room, where we zonked out until it was time to dress for the concert. This performance, despite its messy opening, is the one I decided to include on an LP of live performances that I later made for publicity use.

My final Melbourne engagement was a Saturday afternoon family concert, where I played Griffes and Hofmann. I found the circumstances odd. They had started the series as an alternative to the football games, but people were constantly telling me that nobody came because they were all at the football. Because nobody was interested, the ABC didn't advertise. Talk about defeatist!

Once again, my feeling about my performance for the modestly-sized audience was contradicted by the critic. He missed the Griffes (at the footy?) but called the Hofmann "a brilliant and attractively lyrical work," and noted that I played it "with effortless virtuosity and a glorious tone, impeccable phrasing, admirably subtle dynamics." I clearly recall how badly I felt about what I was doing.

Social things were now getting frantic, as our trip was coming to its end. I had one more journey, alone, back to Sydney for a bunch of meetings, then to Canberra for my final performance, the Ibert again — and again not so good. I flew back to Melbourne for family farewells, then, joined by Vicky and the boys, to Hawaii for a needed rest.

Opera rehearsals began, as usual, in mid-August, and included Bizet's *Pearl Fishers*, a first for us. The season would prove to be most harrowing for me. My hand was so problematic that I had to go into the pit before each act of every standard opera – those ones that we barely rehearsed, if at all – to see what previously routine solos I would now have to pay increased attention to and learn to negotiate. One such moment was in the opening of the fourth act of *Bohème*, a solo that starts with a quick E major arpeggio, now more of a scale. This reminded me that when I played *Bohème* at the Met, the concertmaster, Ray Gniewik, a Newport colleague, commented on how nice it was to hear this solo played so cleanly. When my predecessor played it, it sounded more like a scale.

I phoned Victor Just – yes, he had suffered for years just the kind of dysfunction I was experiencing. He had kept his problem to himself and been finally forced to retire. He had no suggestions for me.

I was excused from two days of opera rehearsals to attend the Boston flute convention, where I now participated as a board member in the running of this organization. All the decisions needed to guide the NFA through its next year were made at the breakfast and luncheon meetings on each of the three days. Ron Waln was now the president, and he handled the proceedings in a quietly efficient way. Erv Monroe, as program chair, had given me two assignments – to play the Molique *Quintet*, which I did with colleagues from the opera, and to participate in a panel on opera. With Harold Bennett, former principal at the Met, as the senior member, we engaged in a lively and humorous rather than an educational hour.

The highlight of the fall opera season was the televised gala farewell to Beverly Sills. It was staged as the second act of *Fledermaus*, currently in repertoire, into which were interpolated a whole raft of guest appearances. Carol Burnett led the proceedings and introducing Sherill Milnes, Eileen Farrell, Placido Domingo, Mary Martin, Renata Scotto, and Ethel Merman, Bobby

Short, and James Galway, who played "Danny Boy." I went to the post-performance party in a tent on the plaza, in the hope of meeting Galway. If he came, it was after I had given up and gone home.

In October, the Queens Symphony played a special concert at Carnegie Hall, repeating the weekend's concerts in Queens. The program contained the *Leonore Overture Number 3* and the Brahms *Fourth Symphony*. If I didn't know it before, this experience clarified that my problem was not just a matter of nerves. The solo in the last movement of the Brahms went very well; the *Leonore* with its arpeggios was a strain.

I was seeing my psycho-therapist twice a week, but I clearly either had to take an extended break from playing, or I had to find a physical therapist with a solution to my problem. Instead, I was busy planning to return to Australia the following summer, having been invited to participate in "Music 81," a yearlong celebration of music in the state of Victoria.

Ahead lay uncertainty, as I sought to extend my playing career. The goals would become more modest; the achievements frustratingly erratic. I would find different outlets for my energies.

At Doyle's on the Beach, Watson's Bay, with the Sydney skyline in the background.

Reassessment

1981

As I look back at the 1980s, I find it hard to reconcile the number of performances I played with my memory of being incapacitated. Although my tendinitis had eased considerably from the previous year and eventually disappeared, allowing me to function reasonably well in many situations, I was still suffering. A performance medicine practice didn't exist yet, but the term that was finally given to my dysfunction was "focal distonia." At first it seemed to be a catchall for any condition that couldn't be otherwise explained. No treatment existed. Recently, a flutist/doctor in Germany claimed some success using drugs to help stimulate the formation of new neural pathways. In a certain sense this is what the Alexander Technique encourages, but without drugs.

As the medical profession developed its ideas about this, I was clutching at any recommendation at all. If I was playing duets with Eddie Daniels and he said to try some "guru," I did. If pianist Seymour Lipkin said some doctor was helping musicians, I made an appointment. Over the next years I saw dozens of experts, not just surgeons and nerve specialists but all kinds of healers and a few quacks. I had hair analysis, parasite testing, and iridology (a study of the iris that showed I should become a vegetarian). I spent a long time with a kinesthesiologist, and I had garlic put on my chest. I spent extended time at Rolfing, Feldenkreis, and other less specific physiotherapy, with chiropractors, psychotherapists, holistic and biofeedback practitioners, and hypnotists. My treatment was totally haphazard and largely unhelpful, though I did begin to develop some techniques for lessening the physical and mental effects of my condition. Too often, what I found was egotism bordering on arrogance, as person after person knew exactly what was wrong with me, though somehow I was still unable to perform any better.

During all this time, I was simultaneously experimenting with modifications to the instrument and in the way I held it. The former led to left-hand key extensions that helped but created a counter-problem when the weight of the G♯ extension led to an unsatisfactory F♯ to G♯ trill. The better solution turned out to be moving the whole hand down the flute body by extending the C♯ finger button and eliminating the awkward stretch between the first two fingers. With the hand at last comfortable, it became more apparent that the coordination problem was largely in the contrary motion that occurs particularly in the top octave, and was compounded by repetition and speed. In addition, tension was created whenever the thumb left the flute, probably from a latent fear that the flute would fall. Even as I learned to support and balance the flute better, the reaction remained. I could play a scale to the note preceding the thumb-lifting without tension, but add that note and the hand cramped in preparation. In Alexander terminology, I had to learn to inhibit that response, but this knowledge lay a few years down the road.

As I prepared assignments over these years, I would reach the point where I would have to admit that a particular passage was not going to work, usually the day before or even of the performance. I began accumulating a bag of tricks – alternate fingerings, harmonics, even a G to A♭ trill played by the first finger of the right hand. I discovered a strange relief from dropping the left pinky when it was not needed and found this saved innumerable top octave disasters. A few years later when preparing for the New York NFA convention, I took James Galway and Ransom Wilson to the room where they would be playing to ask their opinion on the set-up and accoustics. To my surprise they both dropped that pinky when not needed, and neither was aware of it. Yet we are always taught to keep this finger over the key, ready for use at all times.

During all this time my professional life continued. At the opera, in addition to a repeat of Maralin Niska's fabulous *Makropoulis*, we were introduced to Verdi's *Attila*, with Sam Ramey as the Hun and Sergiu Commissiona making magic of the instrumental interludes, Thea Musgrave's powerful *Mary, Queen of Scots*, and the delightful charm of Janácek's *Cunning Little Vixen*, with Gianna Rolandi as the Vixen and Michael Tilson Thomas conducting.

I played other interesting concerts during the spring. Apart from my continuing association with Musica Sacra and QSO, our orchestra was hired for another Pavarotti telecast. I believe this was the year he insisted the orchestra arrive for the concert early, to run through the half-step-lower transposition of his "*Che gelida manina*." I participated in my friend Livio Caroli's 40th birthday present, an oboe recital at Carnegie Recital Hall, in the Ginastera *Duo*. With the Bronx Arts I struggled with the awkwardnesses of the Arthur Honegger *Concertino for Flute and English Horn*, as well as those of the Hofmann *Serenade*. We were preparing to record the latter along with his *Octet* for Musical Heritage, and with happy Newport memories of both, I knew I had to deal with a couple of tricky spots I could no longer play with ease. Still, the players were excellent, and the recording, when we finally made it in the following year, was lovely.

I developed a new medical problem, angioedema. This swelling, something like hives, has no known source. In my case it happens around the mouth. If the swelling is in the cheek, it is only embarrassing, but when it hits the lip, I can't play. Episodes seem to be somewhat seasonal and will often not occur for a few years. The best description I got from an allergy specialist was that the histamines build up from a number of different sources, and sometimes the body can't handle them anymore. She said that in addition to the effect of stress, twenty-five percent could easily come from the pressure of the flute on my lip. Add in a very strong reaction to dust mites and some seasonal airborne allergants, and off I go. Not surprisingly, the feeling of a swelling coming on created its own anxiety as I looked at my upcoming schedule.

In twenty years, however, I only recall two collisions. One was an opening night of *Lucia*, when I felt the tingle during Act 2. I raced out during intermission to try and find an open drug store for an antihistamine. When I returned, unsuccessful, Beverly took one look at my triple-sized lip and gasped. With great aplomb, Florence Nelson moved over to play the mad scene. I awaited the second performance with great anxiety, fearful that the condition was psychological, but I had no problem. Another was a decade later, during a recording session of the C. P. E. Bach unaccompanied *Sonata*. The swelling was not really bad, but it minimized my tone control. I listened to a playback and cancelled the session – it was easy enough to reschedule.

With the spring opera season over, I had time for some concentrated stretching and movement work with a physical therapist, before leaving at the end of May for "Music 81." I had been invited the previous year to participate in this yearlong celebration by the state of Victoria. As with all my Australian experiences, it had taken months of back and forth, crossed letters, and changed plans before the itinerary was finally settled. I would be in residence for six weeks, with a variety of activities both in Melbourne and throughout the state. I would in fact visit thirty high schools, the tertiary institutions, and some adult centers, playing recitals and teaching but mostly offering some mixture of the two in an informal setting. I would be a resident at the annual weekend camp of the flute society and play a recital for them. For this latter, I had again the wonderful collaboration of Stephen McIntyre in performing Schubert, Poulenc, Prokofiev, Mozart K 13, Böhm *Elegie*, and Bach *Partita*.

This was the first time I used a beta-blocker. A visiting clarinetist told me that this hypertension medicine was being used by performers in tiny doses to control the flow of adrenalin before a concert. He gave me a couple of tablets and suggested I try it some time beforehand to make sure I had no adverse reactions. I chose the dress rehearsal. I hate rehearsing anyway, and certainly didn't enjoy a further lowering of my adrenalin. Game for anything that might help, I still took a half tablet just before the recital, as instructed. I found that it did stabilize my breathing but had no effect on my hand problem. I got a prescription from one of my doctor friends, and since that night I have taken this minimum dose before any solo concert or speech. I have never quite understood some people's reaction to use of this drug, as if it were somehow cheating. I see it as just another tool like meditation or a banana to help one produce to one's capability. I only wish I had had this option earlier in my career, particularly at auditions.

With Les Barklamb at the Victorian Flute Guild weekend, 1981.

For our summer family trip this year, we took the boys to England and France. A highlight of the former was the Cotswolds, and of the latter the castles of the Loire. The trip then took us via Carcassone to Nice, where Vicky's folks had taken a house.

My association with the NFA deepened when President Dick Hahn phoned to ask if I would take over the administration of the Newly Published Music Competition. In typical fashion I was initially overwhelmed, but as he gently took me through the responsibilities, I began to see how I could handle the assignment and agreed.

This first year, a few dozen new publications were forwarded to me for my committee's inspection and evaluation. I would write a report for *The Instrumentalist* magazine, and forward the winning publications to the professional flutists who had been chosen by another committee to play them at the next convention. By the time I passed the responsibility on to my colleague Florence Nelson a few years later, the number of publications being reviewed had risen to over two hundred. All of this material eventually became a part of the NFA's library. More important, I was able to arrange for the winning publications to be used as requirements in the various performing competitions for the following year. I believed this would encourage publishers to participate in our competition and offer some tangible reward in increased sales and exposure.

At the convention itself in Detroit, I continued my service on the board of directors, attending the daily breakfast and lunch meetings where plans and budgets were discussed and approved. I also played the Romberg *Concerto*. This was the first time the NFA had felt it could afford an orchestral accompaniment, and the program chair, Alex Murray, had honored me by asking me to join William Bennett, playing Theobold Böhm's *Grand Polonaise*, and Bob Aitken and Per Oien, playing the Franz Doppler *Double Concerto*. This should have been a high point for me, but I was disappointed not to have the technical mastery of my 1976 recording. I was less traumatized than I was the previous year in Australia and believe I gave a decent account. One reported audience comment (female) was, "well if you didn't like the music, he was fun to watch."

The fall was comparatively quiet after all this activity – the opera, Musica Sacra, QSO, and teaching. New at the opera were Verdi's *Nabucco* with its fabulous "*Va, pensiero*," and Weber's *Der Freischutz*. For a few weeks during this season, I took some biofeedback sessions intended to help me relax. After being wired up and led to an alpha state, I was presented with a math problem or something similar. The level of brain activity and time taken to relax again was measured. The therapist began commenting on how well I handled this stress and how unusually quickly I was able to relax again. Sitting in the pit later, I realized of course that this was why I was successful at my job. A study at this time had shown that the level of stress on an orchestral soloist was similar to that of a pilot landing a jumbo jet – and we were handling this three hours a night! The thought occurred to me that the therapist should be paying me to be his guinea pig, and I stopped the sessions.

An amusing incident arose from a fall performance of *Rigoletto*, one that I didn't play, on a Saturday when the Met also performed it. Andrew Porter, the extraordinary critic then at *The New Yorker*, attended both performances and wrote a major article about the opera itself, as well as comparing different aspects of the two events. Commenting on the important role of the flute, he praised Michael Parloff's contribution at the Met, while offering that his counterpart at City Opera had been less successful. I wrote to him, explaining the situation, and pointing out that anyone reading the article would assume he was referring to me. He wrote a lovely reply, admitting that his general principle of naming performers in positive references but not in negative ones was not appropriate in this situation. However, he said, he could hardly now write a follow up saying the flutist was actually _. There I thought the matter finished, until *The New Yorker* published his review of a concert the following year. The piece was the Berlioz *Requiem*, and the location the enormous, reverberant Cathedral of Saint John the Divine. Referring to a movement where I played a slow theme along with the violins (my only quasi-exposed moment at all), he made special mention of "the lines of the solo flute (John Wion)."

The year ended with a family vacation to the Yucatán Peninsula in Mexico.

1982

In January I was recommended to Dr. Heinz Lippmann at the Albert Einstein College of Medicine, who had had some experience with musicians' injuries. He noticed the constricted position of my left arm and the way my fourth finger made "a forceful extensor movement" whenever the third finger was raised. His basic advice was a daily routine of swinging the arms forward and back, something I still do. When I saw him a month later, I could report some improvement. Problems during all these years were the vagueness of my symptoms and the fact that I could sometimes have minutes with no problem at all. The slightest change in hand position might lead to the latter, to be followed by a relapse as the hand somehow compensated once again. A recent medical report noted that just the thickness of a latex glove could make a temporary difference to someone with a problem like mine. I soon realized that I had no dysfunction with my fingers themselves – only when they were in flute-playing position. Dr. Lippmann's final report said my anxiety "which was undoubtedly a factor has largely vanished with his understanding of the problem. I believe this [meaning the arm swings and more relaxed position] basically solves his problem." A few years later his speech at the first conference on performers' problems at NYU cited my case (not by name of course) as one of his successes. But in fact I was still struggling on a daily basis to keep functioning.

The spring opera season began on a strange note with a concert performance of Wagner's early *Die Feen*. The stage at the New York State Theater had been designed to muffle the sounds of dancers; this, my only time playing on it, gave me some idea of what our singers struggled with all the time. Even with an improvised shell it was a dismal experience.

The season proper introduced Italo Montemezzi's *L'Amore dei Tre Re*, which I thoroughly enjoyed, and continued our traversal of early Verdi with *I Lombardi*. This was largely distinguished, in my memory, by the minimal production – a set consisting of a circular staircase going nowhere. At the end of a scene, to giggles from the audience, it rotated to a new position. Finally, the production was modified to pull down the curtain between scenes. But I remember thinking that Rudel would have seen this coming in a flash. Luigi Cherubini's *Medea* with its extended flute solo was always fun for me, and *Lucia* was revived. This time the soprano was Gianna Rolandi, and one of the performances would be telecast.

The flute part in the mad scene in this opera had been written originally for glass harmonica, an instrument of tuned glass discs, over which the performer rubbed wet fingers, producing the eerie sounds familiar to anyone who has rubbed the rim of a crystal wine glass. When Beverly Sills recorded the opera in Europe, this instrument had been used. She now had the idea of making an intermission show out of this subject. The best she could manage for a demonstration was someone who played across the rims of tumblers that he tuned by adding different quantities of water. The day before the telecast, we all assembled with Kirk Browning, the producer, and had a wonderful, enthusiastic, spontaneous chat. This sapped everyone's interest in the subject. The next night, I hurried backstage during intermission to join the already started session. As I approached, Beverly gave me a kind of relieved, exhausted welcome, and basically said, "what do *you* think, John?"

Beverly continued her kindnesses to me during a radio telethon this season. I had put together a recording, *John Wion Live*, of concerto performances from my Australian tours (Ibert, Mozart, Saint-Saëns, Hofmann), to be used solely for publicity purposes. I offered a number of copies for auction. She gave a lovely promotion and later sent me a note saying the copies had disappeared very quickly.

This spring's concerts included a fabulous *Matthew Passion* with Musica Sacra at Lincoln Center, and performances of the Kennan *Night Soliloquy* and Hanson *Serenade* with the QSO at Merkin Hall. At the close of the spring season, I began taking ear-training lessons. I always felt my Australian training had been inadequate and that some intensive study could only be of benefit. I found a terrific teacher, organist Ford Lallerstedt, who drilled me relentlessly but with amazing patience, twice a week. This went on until my involvement in an orchestra negotiation the following year got in the way of everything else. When I finally was able to think about starting again, Ford wouldn't return my calls. I imagine he had written me off as not serious. Unfinished or not, the experience was invaluable, and I was able to hear intervals and follow musical lines with more clarity.

In July, with our boys in summer camp, Vicky and I spent a month in Tuscany. We had been looking into home exchanges as an affordable way to stay away for an extended time, but nothing in our chosen area worked out. One respondent, however, explained that their listing was an error, that they actually rented some properties on their Chianti vineyard. Our friend Livio was kind enough to phone them to get a sense of the advisability of pursuing this, and he gave a favorable report. They would rent us their son's car, and further, they would pick us up in Rome. It all sounded too good. Yet they did indeed meet us, Signor and Signora Lucarelli – he a former schoolteacher, she his student. Their estate, Malfiano, had been in her family for generations. Exhausted by the overnight flight and wanting nothing more than to lie down somewhere horizontal, we were dazed when our hosts said they would take us to lunch first. Driving across Rome, the signore confided that we would be having lunch with his sister, and a bit further on told us his sister was a nun. Strike three!

To the contrary, the experience was memorable. The sister was a teaching nun and school was out for the summer. The other nuns cooked and served, while we five had a true Italian feast. We had no idea what to expect, our first surprise being the copious flow of wine. When our host said after the antipasto, "a leetle more, signore," well, it was so good. And after the pasta, which I assumed was the main course, "a leetle more." But then came the veal scallopini, the vegetables, the cheese and dessert. After a compulsory tour of the empty classrooms, we collapsed in a stupor beneath a pine tree, as our hosts took the traditional siesta indoors. A couple of hours later we heard stirring, we politely declined lemonade, and eventually, with an espresso stop, we reached Malfiano. Our two-bedroom apartment was the second floor of a recently built unit – simple but elegantly Italian. Sitting on the deck, we had a view that stretched across the vineyard, across Tuscany, until it blurred into the horizon. We were always being encouraged to take more wine for our room, vegetables from the garden, fruit from the trees. They made sure we always had a small pitcher of their precious olive oil – not for cooking! Late each afternoon, Raffaele (the signore) would appear at the "library," a garage used as the wine cellar. He would hang around, rinsing some bottles or something, until one of the guests would appear, "a leetle wine, signore?" And so the party assembled. We made close friends and have returned to Malfiano many times since.

That first year it was a great base for discovering northern Italy. So much could be covered in a two-hour radius: Pisa in one direction, Perugia the opposite. And yet, we felt such bliss just sitting on our balcony in Casa Elena, that we settled into a routine of being tourists only on alternate days. We frequented the local restaurants. Raffaele would ask how much we paid, and if he felt it was too much, would phone the owner and complain. The nearest village, the hilltop Civitella della Chiana, was pretty sleepy at that time – a bakery, a general store. Now the smart set drive up from Arezzo for pizza on the piazza overlooking the valley or dinner at the elegant new restaurant in the old olive press. Germans are still not welcome. During the war, the partisans killed three German soldiers. The Germans retaliated by lining up three hundred male villagers against the church and killing them. Our signora, Lara, twenty on that day, survived the smoking-out of villagers from hiding, and has written down the story for future generations to know.

We were paying so little for our apartment that we felt we could stay away overnight without feeling too guilty. We drove across the Appenines to see the stunning mosaics at Ravenna and then drove up the Adriatica to Venice, to stay with friends from 180 Riverside Drive who had taken an apartment on Giudecca. The Adriatica is a three-lane highway. I was crawling along in the right lane, watching cars and trucks zoom up and down the middle lane. After a while, I asked Vicky where we were on the map. She checked off a tiny fraction of our necessary itinerary. Out I zoomed and started playing that terrifying game of chicken, driving up the center lane with one eye on the approaching vehicle and the other on the last possible car to veer in front of. We did get to Venice, but I will never do that again.

The view from Casa Elena, Malfiano, Tuscany.

On the way back, we circled via Verona to catch a performance of *Aida* at the Roman amphitheater. The audience for the unreserved seats in the rings arrives early and waits for the gates to open. Then a natural but scary pressure is felt, as everyone converges on the nearest entrance. Entry is by batches for security check. You get your cushion and a little candle, and wend your way up. The place was jammed. Lines of people circled the rings in both directions, pleading with someone to move a little and make an extra space. Night fell, and, following a speech in Italian, everyone lit their candles. We didn't understand the significance, but it made for a lovely sight. The performance was a true event – no amplification but a double orchestra and chorus. At the end of an act, the leads bowed at the left, center, and right of the stage and had quite a little walk between bows. The triumphal procession with its chorus of trumpets and line of elephants was spectacular.

At the August NFA convention in Seattle, I was asked to present a lecture on musicians' injuries, a version of which was then published in the association's newsletter. The presentations at this convention marked an important beginning in awareness, discussion, and dissemination of information about injuries by the NFA.

The highlight of my fall was Musica Sacra's memorable performance of the B Minor Mass at Philharmonic Hall. The opera orchestra had postponed a difficult negotiation by settling for an extension of the existing contract to cover the fall. The season offered two flute moments – Ambroise Thomas's *Hamlet*, a vehicle for returning Sherrill Milnes, and Christoph Willibald Gluck's *Alceste*. The former includes the soprano mad scene which I had played in the Pavarotti/Sutherland concert, while the latter contains a dance solo, charming if not as poignant as the famous *Orphée* one.

The year ended with our final Los Angeles season, something that added to the overall gloom prevalent among us. With a new summer/fall format ahead, the orchestra would have no work for the entire first half of the year. When work began in mid-July of 1983, it would consist of a single rehearsal week and a continuous nineteen-week season. Without Los Angeles, these twenty weeks would be all the orchestra had to look forward to in the future. The question in every mind was how long would the strike last?

1983

A large part of my energies this year would be devoted to negotiating a new contract for the opera orchestra, as a member of its five-person committee. Additionally, I had been asked by Ms. Sills to be the orchestra's representative on the opera's board. She felt that having someone from each area participate in the meetings would somehow instill a new sense of cooperation. However, the level of antagonism in the orchestra was too high for this to have any impact. Not only would we have seven weeks less work to look forward to; no one seemed to understand the consequences of moving work from spring to summer. Many orchestra members subsidized their opera income with summer jobs at New York's Mostly Mozart Festival, or out-of-town locations such as Aspen or Chautauqua. Now they would have to relinquish these positions. In addition, the New York freelance season was fall/spring, and it might not be easy to pick up work in just the spring part. This was what my colleagues were grappling with, and they were in no mood to compromise.

I, on the other hand, saw that my life was going to be easier. Most of the opera rehearsing would be completed when the fall semester at school started, and the season would end before Thanksgiving. In the spring I would have no conflict with my teaching schedule.

In this my opera-free spring I was seeing doctors, taking ear-training lessons, spending two days a week at Hartt, playing orchestral concerts with Musica Sacra and Queens Symphony, subbing on Broadway at Anthony Quinn's *Zorba*, and playing chamber music concerts with Bronx Arts. At these latter concerts, we played the Hummel *Septet* with pianist Eugene List, and introduced the *Nonet* of the nineteenth-century French composer, Louise Farrenc. This latter made an excellent recording, along with the Josef Rheinberger *Nonet*. I also played a recital.

I had been invited by the New York Flute Club to play the March concert of their Cami Hall series and felt good enough about the state of my playing to accept. I was getting a better sense of which pieces I could negotiate without too much anxiety and chose Bach B Minor *Sonata*, Rheinberger *Rhapsody*, Copland *Duo*, Messaien *Merle Noir*, and Prokofiev *Sonata*. I also felt enough time had passed since 1978 that I could ask Gil Kalish to join me, and he accepted. This would be our last concert together, and in many ways a memorable one for me.

SUNDAY, MARCH 27, 1983 AT 5:30 P.M.
CAMI CONCERT HALL, 165 WEST 57th STREET, N.Y.

JOHN WION, Flute   GILBERT KALISH, Piano

Sonata in B Minor BWV 1030   J. S. BACH (1685-1750)
    Andante
    Largo e dolce
    Presto

Rhapsodie in B Major   J. RHEINBERGER (1839-1901)

Duo   A. COPLAND (1900-   )
    Flowing
    Poetic, somewhat mournful
    Lively, with bounce

INTERMISSION

Le Merle Noir   O. MESSAIEN (1908-   )

Sonata Op. 94   S. PROKOFIEV (1891-1954)
    Andantino
    Presto
    Andante
    Allegro con brio

NEXT CONCERT: Sunday, April 24, 1983 at 5:30 P.M.
FLUTE CLUB COMPETITION WINNERS
At Trinity School, 139 West 91st Street, N.Y.

In May, I made a quick two-week trip to Australia, mostly to see my mother. With her now in her eighties, I felt it important to make this trip each year. My only performing was to make a tape of the Bach *Partita* and the C. P. E. Bach unaccompanied *Sonata* for the ABC – no rehearsing required. Back home, we made an interesting trip to the West with the boys, to visit an array of parks. We found ourselves with a congenial group, led by an enthusiastic young couple who cooked, guided, helped pitch tents and navigate white-water, and made us all feel thoroughly comfortable.

Then, with Anthony in summer camp, Vicky and I left Russell in New York and took off for Italy. The highlight was definitely our visit to Lake Como, surely one of the most magical places in the world. And the most memorable moment was a dinner on the little island of Comacina. As light fell, our (powered) gondola slid across the lake to the restaurant in the only villa on this island. Dinner was served on the patio – no menu, but an endless procession of dishes ending much, much later with flamed coffee, and our boatman waiting to glide us home across the starred lake.

The Wion family at the Grand Canyon, 1983.

Between these relaxing interludes, we had negotiation, or rather non-negotiation meetings in New York. The orchestra had voted not to accept the management's offer, as was clearly expected, and the season did not open in July as scheduled. In fact, the entire summer season was lost. A period of much anger, frustration, and soul-searching had to pass before a depressing three-year agreement was reached at the end of August. The committee had to sit through endless meetings with mediators, lawyers, and union officials, since the time when we could actually sit across the table from the management had long passed. I was still attending board meetings, and at the June meeting said how disturbed I was at the lack of progress in negotiations. No one seemed interested. Then the board meetings were canceled for the length of the strike, and I realized that the board had no part in anything but fund-raising; the decisions were being made by the executive committee.

The chairman was the millionaire Robert Wilson, who had cordially invited me to lunch earlier in the year when my tenure on his board started. I prepared statistics for him to show how our orchestra's compensation was falling behind other orchestras', even the NYC Ballet, and even in real terms, when inflation was factored in. He found them interesting but added, quite correctly, that they couldn't affect the current negotiations. The board had approved an inadequate budget, and this was being used as the yardstick to show how preposterous our proposals were.

After we started back in the fall and the board began meeting again, I asked to address the gathering. I prepared my speech carefully, outlining the issues of the strike and its impact, and basically urging the board not to let this happen again. The speech was not long – five pages, maybe ten minutes – but in the middle, the chairman interrupted, and asked if I would be finished soon. He went on to ask, if I was so unhappy in the orchestra why did I stay? I was stunned. Beverly smoothed things over and said with her big smile that they should let me finish. Thoroughly deflated, I did. I wished I could have composed a proper answer to his question. Instead I resigned from the board.

I also resigned from any further committee work. Two situations in particular left me feeling particularly inadequate. The first consisted of a private meeting with Beverly Sills. Our committee had come up with a bottom line proposal, and I, because of my relationship with her, had been assigned to ask – totally off the record – if this were offered, would it be accepted? Boy, was I naive! She immediately called in one of the management team to write down my proposals. And of course that became a new level from which to beat us down.

The other incident, mentioned earlier in this story, occurred when an orchestra member approached me after a mid-strike meeting to ask why we were on strike when we were all out freelancing for less money than we earned at the opera. He had a point, because our strikes did not in fact lead to any substantial gains. For instance, an important issue in this negotiation was extra weeks of work, to compensate for the shortened new format. Just not possible we were told, until, miraculously, after nine weeks of strike, nine weeks of extra work over the life of the contract were offered as part of the final package.

In truth, this was the end of the NYCO orchestra as a body that had dreams of full-time employment. It now became the best freelance job in the city. The new players coming into the orchestra saw it as a summer job that extended into the fall, until the regular freelance season got into full swing. They treated it as a freelance job too, manipulating their schedules to be able to play outside engagements. Over the years, we had argued that we were working too hard, that other orchestras, including opera ones, played four performances a week, not six or seven or eight. But now, with members freelancing at every opportunity, seven days a week if possible, how could we argue this? And who cared?

In the meantime, I was still trying to deal with my hand problems. One of the first performing arts clinics was at the Massachusetts General Hospital in Boston, and with considerable optimism that fall I arranged appointments with Dr. Leffert, a surgeon, and Dr. Hochberg, a nerve specialist. The former, however, could only suggest minimizing the bend of the left wrist. The latter, with no real measuring instruments, was even less helpful, proposing only a regimen of drugs and swimming.

The fall "freelance" season introduced me to Massenet's charming *Cendrillon* at NYCO and included a repeat of the *B Minor Mass* with conductor Richard Westenburg.

At the NFA convention in Philadelphia, during our strike, I was elected to the vice presidency, president-elect. The concept of this three-year tenure was to allow one year of learning, one of doing, and one of advising. I learned in the coming year that the NFA was a solid organization that could survive an inadequate president for a year without self-destructing (no reflection on my predecessor). That made me feel less overwhelmed, and I started to wonder if I might in fact be able to be of some service when my time came.

NFA Years

1984

The "operaless" spring once again gave me the opportunity to focus on therapy, a series of Rolfing sessions for the physical angle, and a psychologist for the mental side. I had been asked to play a concerto at a Bronx Arts Ensemble concert in February and preparing for this occupied the early weeks of the year. *Turns and Mordents* by the New York composer Bruce Saylor was the choice of the conductor, John Demain. I did not learn till later that he had intended to have it played by Linda Chesis, with whom he had performed its premiere. BAE's director Bill Scribner insisted that I be the soloist for this concert – another example of his continued loyalty to our longtime friendship. I was able to make it up to Linda a couple of years later by asking her to play this excellent concerto at the New York NFA convention.

Also in February, I went to Boston to pick up my new Brannen flute, in silver, number 500. My serious hand troubles somewhat coincided with getting my first gold flute, and it seemed sensible to try using the lighter weight of silver. The event, which was of some significance to the Brannens also, became an occasion for a little surprise party for Bick Brannen. I had requested number 500 and later similarly asked for number 1000. That, however, turned out to be too significant, and they asked if I would relinquish my request so they could keep that numbered flute for their own archive. When I did order a second silver flute to take advantage of technical improvements, I secured number 1992, the only flute ever to carry the serial number of its year of manufacture.

In an effort to provide some work in the first half of the year, the opera arranged a recording of Philip Glass's *Satyagraha*, which oddly was not yet in our repertoire. This experience was surrealistic in every way, and not something I would ever want to be involved with again. The decision had been made to record the music by building up layers of sound. The strings would be first. We started hearing horrific stories about insistence on metronomic exactitude and technical perfection in this minimalist music of endlessly repeated arpeggios. Under normal performing circumstances, this kind of detail would be lost in the overall blend of sounds (opera is not an exact art!), but here everything was transparent. The concertmaster had finally resorted to tuning each string chord by going back through the ranks. When everyone had their fingers exactly set for the particular arpeggio, that section would be recorded. Now came our turn.

We spent a whole week at the RCA studios playing repetitions of arpeggios, the worst possible activity for my tendinitis-prone state. A synthesized version of the music had been pre-recorded and a click track added, and we had to conform to this via our headphones. You might wonder at the need for a conductor, but Christopher Keene was up front waving his arms around. Actually, by the end of our week he had called in sick, and the remainder was "conducted" by one of the engineers.

We spent the entire first morning playing three chords. A page of music was called and rehearsed. It consisted of one arpeggio a number of times, then a second, then maybe the first again. This section of music took a couple of minutes. Problems needed solving. Breaths for example – can't have those. The two flutes could take alternate breaths, but what to do about that single piccolo — and on top too? When we finally got these couple of pages recorded, we were given another section to rehearse, exactly the same chords at the same tempo, but we spent another hour recording them all over again. Then a third section! It was mind-boggling. To top it off, we returned from lunch to find that the producers still weren't happy. However, they had a creative solution. We would re-record the same sections of music but only play every second bar. With their digital editor they would stop and start the recording. Then we would repeat the process, filling in the "even" bars. The playback was sensational, impossibly perfect. Could have been a machine. Should have been a machine.

Much more interesting was a concert performance at Carnegie Hall of Dvorak's *Dimitrij*. This was the kind of freelance activity that I could now fit into my schedule. Even if the operatically untrained musicians were not as adept at this kind of material as our opera orchestra, the variety made it fun — and Andrew Porter mentioned me again in his *New Yorker* review! Subbing on Broadway was also enjoyable. I now added *On Your Toes* to *Zorba*. One way or another, March was just as busy as when I was playing the opera. Its high point was a second *Matthew Passion* with Westenburg. Apart from the profound satisfaction of the opening and closing choruses and the wonderful "*Aus Liebe*" obbligato with its two English horn accompaniment, I had the pleasure of listening to the instrumental solos of my colleagues, most notably Ronnie Roseman's oboe and Jean Benjamin's violin. This is not to diminish the overall level of all involved — soloists (particularly Charlie Bressler as the Evangelist), chorus, and conductor. This was a deeply moving performance of a transcendent masterpiece.

Just as things were easing up in April, Sam Baron had a heart attack and I was asked to cover his class at SUNY Stonybrook for the rest of the semester. This made for a long day, too much of it on the Long Island Expressway, but it proved to be an interesting experience. Although I found the students less technically polished than expected, it became clear to me later that Sam had a gift for recognizing interesting students with intellectual curiosity. Several of them went on to have successful careers, notably Laura Gilbert, Tara O'Connor, and Alexa Still.

In May I went once again to Australia, this time with better preparation resulting in more engagements. In Melbourne I played three recitals, one unaccompanied, one with harpsichord, and one with piano. Moving up to Sydney, I did a week's residency at the conservatorium that included a recital. It was a strange experience. I enjoyed working with the students but didn't feel particularly welcomed by the administration. On my last day, having not yet met the director, I asked for an appointment. He was perfectly pleasant. When I expressed a sense of being ignored, he recalled how welcome he himself had been made to feel when he had been a guest in the U.S.A. Somehow it had not occurred to him to act the same way.

I spent the weekend in Brisbane teaching a class and participating in a concert in which I played the Quantz *G Major Concerto* with an amateur orchestra as well as the Prokofiev *Sonata*. After flying back to Melbourne, I made a tape for the ABC of Copland and Rheinberger. My lively associate was Dobbs Franks, who had conducted my Reinecke and Molique on earlier tours. Finally I traveled to Adelaide for a weekend with the local flute society — a seminar, a class, some private lessons, and a full recital with piano. My repertoire for all these concerts was a combination of my New York recital and my bag of unaccompanied pieces, and it worked pretty well for me. I even garnered some nice reviews in Sydney and Adelaide. The Quantz was a problem; some of the extended technical passages were too awkward for me and sent my hand into spasm with rather messy results.

June saw Russell's graduation from high school. He had had a nasty shock in the spring when his first college letter was a rejection from The University of California, his safety. His advisor phoned the school and it seemed a mistake had been made, but in the meantime some other acceptances had come in. He chose RPI's computer science degree. Rensselaer was one of the first colleges to develop a profile of "computer kids," bright students with excellent math skills, who did not always have across-the-board As.

Russell's graduation from Columbia Prep, June 1984.

By the end of the month the opera was back in session. First was a week at Artpark at Lewistown near the Canadian border, then the first nineteen-week New York season. Interesting were Stravinsky's *Rake's Progress* and Delibe's *Lakmé*. A strange *Carmen* set in the time of the Spanish Civil War and full of gunfire was also offered. This was PBS's choice to telecast. I watched the beautiful third act entr'acte, wondering if I would be on camera. Instead the camera focused on the conductor's back throughout, and the audio pickup favored a single string on the harp. An excellent production of *Sweeney Todd* was marred only by the odor of whatever smoke device was being used on stage – unpleasant, given the association with pies made from the barber's victims. At one of the later performances of this work, Sondheim sat in the pit. I remember thinking that this was my equivalent to Mozart watching a performance of *Magic Flute*. With the experience of recording Philip Glass's *Satyagraha* clear in my mind, I excused myself from performances of the same composer's *Akhnaten*.

Every now and then things fuse in an opera house and sheer magic is the result. This season it was Puccini's "failure," *La Rondine*. He wrote this for Vienna, and filled with waltzes it is. But when Austria and Italy were on opposite sides in the First World War, the commission was unfilled. Instead, it finally appeared in Milan. Being so different from Puccini's other operas, it was misunderstood and did not enter the repertoire. Things had conspired against it at City Opera too – first the tragic death of Cal Simmons, the scheduled conductor, and then one of our strikes. Now the conductor making his debut was Alessandro Siciliani, and did he ever make music! The rubati were extreme and omnipresent as he milked every nuance from the score. The singers hated him because he led instead of following. At the dress rehearsal, in the final scene, the tenor walked off the stage in frustration (so they said). But the opening was electric. The second act contains a grand sextet with chorus set in a Parisian restaurant straight out of Renoir. At the end the audience erupted, going on and on, and the conductor didn't know what to do. My Italian friend Livio, perhaps in jest, said to him, "Bis" [Again]. Siciliani swept his arms at the orchestra and launched into a repeat, unheard of at NYCO. Everyone scrambled. I can imagine the confusion and regrouping on stage. Every performance was received with the same enthusiasm, but the conductor had been given strict instructions; we would have no more repeats.

My downer during the season was an incident involving our music director, Christopher Keene. With a crisis in one of the sections of the orchestra, he was making a move towards a firing. I had been asked if I would act as an informal mediator, and I participated in a couple of sessions with the parties. My meetings with Christopher were amicable. He was brilliant, articulate, and had a good sense of humor. Then at a one-on-one meeting before a performance of *Carmen* that he was conducting, he lit into me in an extraordinary way, as if I were somehow responsible for his problem with these players. I was flabbergasted. During the first act, it was all I could focus on. Then a day or two later I received a formal letter from him complaining about my performance that night. I quickly phoned a number of my colleagues to see if they had noticed anything about my playing. Nothing had been noted, indeed one colleague said he thought I had played particularly well that night. Yet, the more I thought about it, the less I thought could be achieved by responding. Instead I wrote down all the facts in a letter to the union, just to match the one that was now on file at NYCO. Years later that I learned that Chris had a serious drinking problem, and I was glad in retrospect that I had let the matter die. We had a good working relationship for the rest of his life, but I made a point of avoiding any one-on-one situation.

Since the end of the Chicago convention in August, I had been president of the National Flute Association and would spend much time over the next twelve months dealing with its activities and problems. My predecessor, Erv Monroe, had dealt with the first of these, changing the newsletter to a new, enlarged format called *The Flutist Quarterly* and appointing a new editor. This was before the NFA established a policy of rotating chairs on a five-year basis, so it was difficult to ask someone to relinquish a position without it seeming like dissatisfaction. My responsibility was to work with the new editor and help develop this new format. Erv had made a good choice in Glennis Stout, and after she got over the typical sense of being overwhelmed, she proved to be a good editor. Most people joined the NFA to attend a convention, and then many, particularly students, would not renew their membership. (And we didn't even have a system of reminding them!) I felt it was important that the *Quarterly* be seen as reason in itself to maintain membership. I thought, for example, that an ongoing listing of flute recordings, a couple of pages a month, would be a good hook. So we found a member with an amazing database he was willing to share and began the series.

With outgoing NFA President, Erv Monroe, August 1984.

The second problem I had to deal with myself, although it did not originate with me. This was the appointment of the program chair for the upcoming Denver convention. The local flute club in Denver had worked hard to get its city chosen, and they expected that their president would be appointed to the run the convention program. Many former administrators had strongly advised me that this would not be a good idea because local politics would inevitably get in the way, and the program might tend to lack a national appeal. All of this made sense to me, and I decided to ask Bill Montgomery to serve as program chair. Bill had chaired the early Atlanta convention, and I thought it had been imaginative and well organized. He gave it long thought and, believing that he could in fact offer some new twists and improvements, agreed. I then had to deal with Denver. Although feathers were ruffled, everyone ended up providing terrific support, both in ideas and the implementation of ideas, and for the enormous, thankless burden of actually manning the convention. An outside director was a good idea, and one that became a general rule for the NFA.

I became an exception to the rule in the fall, however, when newly elected vice president Felix Skowronek phoned to ask if I would create the program for the New York Convention, set for 1986. Feelings were that New York was different – that only someone living there could manage the event. I believe this proved to be true, and the NFA made another exception ten years later when the convention came again to New York. I was an exception in the NFA anyway; the normal progression was for a program chair to later become president. With this confluence, I was being asked to run the organization and at the same time spend two years preparing the convention program. Vicky and I spent some time thinking through the ramifications. I decided first that I could handle it, and second that it would be hard to find anyone else who could do better, if indeed we could find anyone at all. Before accepting, I met with the board of the New York Flute Club, to see if they were prepared to do all the "dirty work." I actually had a difficult time, as few of its members went to the conventions. However, they did agree, and in the end provided wonderful service. So I too agreed. 1985 would be a busy year. I was already preparing a recital program for February and another Australian tour for May.

1985

Compared to the previous spring, my freelance activities were minimal. Vicky and I made an effort to schedule some free time around my set commitments. In February, we spent a week in Martinique and in March took advantage of Hartt's spring break to spend a week in Paris. In addition, we were able to spend some weekends at our cottage. In terms of my hand problem, I had been recommended to another physical therapist and spent the spring working with him without success.

I had planned a recital program to present at Hartt, feeling that this was the only way I would force myself to learn some new repertoire. My pianist was Bridget Castro, wife of a Hartt faculty pianist. Her initial enthusiasm had prompted the recital. I was nervous when I learned she would be away over the winter vacation, but she turned out to be a fast learner. In addition to the Bach *A Major*, which I had never played in public, and the Taffanel *Andante Pastorale et Scherzettino*, which I had learned for my recording, but also never played in public, I learned the Robert Muczynski *Sonata*, the Schubert *Arpeggione Sonata* arranged for flute, *Goldfish Through Summer Rain* by Australian composer Anne Boyd, and *Five Preludes* by the Hartt composer, Stephen Gryc.

This latter had been performed by one of my undergraduates a few years before, and I had been sufficiently impressed to want to add it to my repertoire. Each unaccompanied solo captured a distinct mood with great effect, from the first "Fish in Shallow Water," with its darting shimmers, to the final "Calm Lake and Autumn Moon," with its mesmerizing sustained progression ending with the long high G produced by alternating different harmonics. I would go on to give many performances of these wonderful pieces and to record them, but the first spin-off was that Steve proposed writing a concerto for me. That composition, *The Moon's Mirror*, evolved over the year and premiered at school in the fall. The Muczynski proved to be too stressful for my hand and was soon dropped from my repertoire; the *Arpeggione* created serious breathing problems and, although I enjoyed playing it, I decided I would rather hear it on cello. The remaining three pieces, Bach, Boyd, and Taffanel served me well in future recitals.

Also this April, I had the thrill of performing the Foote *Night Piece* and the Mozart *D Major* with the Emerson Quartet on one of their Hartt programs. These four outstanding musicians are also four extraordinary people, and making music with them was a joy. They are very relaxed and laid back and funny, but that does not mean their preparation and performance are casual. The concert was taped and played over PBS. If I had one reservation, it was about their wish to play the Mozart *Adagio* very slowly. They had recently recorded it that way.

In the same month, I performed the Telemann *Suite* at a concert in Tappan Zee, New York, as a part of a series organized by Abba Bogin, contractor of the Queens Symphony. Abba had a partnership with the composer Arnold Black who, among his other activities, wrote television commercials of a more classical type for upmarket sponsors like Estée Lauder and Bermuda Travel. He wrote me some nice flute moments for these, and their success led to some good residual payments for a few years.

May was once again Australia, and again without Vicky, who had made her own trip there the previous month to stage a ballet. I had signed an agreement with an agent in Australia the previous year, and for the first time was relieved of a lot of correspondence. Still, I had to deal with plenty of crossed wires, lost letters, and general confusion before the itinerary was in place. In fact the agent had not secured me any work, basically acting as a negotiator/secretary. I had had dealings with many managers over these years, and finally realized that this was all they ever really did do. Getting engagements was always going to be my own responsibility.

As the spring progressed and I worked on my chosen repertoire, I was finding an increased level of dysfunction in my left hand. I knew I could modify my solo repertoire if necessary, but I was having a particular problem with the outer movements of the Reinecke *Concerto*, which I was scheduled to play with the Tasmanian Orchestra on their concert series. The problem, as usual, was certain extended arpeggiated passages. I was trying a large cork spacer between my first left finger and the flute to see if that helped, but I looked for a remedy in a totally different area also.

I had been reading Eloise Ristad's wonderful book, *A Soprano on Her Head*. Hearing that she was in the city giving a class, I registered. She was a warm, enthusiastic person whose life sadly ended too soon when, losing her balance, she fell from a boat and died of hypothermia. Much of what she did was improvisatory, looking for anything that might help a student. In her class she had several routines like ball throwing and dancing. This latter gave me my own opportunity to make a contribution to the class. One of the women in the class, a pianist, was a superb dancer – absolutely natural, sinuous in her movements. Yet, when she came to play the piano, she was rigid and inexpressive. I asked if she could play without the bench. When she did she became a different performer. As she thought on the matter, she realized that when she started piano as a young girl, her teacher had been strict about position and lack of movement. She was carrying this unconsciously into adulthood. In my own demonstration I played some Reinecke, focusing, of course, on trying to get the notes to come out. The class response was "you play fine, but you don't seem involved in communicating music." I explained my problem and took their suggestion that I try again just focusing on expression, in other words performing! I'm a good performer and they loved my second effort, though I knew the notes weren't coming out any better.

So, full of anxiety, I headed off to meet my fate in Hobart. At the concert I "performed" very well, and the slow movement was really quite lovely, but I was depressed by the quality of the outer movements. A longtime colleague, David Cubbin, was in the audience, and without criticizing the performance, observed just how angled I was holding the flute. The value of this observation only took hold when I later began my Alexander studies. After I explained my dilemma, David recommended I see a doctor in Melbourne, Hunter Fry, who was developing an international reputation as an expert in musicians' injuries. He was kind to me and took a good history but used no equipment at all. His recommendation was to take a year away from the flute, after which I should begin again, playing no more than two minutes a day and slowly rebuilding a new approach to the instrument. The problem to avoid was jumping right back in and assuming the old habits. If this wasn't financially possible, he calmly suggested that I consider retiring from playing the flute and directing my life elsewhere. I was shocked. People who are not performers just don't understand the psychological implications of cutting oneself off from a life force that has been growing since pre-puberty.

A Melbourne ABC taping of a program with string quartet was at the last moment rescheduled for Perth, so I had a whole week to enjoy friends and family before flying there for my two-week residency at the University of Western Australia. The taping of Foote and Beach with a quartet from the WASO went well, and I enjoyed working with the students, despite their obvious insularity from international standards. I played some concerts with visiting pianist Roy Howatt, who proved to be an excellent associate and friend who later became involved with the critical edition of Debussy's music.

A newspaper photographer has caught my angled posture.

I learned a good lesson from one of these concerts, where I played on stage feeling miserable and wondered what I was doing half way round the world from my family. A local professional took me to lunch afterwards and started telling me his own woes about having negative thoughts while performing. Then he said, "And then I go to your concert and you're up there having such a good time." I had to share the irony with him.

I felt even further from home when I got a call from Vicky to tell me that she had been mugged on our street in New York. She had been pushed from behind onto the pavement and probably momentarily blacked out. Sixteen-year-old Anthony had been home and had gotten her to the emergency room and back, and helped her through the immediate trauma. I felt so helpless and far away for the rest of my tour; somehow the telephone was not enough.

I participated in a festival in the nearby town of York, gave a class for the flute society, and another for the conservatorium. At the latter I met Brian Warren, British flutist and Alexander teacher. I explained my problems and he recommended me to Judith Youett, an English clarinetist and Alexander teacher who had recently moved to New York. I filed this information away, little knowing how it would affect my life.

Back in Melbourne, I was a guest at the flute club's annual weekend out of town, and then prepared for my important recital in the city, which they were sponsoring. I intended to play my Hartt program, but the thought of playing Muczynski was discouraging. When the pianist, Nahama Patkin, expressed some reservations about its content at our first rehearsal, I happily proposed changing to Copland. I have not had many fan letters in my life and was extremely touched by the adult student who wrote: "Thank you, thank you for a wonderful evening of beautiful music. The last note of 'calm lake and autumn moon' still haunts me. I just wish the two hours had not gone so quickly." Following this concert I flew to Hawaii, and a needed reunion with my bruised Vicky.

We arrived back in New York on Sunday morning for the opera season which began its week of rehearsal the following Tuesday. I also made immediate contact with a highly recommended chiropractor, with whom I met weekly for the next year. I had seven weeks until the Denver convention to see that all was going as planned and, more important, to prepare for my duties as president. I had made a quick trip to Denver the previous winter to get a feel for the facilities at the Fairmont Hotel and around the city and was confident that good choices had been made. Bill Montgomery, although needing to be pushed to meet deadlines, came through with an imaginative program with William Bennett as the headliner. Montgomery took advantage of a nearby church to use as the principal concert hall. That meant we had to concern ourselves with the question of safety for the audience walking from the hotel and back. The opening night would be at an outdoor amphitheater – a picnic and a jazz concert with Steve Kujala. In an effort to get people to pre-register, we gave several incentives, including ten free convention registrations. My assignment on opening night, apart from welcoming everyone, was to draw the winners of this raffle. We also made an arrangement with an airline to sponsor the convention flyer and offer a special discount fare.

I didn't see too much of the convention itself, being otherwise engaged with administration. But still engraved in my mind is the exquisite performance of Charles-Marie Widor's *Suite* by Marilyn Prestia. Marilyn's father, Ross, as NFA Exhibits Coordinator, was a cornerstone of these early conventions. He became a trusted advisor and dear friend.

Two things concerned me as I reviewed the NFA's state during the year. The first was the fact that we were running an annual profit. I was not sure how long this was acceptable to the IRS in relation to a nonprofit organization. Beyond checking with our lawyer, Doug Royal, I proposed we spend a bit more, specifically in commissioning a new work for the annual Young Artist Competition. The new work would become a compulsory part of each semi-finalist's program.

The second matter was administrative. I read through all the minutes of board meetings since the founding and discovered that the board regularly proposed a directive affecting some part of its activity. However these directives were never incorporated into any document. As the administration changed totally every three years, the directives passed into history. I therefore spent a lot of time at the daily meetings reviewing each directive and asking the board to pass it up or down. I then arranged for those pre-approved directives to become a part of the bylaws. And finally it was my duty to prepare and present for approval the budget for the following year. I spent much time agonizing over this but was assured by my predecessor not to worry, it would all fall into place. I had a double interest here because a large part of the budget would be devoted to "my" New York convention. This would obviously be our biggest event to date, but I needed to be conservative regarding the expected attendance. Ross Prestia helped make the assessment relating to income from the exhibitors, again our largest number.

My presidential welcome.

I believed that the entire income from the convention should be available to me, to ensure that it would be our best program yet. I also called a meeting of past presidents, feeling that we were losing an important resource by not keeping them informed and not seeking their perspective and advice.

I enjoyed many wonderful moments between meetings. I had the presidential suite on the top floor – in Denver that is pretty spectacular. I hosted parties, and I got to conduct the traditional Bach *Air* at the final gathering. Then I finally handed over my responsibilities to Felix Skowronek and relaxed. I also met people like Geoffrey Gilbert, who sent me a lovely note afterwards, thanking us for inviting him. I met Michael Emmerson, James Galway's manager, who attended the convention as a judge and lecturer. I had been in touch with him immediately after being appointed program chair for New York, to see if Galway was a possible headliner, but had not heard back from him. Now, introducing myself, I mentioned this, saying I assumed his silence meant no-go. He looked me straight in the eye and said, "To the contrary, I think we should talk." And talk we did. By the end I knew New York couldn't fail.

Having been given a week's leave from the opera, I picked right up again for the week before Labor Day. Then my teaching began and I was back in full swing.

Vicky was also busy. With Russell at college and Anthony grown up, she had allowed her staging assignments to grow to a point where her fall and spring were filled with five-day trips around the country separated by weekends at home. Her break came as companies swung into their holiday *Nutcracker* productions. The week after the opera season ended in November, the orchestra was hired to play a concert performance of Donizetti's *Anna Bolena*, an opera Beverly Sills had had such a success with. This time the queens would be Joan Sutherland and Marilyn Horne, with Richard Bonynge conducting. I had fun working with such high-profile performers again, and felt thrilled to be participating in their great art, as well as an operagoer's "event of a lifetime."

After handing over responsibility to incoming NFA President, Felix Skowronek, August 1985.

I also had my music for Steve Gryc's *Moon's Mirror*, and was working out the technical difficulties. The third movement was built around extended running sixteenth note passages, some of which I found awkward. I had to work slowly at finding ways to stop or minimize my hand spasms. I was excited to finally hear the piece with the school orchestra in November and enjoy the sensitive coloring of the strings, percussion, and alto flute accompaniment. The performance went quite well.

The busy part of my fall was, of course, developing the program for August's convention. I had free rein from President Skowronek, although I always ran my ideas by him before proceeding. I also had the input of the enormously creative Michael Emmerson, and not only in relation to Galway's part. My first priority was to set the principal evening concerts in place. The gala opening of the convention on Thursday would be a full concert by James Galway with orchestra. Friday would be a chamber music concert. Saturday would be a full recital by Julius Baker. Sunday would be the closing concerto concert.

I made two early decisions. One, I saw this as a New York performers' convention. I had previously sent out feelers to some high-profile European flutists, none of whom was available, and I was now actually thankful for this. The talent in New York was extraordinary – so many people actively pursuing creative lives as soloists, chamber musicians, composers – and it seemed almost insulting to be looking elsewhere. Galway was in another category of course. I did not mean to be parochial about this, and in the end a number of non–New Yorkers did participate in one way or another, but I felt it was a good working principle.

My other decision was that I wanted certain pieces, my repertoire, on the program. In some cases I could tell someone, "This is the piece I want you to play," and that was the end of it. However, I was also dealing with some big names where it was more a matter of asking politely and accepting a rejection. I was particularly anxious to get the concertos of William Lovelock, Heinrich Hofmann, and Bruce Saylor onto the final program. I had my own tapes and scores of these and began circulating them among the flutists I wanted to play them – Paula Robison, Carol Wincenc, and Jeanne Baxtresser. They politely declined for one reason or another. Jeannie sent me a lovely note saying how much she enjoyed the music, even proposing I should play the whole last concert myself!

The next decision would be about the alternative contribution of these key performers. Paula asked to play a late afternoon recital, and Carol then decided similarly. With wonderful advice from Michael Emmerson, I had several meetings with Jimmy Galway (who was in New York quite a bit that fall), helping him to understand why Mozart was not the best idea for his gala and selling him on a couple of less often played concertos. As ideas fell into place, he mentioned he would like to play a double concerto with Jeanne Baxtresser – so her contribution was settled. A wrinkle was created when Julius Baker asked me what Galway's program would be. Jeanne was Julius's protégée, and I couldn't lie to him. When I mentioned the duo he was silent for a long moment, then said he would like her to play on his recital also. She gracefully agreed to play twice.

Ransom Wilson had agreed to conduct the gala concert and asked to play the Carl Neilsen concerto on the final concert. I still had to find soloists for "my" concertos. I got a terrific break when Jimmy came round one night and listened to Hofmann. He enjoyed it and agreed to end the convention with it. He would later add it to his concert repertoire, though a planned recording didn't happen. I decided to break a rule on performing at consecutive conventions and ask Linda Chesis to play the Saylor. It was her piece before it was mine. This left only Lovelock and I was determined to have it heard. I finally approached Elena Duran, Michael Emmerson's wife. He had asked me to try and find a place for her on the program, but neither of us had something like this in mind. I didn't know her playing, but had been struck by her personality and quiet intelligence. I reasoned she would not accept unless she felt she could handle the assignment. She enthusiastically accepted and worked conscientiously over the next months to master its challenges. I hoped to get Geoffrey Gilbert to play the rarely heard little Weber *Sicilian Romance*, but he firmly said his days of playing in public were over. So to round out the program, I added as an overture the delightful flute and oboe "Rondeau" from Mozart's *Posthorn Serenade*, thinking to throw a light on the orchestra's principal flute.

It only remained to set Friday's chamber concert. I wanted "my" Beach, Molique, and Hofmann on the program, and thought that André Jolivet's *Chant de Linos* in its string/harp version should also be heard. My final choice was the *Rhapsody* by James Hosmer, longtime second flutist at the Met. Leone Buyse signed on for Molique, Michael Parloff for the Jolivet, Eugenia Zukerman for the Beach, and Judith Mendenhall for the Hofmann. I owed Bill Montgomery a favor, and he kindly agreed to play the Hosmer. I was able to hire the wonderful Alexander Quartet for the evening.

I needed only to talk to my many friends and colleagues in New York, and their imaginative proposals, often New York compositions, quickly fleshed out the program. I called their concerts "Bites of the Apple." One of our great assets was that we could draw on local non-flutists in a way not normally possible. So we could have eighteenth-century concertos on period instruments, (including strings) and draw on singers of the Bach Aria group (for Sam Baron's program), pianist Ruth Laredo (for Paula Robison's recital), the Dorian and Boehm Quintets, Robert Dick's avant-garde New Winds, two different orchestras, and a host of accompanists for the many soloists.

New York was a jazz center too. Legendary "Magic" Frank Wess, Lew Tabackin, and Dave Valentin would perform with "Fatha" Tommy Flanagan on piano, "Smitty" Smith on drums and "Bulldog" Drummond on bass.

For the classes, I wanted teachers who would address the question of style, feeling that this was a singular lack in young performers. So I picked a seminal work from each historical period from Bach through jazz and a matching teacher. Louis Moyse, for example, would work on a French solo with a young performer; Claude Monteux who had played the Poulenc *Sonata* with the composer would coach that; Robert Dick, his own *Afterlight*; and so on.

The convention had the potential to be so huge that I decided to run four events at a time during the daytime sessions. With this in mind, I tried to make four categories of interest, hoping that this would help each individual choose an event. I hoped someone who was interested in a historical subject would not mind missing a lecture on developing a career, for example. Whether the idea helped or frustrated I don't know. Ross Prestia proposed industry showcases where an exhibitor could demonstrate a product; we developed this idea and worked it into the schedule. With such a complicated agenda I knew it was imperative that things run on time. Not only did I need honest performing times, but I needed to build in set-up time, audience movement time, rehearsal time. A myriad of administrative details and minor program changes would absorb me throughout the first half of 1986, but by year-end I could report that the program was largely set.

With James Galway and Ransom Wilson, October 1985.

In October, I took advantage of the availability of Jimmy Galway and Ransom Wilson to check out the Imperial Ballroom at the Sheraton, our principal performing space. Newer hotels were never designed for flute concerts, and finding places that were at least adequate was always a major problem. The responsible committee had decided that the Sheraton was the best compromise for our many needs. I now wanted a sense of whether the performers would agree. We had already investigated New York's concert halls for possible sites for our major concerts but had drawn a blank. Carnegie Hall was closed for renovation, and Lincoln Center was fully booked. We even tried Radio City Music Hall for the Galway concert. I was now concerned that if he was unhappy with the Sheraton he might back out.

He and Ransom alternately took the stage and played while the other joined me in assessing. The room was large, and long from front to back, with entrance doors along one side. Not happy with his sense of projection and intimacy, Jimmy suddenly said, "Let's try playing from the middle of the far side opposite the doors." They both seemed happier with the sound and in feeling closer to the audience. The next question was, could we make it work? The hotel would have to build a stage that would support not only a grand piano but a symphony orchestra. The stage would have to be lit and would need a back stage area screened off next to it, with a corridor back to the true backstage. The hotel staff felt it could be done, so we settled for it. The one thing we couldn't predict was that in the middle of summer the room would need to be air-conditioned, and the air conditioner would be noisy.

Taking advantage of the end of the opera season, I began a new round of therapy with the Feldenkreis expert, Anat Baniel. Over the next year she would help me understand better body use, and I came out of the lessons feeling I was functioning with greater integration and ease. But she seemed uninterested in incorporating my flute playing into the therapy, so I would go home and practice in my habitual ways, unable to make the connection myself.

Then the Wions were off to London. Our friends Livio and Betty Caroli had been offered a "house-sit" in the Victorian home of actress Miriam Margolyes, whom they had met in Tuscany. She had properties in different parts of the world and was delighted to have friends keep an eye on them in her absence. I arrived ahead of Vicky and the boys to find a slight problem. Two other friends of the owner who had been living on the ground floor had failed to depart, and the remaining space was not adequate for another four people.

A second problem was a stomach flu that seemed to be generated somewhere in the arrivals area at Heathrow. At first I thought I had food poisoning from my first dinner out, Chinese. But twenty-four hours after Vicky and the boys arrived, they had the same problem. The boys had been at the theater with the Carolis when Russell said they had to leave. Betty thought they were just jet-lagged, but Russell arrived home very green, having vomited on the train. Then I was up all night with Anthony. Through all of this they were sleeping on the living room floor. Things finally did settle down. A discreet word to the owner's secretary led to the vacating of the ground floor, and we had a lovely holiday, including English plum pudding with our Christmas dinner.

New Year's Eve, Vicky's birthday, was even more magical. Michael Emmerson had used his influence to get us all a table at the Dorchester. We six dressed up in our best — gowns for the ladies, tuxedos for Livio and me, new suits for the boys — and had a superb, perfectly timed four-hour dinner with dancing before the traditional silliness of midnight. I felt I deserved this break, but I knew I was heading right back to a new year that would be at least as stressful as the old. I wondered what shape I would be in after those twelve months.

1986

My year began with another Pavarotti concert/telecast, followed by a similar gala with Marilyn Horne and Monserrat Caballé, both at Lincoln Center. The performing part of my spring activity was fleshed out with the Bronx Arts and Queens Symphony concerts and a three-week run of *Brigadoon* at NYCO.

I had a new round of doctors to explore, my continuing Feldenkreis lessons and, of course, my own teaching. Vicky and I also made time for two short vacations, the Caribbean in February and London in May.

But all of this seemed like background to the continuing preparations for the convention. Apart from dealing with the occasional cancellation, I mostly refined details and dispersed information. Continuing our effort to encourage pre-registration, we offered, in addition to the previous year's raffle, a pre-mailing of the detailed list of works to be performed, such as was not normally available until one picked up the program book on registration. We thought this would help people bring copies of music they might like to follow during a performance.

I sent logistical information to performers (concert dress and rehearsal time for example) and made requests for their needs. The hotel needed lists, such as our lighting and sound requirements. I had to hire instruments. I made an arrangement with Baldwin to provide basically free pianos for the performance and rehearsal spaces, but we also needed music stands and percussion instruments. All these things had to be delivered, in coordination with the hotel's loading-dock, to be sure they would be accepted and moved to the reserved rooms. I had to track down and hire tuners for pianos and harpsichords, and make space in the schedule for them to work. I had to locate orchestral parts, hire or borrow them, then deliver them to librarians. Unexpected problems had to be solved. The lighting manager worked in an office far from the ballroom; if we wanted lights to go up and down during concerts we would have to give him an exact timing chart. In this time before cell phones, it was impossible to whisper, "Raise the lights now, please." Given performance vagaries, it finally seemed best to leave them set throughout. I was lucky to find an excellent assistant in Dierdre Manning who, in addition to taking care of a myriad of small things, acted as a liaison with the New York Flute Club volunteers.

I was reluctant to make an Australian trip this year, well aware of my NFA duties, and advised by my predecessors how busy this period would be. But I felt obligated by an Adelaide residency which had been postponed from the previous year because of date conflicts. As usual, it seemed to take forever to define the project and set repertoire, and the tour only started to come together in April. Support for the five-day residency of six-hour daily sessions would come from the three tertiary institutions and the local flute club, so everyone needed a piece of me. The result was a number of classes and coachings scheduled around rehearsals for a single concert. In the latter, I would play double concertos by Antonio Vivaldi and Domenico Cimarosa with a local flutist, Louise Dellitt, and the Arthur Foote and Kent Kennan solos by myself. I would also coach the orchestra in these latter two pieces. For the remainder of the program, I would play Bach and Boyd with piano, and Gryc, Debussy and Varèse unaccompanied. It was a program I thought I could handle. I had been eliminating more and more Bach as my hand worsened and was by now pretty much down to B Minor and G Minor, the latter of which I chose here.

Thus, at the beginning of June, confident that all my NFA responsibilities and deadlines were in order, I flew to Melbourne to spend a few days with my mother and brothers before going on to Adelaide. I didn't feel particularly good about the residency, and somewhat out of my depth coaching Schubert's *Shepherd on the Rock* for example, and under the eye of the legendary oboist Jiri Tancibudek. Nor did I think much of my conducting skills as I tried to inspire the young string players in the Foote. I was definitely not feeling good about my playing either and was pretty happy when it was all over.

Returning to New York, I had only a day to touch base with everyone involved with the convention and then I had to leave for Saratoga, where the opera was about to begin a residency at the outdoor performing arts center. This theater was already the summer home of the Philadelphia Orchestra and the New York City Ballet. Unfortunately, those seasons, combined with the opera's summer season in New York, meant that we could be scheduled only in the early summer, when the nights could be cold and the summer residents had not yet arrived. This first year was truly uncomfortable, trying to play in the damp, chilly, June weather, and the added stiffness in my hands made *Carmen* a real trial. A number of years would be required to build an audience of local residents. But with a large grant, we were able to continue and grow for several years, until the management of the facility decided they could make more money from a single rock concert than they could from a week of opera.

The following week, opera rehearsals began in New York, and I began what would become a seven-day-a-week regimen that would continue until November. I resumed my Feldenkreis lessons and chiropractic sessions, and made an appointment at the new performing arts clinic at nearby St. Luke's Hospital. The nerve doctor there had equipment for measuring activity, and after several tests concluded that I had a very slight impairment of the left ulnar nerve at Guyon's tunnel in the wrist. With this knowledge, he prescribed a brace to hold the wrist in a neutral position. I wore this for the next months except when sleeping. During that time I had some exciting moments when my finger dexterity was totally normal, but those moments were erratic and didn't last.

By far the most engaging opera this season was Massenet's *Werther*, with Sergiu Commisiona conducting. It was also the most stressful. The score is more like a symphony with vocal obbligato, so rich is the instrumental writing. Commissiona was most demanding in rehearsals, and opening night was particularly tense. In an ill-advised first intermission meeting of the principal winds, he complained of poor intonation and advised us collectively to try harder. Since we all did nothing less than our best on opening nights, the result of this speech was that we all went back to the pit wondering if the comments had been directed at one of us in particular.

In unusual programming, the season then went on to include Massenet's *Don Quichotte* and *Cendrillon*, both filled with charming music. The telecast of the year was Leonard Bernstein's *Candide*, with Erie Mills as Cunegonde.

As July passed into August, I was running more and more between the theater and the convention hotel a half-mile away. Finally, it was convention week, and everything came together. At the begining of the week, key administrators arrived and settled in. I met with all of them, as well as with members of the hotel staff. Instruments were being delivered, including five grands from Baldwin, music stands, and percussion instruments. The full-sized grand would have to use two separate elevators to get to the ballroom; the one directly at the loading dock was not large enough. And everyone needed to be doubly reassured that the newly constructed stage would support it as it was rolled up and across – tense moments! I met with the volunteers from the NYFC who needed instructions on guiding audiences, keeping doors closed during performances, and minimizing the conversation of those waiting to be admitted. Concerned about instrument safety, we developed a system for people to check them whenever they wouldn't be in use. As the guards would not be musicians, it had to be made clear that they would only be responsible for the container; someone could not check an empty flute case and later claim it had contained a platinum flute. The supplies, badges, programs, and inserts had arrived, and relays of volunteers assembled packages for the registrants. Disturbed by long lines of people waiting to register at past conventions, including the founder, Mark Thomas, we devised a system for processing pre-registrants and a special line for VIPs.

On Wednesday, the day before events started, James Galway gave a double master class, divided by an open orchestral rehearsal for his gala concert the next day. He wanted to work with some international students, and I devised a plan with Michael Emmerson. A student from each of the United States, Britain, Japan, and Australia was chosen to have this wonderful opportunity. I was particularly happy with the Australian inclusion, as I had been approached early in the year to see if the winner of the Australian Young Artist Competition could be offered, as a prize, an appearance at our convention. As was the case for most of the convention, I was only able to poke my head into his first class for a couple of minutes between meetings. I overheard him tell a student, "the difference between you and me is not that I play the flute better, but that I have more confidence."

Ross Prestia had come through with his part of the financial equation, selling a hundred booths, which were being set up under the watchful eyes of our uniformed security guards. We had yet to see if we would meet our attendance projection. Trusting that the evening class, orientation, and registration were in good hands, I hurried back to the theater for the evening's *Butterfly*.

The next morning, the nonstop madness began. For the conventioneers it was 8 AM to midnight. But for others of us, the day started earlier and went later. My detailed schedule for each room began with the sound setup at 7 AM, followed by the day's events starting at 8 AM and scheduled to the minute throughout the day. Only at night, when I had scheduled a single event, was a little more leeway in timing possible. At 7 AM I attended the board's breakfast. As chairman of the board, my role was advisory rather than administrative, but some important discussions were taking place from which I had to excuse myself to attend to some aspect of the day's activities. How a cell phone would have helped! Vicky and I had moved into the hotel, realizing the impossibility of getting home. She was a great help in many ways, including just keeping me together. Our son Anthony also volunteered for the duration and made himself quite popular.

For Thursday and Friday, I was able to excuse myself from the opera. But I couldn't get out of the Saturday matinee or a Sunday afternoon dress rehearsal of a new production of Victor Herbert's *New Moon*, for which I was able to get passes for some of our attendees.

The first day seemed to go smoothly, and it was time for the gala opening. I wanted to create a festive atmosphere, apart from what I knew would be a sensational concert, and proposed an intermission reception. To finance this, I approached Mr. Osama Muramatsu, who graciously agreed after being assured that his action would not be misconstrued by the other exhibitors. And so, in mid-concert the audience of some two thousand moved to the adjacent foyer for wine or soft drinks. Keeping to our schedule, and budget, meant getting the throng back again into the concert hall, and my assignment, with borrowed triangle, was to ensure this.

Michael Emmerson gave me good managerial advice, which helped me stay afloat for these four days. He said, "You have only to get your artists onto the stage, and be there with a big smile when they come off. You don't have to stay and listen." I learned to trust my managers in each of the rooms to see that the schedule was followed and people were kept happy. I had too many other things to take care of to keep ahead of impending snags. But in the relative repose of the evening concerts, his advice helped me go to my room for a few minutes of rest or even a shower. When I finally got to bed after midnight, despite my bodily exhaustion, I had to take a sleeping pill to stop my mind from racing.

The noisy air conditioner in the main ballroom was a problem which couldn't be fixed because we were using the space continuously. We decided to let each evening's performer decide whether to have it on throughout or switch it off during the performance. This was a particular problem for Julius Baker's Saturday recital. He decided just before concert time, when the hall was empty and cool, to have it off, underestimating the effect of two thousand bodies in August. Removing his jacket probably didn't help that much, and we finally had to turn it on.

I was trying hard to stay calm and smile a lot, but inside I was starting to lose my cool. Too often, as I would be pushing some dolly though a corridor, a colleague would pass by and make some jovial comment about how hard I was working, but never offer to help. People would arrive for an evening concert, ignore the closed doors and rehearsal in progress, refuse to leave their chosen front row seats when asked, and then be indignant when, needing more chairs, we added some extra rows in front of them. One attendee, irritated at being kept outside when those others had gotten in, said, when I suggested he might volunteer to help keep the doors closed, "I'm not paid to do that." I never fully recovered my love of the NFA after this experience.

Sunday night arrived, and Jimmy Galway was dazzling his way through the finale of the Hofmann. There followed the incredibly moving Bach *Air* played by all the attendees and the president's closing party. Some hundred events had taken place during the four days. Next day was wrap-up, pack-up, move-out time – time to settle all the hotel bills, decide and pay all the tips to the hotel staff. Time for hugs and tears, and back to the prosaic run of *New Moon*.

With James Galway after his concert at the 1986 NFA convention.

The biggest hug was for Myrna Brown, the NFA's Executive Coordinator and its only employee, though her salary would surely have been less than minimum wage if one counted the number of hours she devoted to the organization. She was everywhere and everything, the one constant in an ever-changing administration. During my presidency, I could and did call her continually for advice. She could always lead you to the right solution and make you believe you had arrived at it yourself. She was full of humor and wisdom, and was an indefatigable worker. She was the first to arrive at the convention, and the last to leave. She arrived with every necessary item to manage and process the attendees, continually charmed the irritated, and smoothed over the awkward with tact and sensitivity. I could not have survived this week without her. She was my age, and I felt a great personal loss when she died four years later. Although our paths would cross at conventions during those years, my last correspondence came that October: "Rejoice and sing! We made money!!" My original budget was based on attendance of 2,000, and we had attracted some 700 more than that.

A big change in my life came in the fall when I became a full-time faculty member at Hartt. The two flutists of the Hartford Symphony, Carl Bergner and Stanley Aronsen, had been full-time throughout Hartt's life, and Stanley retired that spring. The dean had promised me that when this happened I would assume the position. However, with Hartt in a period of waning influence in the university, his first thought had been to eliminate the position. Nevertheless, when reminded of his promise, he immediately agreed. His only condition was that I teach only at Hartt. This meant I had to resign from Mannes, Brooklyn, and Queens Colleges. I thought it unnecessary – those schools attracted a different type of student – but agreed. I also agreed to become chair of the wind, brass, and percussion area, beginning several years of growing administrative duties at Hartt.

I became an associate professor, having agreed to be on campus three days a week. In other words, I added Wednesday to my Hartt teaching schedule, in addition to whatever services would be required in terms of meetings, committees, juries, and auditions. Until mid-November when the opera season ended, I would have to juggle things a bit. I would run back from Hartt on Wednesday in time to play the evening performance when necessary and fulfill my performing obligations over the next four days. Occasionally, if a Tuesday evening performance of a new production was scheduled, I would have to split my week's teaching, perhaps going back Wednesday or Thursday to finish up. This routine was tough, but I thought I could manage for the couple of months. Because the season had started in the summer, much of the repertoire was already rehearsed, and I was able to rotate myself out of any new fall productions.

With letters of thanks to all concerned with the convention, written in spare moments this fall, my administrative duties with the NFA ended. I would still perform at three more conventions, and my advice would be sought when the convention came back to New York ten years later. But, coinciding as it did with my new status at Hartt, 1986 marked an end to a significant chapter in my life. With my fiftieth birthday coming in January, a new chapter seems appropriate.

My Fifties

1987

My work year began in mid-January when the NYCO was invited to the new Orange County Performing Arts Center at Costa Mesa, California, for a two-week season. I enjoyed escaping the East Coast winter, but the atmosphere was hardly like our days at Hermosa Beach. We checked into the same hotel as the New York Giants, there for the Super Bowl. Somehow, they got all the attention.

My hand was giving me a lot of trouble. I had a nasty moment in the entr'acte of *Carmen* when the pressure of my grip actually made the flute slip. The bobble led to an unfortunate comment in the newspaper review; I was mortified. Anat Baniel, my Feldenkreis teacher, had given me the name of a hypnotist in the San Diego area whom I contacted full of hope, and with whom I had several sessions. I thought the experience a bit silly and can't imagine I was a very good subject. Once again I received no benefit and was thoroughly discouraged. Thus I recorded my fiftieth birthday.

Back in New York, I played in two interesting concerts, a performance of Barber's *Capricorn Concerto* with the Bronx Arts Ensemble and a televised concert from Lincoln Center with the tenor, Placido Domingo, trying to steal some limelight from Pavarotti. He sang beautifully but he didn't have the same charisma, and the event fell a bit flat, I thought.

The rest of the spring was relatively quiet, apart from my larger involvement at Hartt. We got away for a few days over spring break to Tortola in the British Virgin Islands, and in May returned to our Tuscan retreat at Malfiano.

In June, the opera season started up for the year with a week each at Saratoga and Wolftrap, followed immediately by the combined summer-fall New York season. At Wolftrap, I got permission to play in the stage band for *Traviata* rather than in the pit. I welcomed any opportunity to lighten the strain on my hand.

My colleague at the opera, Florence Nelson, had had surgery for carpal tunnel and recommended her surgeon. He advised against surgery in my case. Then I received a phone call from Judith Youett, an English clarinetist and Alexander Technique teacher who had recently relocated to New York. She had been given my name by Brian Warren after my Perth visit two years before. I explained to her that I couldn't afford to devote time or money to any further treatment, unless it would directly help my flute playing. On this basis we made an appointment, and she told me to bring my flute.

The lesson began with basic sitting and table work, much as had happened when I had taken lessons a decade earlier. Then she said, "OK, let's go to the flute." As I moved, she remarked that as soon as she mentioned the word "flute" I tightened up. She relaxed me again as I put the flute together. She asked me to play some long tones, but again I tensed at the suggestion.

She started me at square one in my relationship to the flute, and over the next three years led me step by step to a clearer understanding of the tension I brought to it. I felt a similarity to psychotherapy, in the sense that as she made me aware of one thing, it led to the discovery of a deeper layer. She could, with the lightest hand on my shoulder, say, "When you play a high note you tighten your neck" or "you raise your shoulder," the kinds of things I was always noticing and correcting in my students. She never told me not to do something, only asked if what I was doing was necessary. Week by week, I found I could handle things better, even sitting in the pit for three hours without a backrest. I had to learn how to inhibit my habit of *making* things happen with my fingers and just *allow* things to happen. I had ups and downs, but I was making definite improvement.

At the end of August, I received permission to take the weekend off from the opera to attend the NFA convention in Saint Louis. Leone Buyse, the program director, had invited me to play Steve Gryc's concerto, *The Moon's Mirror*, on the final evening. The concert in beautiful Powell Hall was lovely. My performance went well, and I received some nice compliments. The other soloists were Jake Berg, principal in Saint Louis, Michel Debost, and Jean-Pierre Rampal — certainly distinguished company. I took the opportunity backstage to thank Rampal for his role in creating the current popularity of the flute. He was modest, but I meant it. In his time, he was the only flutist to earn a living by recording and touring, and winning people over with his artistry and personality. The height of anyone's ambition before him was to play in an orchestra. And now we had these conventions, where thousands of flutists came to listen and learn.

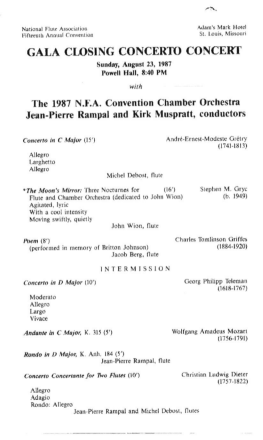

The only opera of interest for me this season was a double bill of Mozart's *L'Oca di Cairo* and Oliver Knussen's *Where the Wild Things Are*, based on Maurice Sendak's book — an enjoyable evening. We telecast a performance of *Magic Flute*, with Comissiona conducting and a wonderful cast that included Faith Esham as Pamina and John Garrison as Tamino.

At Hartt I settled into my new full-time status, working seven days a week between that and the opera. After a decade of living in hotels and eating out, I bought a studio apartment about ten minutes from school, which made things much easier.

In December, the opera opened the new cultural center in Taipei, Taiwan with a two-week season. The theater was spectacular, and a critic from New York who made the trip with us said that it made him realize just how ill-served the company was by its New York theater. The season itself was a bit strange. People trying to buy tickets were told the performances were sold out, but the hall was half empty. Apparently tickets went to important people who didn't use them.

We made the most of our free time in this alien environment with its appalling smog, grey skies, insane traffic, and wild mixes of poverty and opulence. Getting around was a challenge, as few signs in English were posted. At each big intersection on the main street were pedestrian subways, which ran diagonally underground. Before you went down you had to look at a building or advertisement across the square where you wanted to continue. Then, when you came up in the wrong place, you were able to figure out your mistake. We visited the extraordinary museum housing the priceless treasures taken from mainland China when the Communists took over. We were invited to spectacular banquets, were massaged, had our hair dressed (a ritual), saw Chinese opera, and had suits and shirts custom made. I think we took home very little salary.

From Taipei I flew to Tokyo where Vicky had been working and, together with our friends Livio and Betty Caroli, spent a fascinating pre-Christmas week. I was impressed by the way the city worked and thoroughly enjoyed the experience.

We found things harder when we took the bullet train to Kyoto and then to Nara where the English language signs were fewer and fewer. In Kyoto we stayed at a traditional inn, where we bathed in wooden hot tubs and ate and slept on tatami mats in our rooms. We had an amusing experience when the four of us went hunting for affordable sushi. We had heard that it was easy to spend an inordinate amount, so we checked that the restaurant we chose took credit cards. We carefully selected items and kept our own running account. When the bill was presented, however, our credit card was refused. They only took cash. They had only been acting in their typically polite fashion, saying *hai* (yes) to everything we asked that they didn't understand. We pooled all our cash and just made it, though we had to walk back to our inn.

With Vicky at the Golden Pavillion, Kyoto, 1987.

From Tokyo the four of us flew to Honolulu, where we had arranged to use the same house that we had exchanged on a previous visit. This time the owner, now living in New York and about to be remarried, traded the house for Livio's and my agreeing to play at his wedding. The boys flew in from New York (eating their NY deli supplies en route) and we six had another fun Christmas, this time warm and flu-free. We then went our separate ways. First Vicky left for Hong Kong for another job; then I left for Australia, leaving the boys to return to New York a day later. In fact my flight was delayed twenty-four hours, and the boys came to visit me at the beach by the airport. I finally arrived in Melbourne for my first summer visit since I had left thirty years before, and my last visit with my mother.

1988

My Australian trip, barely two weeks long anyway, was shortened even further by my delayed flight from Honolulu. I spent a hot week in Melbourne, staying with my mother and catching up with friends. On the way back I stopped in Sydney for a day of meetings with the ABC and with Virginia Braden, my manager in Australia.

On my return to New York, I found an invitation to apply for the flute professorship at Oberlin College. I seriously considered it but realized, once again, that I was not ready to move from New York. Michael Emmerson, now living in New York as president of RCA Victor Gold Seal (in addition to managing James Galway), helped me come to a decision and draft a gracious reply.

Michael had also brought from London a vertical head-joint I had requested of Albert Cooper. The idea seemed sensible in terms of easing my hand strain, but I found it acoustically unsatisfactory. I explained the problem and he sent me a letter with a sketch of a modified design, requesting me to return the head at my convenience. Nothing came of this but much later Sandy Drelinger in New York did indeed design a vertical head that worked. By that time I was nearing the end of my career.

My comparatively easy spring with only the Hartt teaching responsibilities was filled out by a five-week season of *The Music Man* at NYCO. Still, I took a week off from that over spring break so Vicky and I could go once again to St. Barts.

Florence Nelson, my colleague at NYCO since the spring of 1966, finally decided to move her life in a different direction, and took a position at Local 802. She took all her strengths with her and rose to become vice president of the American Federation of Musicians. Officially, she took a one-year leave of absence and we held auditions to fill this interim position. The winner, through no influence of my own, was Janet Arms, one of my first students at Hartt. Janet had done graduate work at Juilliard and was at that time playing with the San Francisco Ballet. She made a great impression on our music director, Sergiu Comissiona, and the rest of the committee. A year later, when the position became permanent, she won the appointment and went on to become a valued colleague and friend.

In May, the Bronx Arts Ensemble recorded a nonet and octet by New York composer Robert Baksa, a conservative composer through the years of serialism now starting to receive more attention. The recording turned out beautifully. I still listen to it and feel proud of having participated. When Musical Heritage sold the copies they had pressed, they decided not to transfer it to CD. Later, the two pieces were reissued on CD on a different label, with the addition of Baksa's quintet for flute and strings.

Later that month, NYCO went to Tampa, Florida for a week. I felt proud that another of my former students, Linda Toote, at this time principal in Tampa, played with us. More starkly, as I walked her to her car after a performance, some kids jumped out of a car and pointed a gun at us from some twenty yards. After a terrifying couple of minutes, they, for whatever reason, jumped back in their car and drove off.

Back in New York, Vicky and I drove upstate to Rensselaer for Russell's college graduation. After working a short while for a small company, he would be headhunted by Major League Baseball looking for someone young, skilled in a particular computer program, and also a baseball nut.

Vicky and I then took off for Switzerland, where we had planned a trip by train to see as many places as possible. Apart from seeing the many scenic wonders, we were able to catch up with the Galways in Lucerne. When we arrived they were away but kindly offered us the use of their apartment. When they returned, we moved to a hotel across the street, which they called their "guest room," and insisted on paying for. We had a lovely visit.

Once again, the opera season began in June with a week each at Saratoga and Wolf Trap. The repertoire for the season was largely routine for me, with *Lucia* always of interest, and with a return of Britten's *The Turn of the Screw*, his demanding chamber opera requiring me to play flute, piccolo, and alto. For the first time in many years I did not attend the NFA convention in August. As I no longer had an administrative position and would not be performing, I had no justification for requesting a leave from the opera. In the fall, NYCO gave an excellent performance of *Rigoletto* for a *Live From Lincoln Center* telecast. Faith Esham as Gilda, Richard Leech as the Duke, and Brent Ellis as Rigoletto led the cast.

With the Galways at Lake Lucerne, 1988.

With new confidence from my Alexander lessons, I played a recital in October for the Long Island Flute Club. I chose a careful program consisting of the Bach *G Minor* and Martinu sonatas, the Fauré *Fantaisie*, and *Goldfish Through Summer Rain* by Anne Boyd. Pianist Linda Mark gave me wonderful support, and my Alexander teacher, Judith Youett, came for encouragement. I was pleased with the result and began to think that I might consider more solo playing again.

After the opera finished in November, although exhausted from my seven-day-a-week fall, I recorded the *Five Preludes* for unaccompanied flute by Hartt composer, Stephen Gryc. The first, "Fish in Shallow Water," put particular strain on my hand, but I managed somehow and thought the finished product would help him sell his idea for a complete record of his music. That happened, and over the next couple of years, I participated in recording three other works involving flute, including his concerto. Ironically, when all the recording was completed, the producer decided that he didn't like the acoustic quality of the *Preludes* compared to the other tracks, and insisted I either record them again or drop them from the CD. After some soul searching and preliminary practice, I decided I could relearn them and agreed.

Our year ended on a down note when Vicky's stepfather, Philip Jones, died after an extended illness. Phil had been a wonderful friend and support to us, taking care of so many business matters that didn't come easily to us non-business types. A moving memorial took place before the holidays.

Following previously made plans, we flew to the island of Bequia in the Grenadines, where our friends Livio and Betty Caroli had built a vacation home overlooking the ocean. There we quietly celebrated Vicky's birthday on New Year's Eve.

1989

My first engagement of the year was another Pavarotti telecast concert from Lincoln Center, this time with a number of other singers including Shirley Verrett, Sherrill Milnes, and Thomas Hampson. After this I swung into my spring semester at Hartt. The spring musical at NYCO this year was *The Pajama Game*, the music of which I had loved when I first heard it in Australia before leaving in 1958.

In April, I made a ten-day tour of the Midwest with guitarist Lisa Hurlong. I had met Lisa some years before at Newport when she was married to cellist Steve Kates. She remarried an amateur flutist who worked for the State Department, and they began using their contacts to play concerts together in different parts of the world. Now they had separated, and Lisa asked if I would replace him for this already scheduled tour.

We began in Minneapolis, where I stayed overnight with my longtime friend, Basil Reeve, now principal oboe there. Lisa and I had a good time together driving the long distances between concerts. I had not visited this part of the country, and I found it dreary. Lisa's stories of her life on the diplomatic circuit were always interesting though, particularly when she talked of her time in Taiwan. I took her mention of her Chinese language skill with a grain of salt, until one day we were shopping in a supermarket and came across some Chinese students. Lisa immediately began conversing with them to see if they could recommend somewhere to eat. They couldn't of course; the supermarket carried no cheese but Kraft Velveeta, so a gourmet restaurant was hardly likely. In one town we were advised to eat at a quasi-private club. Seeing shrimp scampi on the menu, and forgetting where I was, I placed my order asking if I could possibly have extra garlic. As much as I wanted, said the waitress. The dish arrived with a heavy dose of garlic salt. When we reached the end of our tour at Sioux City, it seemed like paradise.

When the school year ended in May, Vicky and I went to France where, with the help of Basil Reeve's wife, Kathy, we had rented a *gîte* or farmhouse in Provence. When we arrived, our hosts showed us to a lovely cottage surrounded by orchards. First Russell and his girlfriend and then Anthony came for visits, and we managed to survive a lot of driving on the dreadful two-lane national roads in the area. We admired the Roman ruins at Nîmes and Orange, drove as far as Marseille and Nice and Cannes on the coast, and then into the rugged mountains of the Camargue further north. A highlight was lunch in the garden at the famous Oustau de Baumanière. From Provence we went to Paris and on to Giverny to visit Monet's residence and gardens. Then we visited Mont St. Michel, where we had arranged to stay at a small inn. The village streets were magical after all the day tourists had left, and our inn offered a memorable meal, an omelet whipped to great frothiness and cooked over a wood fire. For our final stop we visited the Reeves, who had rented a farmhouse near the Brittany coast. Together we took a ferry to windswept Belle-Ile, where we did some good walking and had yet another great French meal.

In June, NYCO played at Saratoga again, to which it added Artpark at Lewistown near the Canadian border. These engagements led as usual into the summer season.

I was asked to substitute for Sam Baron at the Banff Centre in the Canadian Rockies this year, so for three weeks I would be able to join Vicky, who had been going here every year to stage a Balanchine ballet. Comissiona would release me from the opera only if I agreed to fly back in the middle for the opening of *Don Giovanni*, a new production he was conducting. Banff was sufficiently desperate that they agreed to release me for the necessary three days.

Banff is truly one of the most beautiful, unspoiled places in the world, and Vicky took great delight in showing me the sights, particularly Lake Louise. When one first walks up to the lip of this lake and observes its unreal blue, one cannot but be awed. I enjoyed the teaching and felt I helped the small class, which included Brenda Fedoruk, who has gone on to a successful career in Canada, and Karen Gifford. I was particularly fond of Karen, and we corresponded for some time afterwards. Then, after a long silence, she sent a lovely note with her student Sandy Hughes when she auditioned at Hartt.

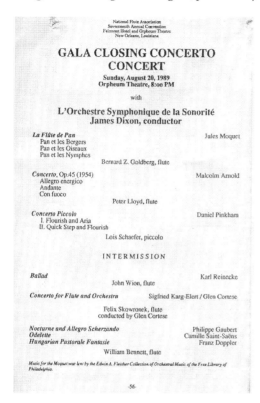

I also performed on one of the concerts with some of the student string players. I felt honored to be in the company of Ralph Gomberg, retired oboist from Boston, and Steve Maxim, retired bassoonist from the Met, and humbled to be treading the same ground as cellist János Starker. As I was only subbing, I had no expectation of being invited back, and I could hardly expect to be released from the opera again anyway. Still, I will always treasure the memory.

I arranged my opera schedule to participate once again in the NFA convention, in New Orleans this year. I flew down on the Saturday and performed the Reinecke *Ballade* with the orchestra at the final Sunday night concert. I chose this piece so as not to stress my hand, and was pleased with my performance and the new sense of freedom coming from my Alexander work.

I had little to fly back to, as the orchestra moved into another of its strikes over the terms offered for a new contract. This time the bulk of the fall season was lost. My friend Mike Elliott was the national photo editor at the *Times*, and he made up and sent a cutely captioned photo of me on the picket line. I was perhaps the member of the orchestra least affected by the strike. Now I could focus on my teaching and did not have to juggle both jobs at once.

In October my mother died, at the age of 91. She had been going downhill since I saw her in January, and finally had a stroke. I had tried phoning her a while before this, but she didn't

On the picket line, 1989.

understand who was calling. I also resorted this last year to sending my monthly support checks to my brother to bank for her. After her death, I got a touching farewell letter she had written, probably soon after I had left. I intended to go back to be with the family and got as far as the airline office, where I had quite a wait. The longer I waited, the more I thought I was making a mistake. I would miss the funeral and would have to turn around almost immediately to return to New York. The following year, we four brothers and our families had an extended visit together.

Marianne Turner Wion 1898–1989.

One exciting night came out of the strike. A televised concert, *An Evening with Alan Jay Lerner*, celebrating the late lyricist, was to be held in our theater, and the contractor had offered to use as many members of our orchestra as he could. The star-studded event included Julie Andrews, Liza Minelli, Jane Powell, and Leonard Bernstein. Jane Powell sang her "How Could You Believe Me" from the movie *A Royal Wedding* with all the energy, enthusiasm and youth of that younger self. Bernstein spoke some dialogue from *1600 Pennsylvania Avenue* and June Anderson sang its "Take Care of This House." Songs were sung from the other Lerner hits, *Brigadoon, Paint Your Wagon, Gigi, My Fair Lady, Camelot*, and *On a Clear Day*. My most memorable moment came from a show I had never heard of, *Carmelina*, with Burton Lane's music. The ballad, for three men, "One More Walk around the Garden" has stayed with me ever since.

Of interest in this otherwise performance-free fall was a concert of the Bronx Arts Ensemble, where I participated in a fine performance of the *Fifth Brandenburg* with harpsichordist Igor Kipnis.

For Thanksgiving we arranged a house exchange in San Francisco. The home was beautiful, and a perfect base for trips up and down the coast as well as exploring the city itself. Our happiness was interrupted, however, when Betty Caroli phoned to say that our dear friend John Palanchian had died. He had been in failing health for a couple of years, but we were still shocked. A very emotional gathering of friends at the Palanchian home took place in December. John's wife, Gloria, wouldn't outlive her husband by very long, succumbing to cancer. Their departure left a big hole in our lives. I had admired John so much during my early years at the opera, and we had spent many wonderful times together.

MY FIFTIES

1990

Vicky and I spent New Year's Eve in Rome, joining our friends Livio and Betty Caroli. The four of us then drove to Tuscany where they had friends, and had lunch in Arezzo with our Malfiano hosts, Raffaele and Lara Lucarelli. From there Vicky and I went by train to Milan, where Vicky would be working at La Scala. A highlight for me was sitting in house seats close to conductor Riccardo Muti at a performance of I *Vespri Siciliani*.

John Palanchian, 1979.

We had flown to Rome via London, where Albert Cooper had made me a curved head joint. Emerson Flutes were making such a head-joint, and I had arranged with Mark Thomas to get an unfinished tube for Cooper to work on. The Emerson head put the blowhole in such a place that the head curved down. When I received my finished head, I found that this curve made the balance unstable. Albert then agreed to cut the head just below the blowhole, and fit it together again with a sleeve. This would allow me to choose any direction for the angle, by adjusting the joint. His solution was brilliant, and I found that having the head-joint curve outwards gave great relief to my neck, by not having to turn to the left. I used the head-joint in several concerts, but the quality of the sound disappointed me, particularly the highest notes. I felt I had bothered Cooper enough and let the project drop.

In February, Pavarotti gave another of his telecast concerts. This year he chose scenes from *Tosca* and *Un Ballo in Maschera*. Among his guests were sopranos Leona Mitchell and Carol Vaness. The spring musical at NYCO this year was *The Sound of Music*. At the same time, I embarked on a recording of unaccompanied flute pieces with a grant from The University of Hartford.

I arranged four sessions spread over the spring semester, thinking this would give me time to focus and prepare the material in small doses. The project was still difficult, and the result didn't please me. I recorded in a dead space with reverberation added. I heard myself through headphones. I found it difficult having no interplay with other musicians and no audience. Also I had no one to hide behind – no moments to take it easy – nothing to mask any blemishes. This led to longer takes to capture whole phrases, and much repetition.

I also arranged to play a recital at Hartt in March. Linda Mark agreed to play the Bach E Minor *Sonata*, the Copland *Duo*, and the Martinu and Poulenc sonatas with me. On my own, I played the Friedrich Kuhlau *Divertimento* I had just recorded. After this, I had a recurrence of my lip swelling – on the date I had scheduled to record the C.P.E. Bach *Sonata*. The swelling was not a major one, so I made the effort. If I had been playing a concert I would have made do, but I just didn't have enough control and knew I would be disappointed with the results. The only good thing about recording alone – I easily rescheduled the session. I saw an allergist about this problem, and she discovered a severe allergy to dust mites. On her recommendation I bought an air filter for the bedroom and special mattress and pillow covers and have not had a recurrence since.

As soon as school ended in May I flew to Australia. Vicky was already working in Perth after having set a ballet in Hong Kong. We arrived together in Melbourne. I had tried for the previous two years to arrange some performances, but my agent had been unsuccessful. When she finally admitted this, we parted ways. I managed to arrange on my own a class in Sydney and one in Brisbane. As a result, I had time to catch up with family and friends before flying on to Maui for a real rest. On the way back through Los Angeles we had lunch with Bonnie and Bill Daniels and spent a couple of days with the Humbles in San Diego.

Immediately on returning to New York, I went to Saratoga for the opera season, which included *Lucia* with Sheryl Woods. Lincoln Center had started a new summer festival, and our orchestra had been hired to play a two-week season of the Bolshoi Ballet. The whole affair was hurriedly put together. The company had by necessity multiple sets of photocopied parts, so that an assistant conductor could proceed to the next town on the tour and start orchestral rehearsals while the company was still performing. These were mostly manuscript parts of variable quality, with previous cuts and players' comments and reminders now permanently a part of the photocopy. We performed *Romeo and Juliet*, *Swan Lake*, an extremely difficult *Ivan the Terrible* (which had started life as a film soundtrack), and a mixed program of smaller ballets. The principal conductor was terrific and the season, although taxing, was most rewarding.

The summer part of the opera season included the *Lucia* prepared for Saratoga and a new production of Janáček's *The House of the Dead*, directed by Vicky's friend from Banff, Rhoda Levine. The season also contained preliminary rehearsals for Schönberg's *Moses und Aron*, which would be receiving its US premiere in the fall. This went well, and, by word of mouth, the audiences grew until the final performance was sold out. With Beverly Sills in retirement and Christopher Keene directing the company, *Moses und Aron* indicated the new focus our repertoire would have.

Also of interest that fall was a production of Sondheim's *A Little Night Music*, based on Bergman's *Smiles of a Summer Night*. PBS chose this as the televised performance of the season. The lead on Broadway had been Glynis Johns. In our production Sally Anne Howes sang the wonderful "Send in the Clowns." The introduction for this is for solo clarinet, but later on it is given to alto flute. At a party some time later at Rhoda Levine's, I thanked the arranger, Jonathan Tunick, for this gift.

In the fall, Larry Alan Smith became the new dean at Hartt and began the process of revitalizing a school which was quickly becoming the music department of a less prestigious university. The university had absorbed Hartt's endowment and now established its budget and provided services such as cleaning and maintenance. If a donor gave a gift to Hartt, the university deducted an equivalent amount from its contribution. Not surprisingly, the school had little incentive to raise funds. Larry re-established Hartt's independence and started aggressively fundraising. Soon things began to improve as money became available for upgrading programs, equipment, and the many things that make the arts expensive.

I had for some time wanted to create a set of opera excerpts to match the nine-volume series of symphonic excerpts created by John Wummer. Unable to find a publisher, I decided to do it myself in partnership with Arthur Bloom, clarinetist with the Lark Quintet twenty-five years earlier, and now a wonderful autographer. He agreed to the project with the understanding, as I could offer no money up front, that he would work when time permitted. Unfortunately, time never did permit. I decided to learn the computer autography program, *Finale*, and took a lesson with David Pogue. David became a guru for anything relating to computers for *The New York Times*. After working for a year, I proudly produced volume one, of which I had a thousand copies printed. Several years later, with much more experience and a more intuitive program, I looked back at this volume with embarrassment at the poor layout and the number of mistakes it contained. After finishing the nine-volume series, I totally revised volume one and republished it, offering to replace anyone's original with this version free of charge.

For the Thanksgiving break, we arranged the same house exchange in San Francisco. What a difference! This time the house was filthy and flea ridden. We found unmade beds and dirty dishes in the sink – and there were cats! We had made clear the previous year that we wouldn't take care of the pets and they were taken elsewhere, but not this time. When phone calls to our apartment in New York did not lead to a correction of the situation, we moved in with Vicky's sister.

In December, flutist Helen Campo asked me if I would sub for her in the revival of *Fiddler on the Roof* on Broadway. This was a nice change, and very enjoyable. More seriously, Steve Gryc had received a grant to record his concerto, *The Moon's Mirror*. He arranged a concert in January with the Hartford Symphony, followed by the recording session. Along with the five unaccompanied pieces already recorded, this would give Steve a good demo to work towards selling a CD of his flute music. Practice for this filled in my December.

1991

My performance and recording of *The Moon's Mirror* went well, although the running sixteenth notes in the third movement were still awkward. My colleague from Hartt, Greig Shearer (the orchestra's principal), played the important alto flute part. Our new dean, a composer himself, came to a rehearsal and seemed to enjoy both the music and its interpretation.

The end of the month brought yet another edition of *Pavarotti Plus*, a televised concert from Lincoln Center. His associates included sopranos Renee Fleming, Cheryl Studer, and Ruth Ann Swenson. Of more interest to the orchestra, however, the conductor was Julius Rudel, in his first association with us since he had left a decade before. At the first rehearsal in the basement of the Metropolitan Opera he seemed not to know anyone, but by the time the rehearsal finished, the old animosities, on both sides, were obvious to all. I could only make the analogy of a parent and grown child reverting to their earlier relationship. During the dress rehearsal on stage, a gaping Pavarotti watched as the conductor took an inordinate amount of precious time to teach the cello section how to play a passage from *Tosca* that they had performed a hundred times. My new colleague, Janet Arms, was speechless too. When she subbed at the Met, he was always such a gentleman, and gracious in his behavior to the orchestra. We were told that the producers were unhappy with the orchestra, and that we were unlikely to be hired again. After some diplomatic discussion to explain the dynamic, we did continue to work with Pavarotti, but with a different conductor.

In lieu of a musical this spring, the orchestra played a February concert at Carnegie Hall – the only time we ever played a concert – in which Renee Fleming sang Maurice Ravel's *Sheherazade*. In

February, I also took a week off from school to play some concerts in Spain with guitarist Lisa Hurlong, now living there. Vicky was already working in Madrid, and Lisa and I used her hotel room for some hurried rehearsing. After a single concert in Madrid, we drove to Barcelona and Valencia for repeat performances.

In Valencia I had an awkward experience. We were invited to act as judges for the local paella competition. This was more a formality than anything else – they all obviously knew much more than we did. At the outdoor dinner we were seated at the table of honor, right in front of an enormous speaker that blasted music. I had no earplugs and just couldn't handle the noise. The mayor took us for a walk around for a while and wondered what to do. Eventually I stuffed some tissue in my ears and ate as quickly as I could.

For our May vacation we went to Scotland, via London of course. We stayed in Edinburgh with our friends Richard and Joyce Milner from Malfiano, and then made a circuit of Scotland by car, seeing many beautiful things and places. We returned home in time for Anthony's graduation from Bowdoin, after which he had planned a long trip to Australia with friends. The month ended with a beautiful recording that the orchestra made with Benita Valente and Tatiana Troyanos of music by Handel and Mozart. Julius Rudel was the well behaved conductor. In June, before my year's work began in earnest, I visited Vicky who was, as usual, working in Banff. We drove as far north as Jasper and saw sights of unbelievable grandeur.

Anthony's graduation, 1991.

The summer season at NYCO was made interesting by productions of Janácek's *Cunning Little Vixen*, which Michael Tilson Thomas conducted, and Bizet's haunting *Pecheurs de Perles*. I popped down to Washington for the flute convention, which was honoring Jean-Pierre Rampal. A new sonata by Lowell Liebermann, played by Paula Robison, impressed me so much that I determined to put it in my repertoire.

In the fall, I began my tenure at Hartt as director of performance studies. The area needed a great amount of reorganization, and I was insane to agree to add this to my already over-full schedule. Apart from anything else, the opera had scheduled Erich Korngold's *Die Todt Stadt* and Bernd Alois Zimmerman's *Die Soldaten*, and I did not intend to give these up. The latter opera was extremely difficult and needed more rehearsing than usual, but somehow I survived the semester intact.

The telecast this season was *The Marriage of Figaro* with Elizabeth Hynes as a memorable Countess. The season ended with a run of *Brigadoon*, a reminder of our Scottish vacation.

Hartt's dean, Larry Smith, proposed that I apply for promotion and tenure. I had been appointed as an associate professor with a three-year contract. I would now be applying for full professorship as well as tenure. I asked Beverly Sills and Christopher Keene, as well as colleagues from the NFA administrations, for letters of recommendation. I also thought it would be good to have support from a former student and asked Linda Toote. She sent me a hysterically funny letter, which I believe was not the one she submitted.

The year ended with a two-month visit from my brother Frank and his wife, Pat.

1992

In 1992 I bought a new silver Brannen flute – the only flute ever made with serial number the same as its year of manufacture. I had been playing Brannen number 500 for a decade and was quite happy with it, but I wanted to take advantage of new developments in both mechanism and acoustics. I used the new flute for several years until, during an overhaul, I needed to use my original number 55 gold Brannen. So many people commented on how much better I sounded that I have used it ever since.

This year also marked my success as a publisher, when volume one of my *Opera Excerpts* was chosen as a winner in the NFA's annual competition for newly published music. I also completed volume two.

My spring energies and time were very much devoted to administration at Hartt, and I felt that even without the opera commitment my teaching was suffering.

I played a few interesting performances. In February, another in the Pavarotti series of televised concerts highlighted June Anderson and Sherrill Milnes. I also signed on to an *Aida* performance in New Jersey. I had played this while at the Met, but NYCO had never offered it, so I didn't want to miss the opportunity.

Vicky and I spent spring break in Sorrento. This was off-season – indeed we were the only guests at a restaurant one evening – which meant we could drive the Amalfi coast without too many terrifying moments.

In April, Steve Gryc arranged to record the final installments in his CD project. First up he scheduled his duo for flute and guitar, *Delicate Balances*, for a Saturday afternoon in the auditorium of a private school. As we prepared for a take, the engineer instructed us to wait for silence from street noise. We started, but were interrupted by noise again. We made several attempts and finally had to give up. As I left I noticed the traffic light outside. Our silences had come from the red light. We rescheduled the session in the basement studio where I had recorded the year before. The environment, while not pleasant, was quiet, and this time I was not working alone. In similar fashion we recorded the very effective trio for flute, oboe, and harpsichord, *Six Mechanicals*, based on the characters in *A Midsummer Night's Dream*.

I had befriended an Australian couple, Cliff and Audley Green, who lived in Hartford. Audley was an enthusiastic harpsichordist who regularly gave concerts in Australia. She asked me if I would join her this year. She had put together a small tour with concerts in Canberra and Sydney and two more in Queensland. The Sydney concert took place in a historic home and was attended by my Sydney-based friends. We stayed with my longtime Melbourne friend Leonard Spira and his wife, Gail. Afterwards, Sandra Leveson, a successful painter and former wife of Russell Meares, arranged a spectacular dinner at her current companion's restaurant overlooking the harbor. We played the final concert in a private home on an estate at Dalby, on the tableland near Brisbane. In this sparsely settled area, people came long distances to listen and socialize.

From Brisbane, Vicky and I flew to Darwin on Australia's north coast, and had an improbably excellent dining experience in a simple place at the end of the pier. The local mud crab was enhanced by a spectacular sunset. We rented a car to drive to the aborigine reserve Kakadu, where we did all the touristy things, including a short flight for an overview. Our hotel was shaped like a crocodile and the menu included crocodile mousse. We drove to a site of ancient aboriginal cave paintings over an unsurfaced and heavily rutted track. Driving my rental slowly in and out of every rut, I wondered if we would actually arrive before sunset. Then a truck full of aborigines zipped past us. I followed suit and learned that at that speed one rode across the tops of the ruts. The caves were worth the trip.

Back in Brisbane, with my hand at its worst, I played a mercifully short recital and taught a class. On the way home, we stopped at Bora Bora in the Tahitian islands. Surrounded by a reef, the water was incredibly clear and the snorkeling magnificent.

Marie and Russell's wedding, 1992.

In August our son Russell married a Long Island woman, Marie, of Italian background. They had an Italian wedding – noisy and fun. In a nod to Russell's Jewish heritage they did stomp on a glass.

Once again the fall brought my triple load – NYCO, Hartt teaching, and Hartt administration. I had been promoted to professor with tenure and was preparing an application for my first sabbatical.

Christopher Keene produced the next of his German operas in the fall, Ferruccio Busoni's Dr. Faustus. I was probably the only member of the orchestra to have played this before, in a concert version with Dietrich Fischer-Dieskau a quarter century before. We telecast a performance of *Cavalleria Rusticana* and *Pagliacci*: Janet Arms commented afterwards that I performed at a higher level with a microphone in front of me.

In September my mentor, Keith Humble, came for a short visit. With Vicky away in South Africa, I alone had the memorable experience of his playing his new *Bagatelles* at my piano.

Our New Year's Eve was a dream. We had decided to go to Tucson for Vicky's birthday and booked for the gala dinner at our hotel. To our delight, we found that the symphony had been hired to play Strauss waltzes for dancing.

1993

For my first project in 1993 I recorded two French pieces with piano, to fill out a proposed CD transfer of my old LP. I had received a grant from the university for this purpose and asked Tom Hrynkew, the original pianist, to help out again. After a lot of thought, I chose the two pieces I thought most worthwhile – the *Concertino* of Alphonse Duvernoy, and the *Ballade* of Albert Périlhou. Much later, when involved with this writing project, I came across a letter from Dutch flutist Franz Vester. I had asked him for suggestions of nineteenth-century repertoire, and he had suggested just these two pieces. I had no conscious memory of this. I had always been unhappy with my performance of Gabriel Fauré's *Morceau* and decided to re-record that also.

A former student, Kim deLuccio, agreed to be my ears at the session, and to make the editing choices. I thought the results good, despite the fact that I was still struggling with technical issues.

By now digital editing was the norm. I had learned a wrong note in one of the pieces I had learned for the original LP. After I became aware of this (from a student of course), I felt embarrassed. Now, digitizing the LP, I thought it might be possible to make a correction. "No problem," said engineer, David Budries. I watched the computer screen as he carefully removed the note in question and replaced it with a copied correct note from the previous measure. Years later, another student made me aware of another wrong note. I can't imagine I will live to see a new technology that would lead to creating yet a third version of my LP. The CD was released later in the year as the first in Hartt's own label.

Becoming more and more disillusioned by my experience as an administrator, my mood only darkened when my application for my first sabbatical was denied. The provost explained that more applications had been received than could be funded, and I had fallen below the line in seniority, not quality of project of course. Still, I felt that my dean had not supported me enough, and it rankled. I felt continually frustrated in my dealings with faculty egos. Basically I was stretched too thin, and something had to go before I snapped. With my thin skin, administration seemed the logical choice, and I resigned from that part of my job effective the end of the school year.

In the spring our orchestra played a season of the Bavarian Ballet, which included a ballet, *Eugene Onegin*, set to music of Tchaikovsky, but not from his opera. We also played a week of *Swan Lake*.

One Saturday morning, I happened to be home when the phone rang. The caller was Eddie Jobson, a former keyboard player for Jethro Tull, now based in Manhattan. He was in the process of remaking a commercial for Bermuda Travel, bringing it up to date. He was using a male voice as the lead but was unhappy with the result. He recalled that a flutist had been used on the original jingle, tracked down the contractor, and tracked down me. Was I free to come down to the studio that afternoon?

At the studio I found only an engineer. Then Jobson arrived and played back the previous day's version. He asked me if I needed music. When I said I would prefer that, he rummaged in his bag for a piece of manuscript paper and wrote out the notes – kind of. We began taping, and he was thrilled with the result. Listening, I thought the engineer had made me sound really good, too. When I left, Jobson hadn't decided if this would be a flute solo or just laid over the voice track. I happened to catch it on TV later and heard only flute. A few weeks later, just after we got back from our annual visit to St. Barts, he called again. The client loved the thirty-second spot and now wanted a sixty-second version. Down I went, but this time nothing I could do was right – I was flat, I was slow, I was unenergetic. I started to understand what that singer must have gone through. I was on the verge of suggesting we just forget about it, when he started sounding happier. Either he picked up my irritation or he had given up and just wanted to ease things over. We quickly wound things up, and I never heard from him again.

I moved ahead with my publishing. Having completed volume three of my excerpts, I decided to publish a flute and piano version of the Romberg *Concerto*. I was convinced that the only reason this piece did not have a place in the standard repertoire was that no piano reduction had been published in the composer's lifetime. Without this easy way for performers to play his piece, it had been neglected and forgotten. One of my early students at Hartt, Elaine Baker, an accomplished pianist, had made such a reduction for me, but I had been unable to find a publisher. With my new skills, I could now publish it myself. The publication sold well and, like volume one of my opera volumes, would win the NFA competition the following year. I proceeded to create an orchestral score and parts for those performers able to play with an orchestra. My print run of a hundred grossly overestimated the demand. Still, a few people have bought sets and given performances, and the piano reduction continues to sell a few copies each year. By convention time in August, I had also completed volume four of my excerpts. I was definitely getting quicker and better. The computer program was also getting better. The staccato dots, instead of having to be placed by hand, for example, now jumped into the correct locations. The slurs too were more intuitive, and more shortcuts were offered.

In May, I played another recital for the Long Island Flute Club. I included the Duvernoy and Perilhou that I had recorded in January, as well as Bach E Major and Schumann's oboe *Romances*. By myself I played Debussy, Varèse, and Berio.

Right afterwards, Vicky and I left for Greece. We had chosen four islands to explore and started on Mykonos where we were charmed by the tiny meandering streets of the town and the signature windmills. On the long ferry ride to Santorini, I met an Australian who knew the property in Dalby where I had played the year before. He had planned to come to the concert, but something had intervened. Small world. We found Santorini absolutely magical and high on our list of places to return to. From the rim of a sunken volcano we looked way down to the glassy blue ocean inside. Ships looked like toy boats I wanted to reach down and pick up. Vicky's friend Olga Evreinov and her husband, Phillipe, were visiting at the same time, and we joined them for a magical sunset drink. Crete involved a much larger exploration, but our most unusual evening occurred on Chios.

Looking for a place for dinner, we enquired at a hotel that doubled as a foreign consulate. The gentleman explained that they served dinner only for the resident guests. We explained that our hotel in Santorini had recommended him. In that case we were welcome to join them. We met the other guests for drinks and were relieved that we would be able to have our own table for dinner on the terrace. A bad pianist on an awful piano played throughout dinner, which was served by handsome young Greeks wearing white gloves. We found everything about the dinner pretentious and felt relieved when it was over. No menu had been offered and we had no idea what the cost would be, so we were even more relieved when the reasonable bill was presented.

The opera season began with the usual weeks at Saratoga and Wolf Trap and moved into uninteresting summer repertoire. In the fall, we had three new productions – *Esther* by Hugo Weisgall, *Marilyn* by Ezra Laderman, and *A Midsummer Marriage* by Michael Tippett. This last proved a real challenge for the orchestra, and one of the most difficult scores for me personally. Music reviews often make one think one has been at a different event, but I was especially irritated by one particular review of the Tippett, which noted the poor ensemble of the flutes. The score specifically notated places where the flutes changed notes at minutely different times, and we had done a good job. The reviewer also wondered how one could take seriously an opera house where the air conditioning was so noisy. A fan was being used on the stage at irregular intervals for a particular effect.

In August, I took a day off to perform at the opening night concert of the Boston NFA Convention. I had been asked to play in Lowell Liebermann's *A Poet to His Beloved* for tenor, string quartet, piano, and flute – a beautiful setting of Yeats's poetry. Robert White was the tenor, and Liebermann played piano. The three of us had preliminary rehearsals at my apartment, and I traveled to Boston with Bobby, who was a totally engaging personality and witty raconteur. When we met for our rehearsal with the quartet in the hotel, he told of the strangest feeling when being taken to his room. He suddenly realized that this was the hotel he had lived in as a child, when a show he was performing in played in Boston before its New York run.

As school started in the fall, I felt enormously relieved not to be dealing with my administrative chores. However, I had agreed to direct a new program the dean had instigated. Called 20/20, it was a tuition-free program for exceptionally gifted instrumentalists. The dean hoped it would raise the level of the applicants. In its first year it attracted a flutist completing her undergraduate degree at Eastman. Later it attracted two terrific high school students to my class. More often, its flute ranks were filled with my own students, whose development while at school justified their acceptance into the program. We developed an ambitious program, which was modified and minimized over the next decade, by which time I had long departed from the directorship.

During the fall, a revival of *Camelot* began a run on Broadway, and I was asked to sub. I went one night to "watch the book" (you didn't get a rehearsal, just a look at the music during a performance) and was horrified by what had been done to the beautiful Robert Russell Bennett orchestration. The harp had gone, the English horn had gone, the string section was smaller and thinner. I found the experience dismal and chose not to become involved. The run was not successful, and I like to think that the thinness of the orchestra was a partial reason. Audiences may not have been able to put their finger on it, but it had to color the experience.

Keith Humble paid another visit in October, this time with his wife, Jill. He told me he had a blockage in his carotid artery and that he would just pop off one day. I largely played down the import of this, as I think one does. At sixty-six he seemed as vital as ever.

Keith had been promising me a flute piece for years and finally wrote his *Sonata* in 1990. He composed two versions, one with piano and one with strings. I offered to publish the flute and piano version and he accepted. On this trip he looked at my efforts and made some suggestions. I published the sonata the following year, and the judges chose it as a winner in the 1996 NFA competition for newly published music.

My dear teacher in Australia, Les Barklamb, died that fall. I had seen him on my last visit, in a retirement home, where I played him some Bach from my new CD. He was desperately unhappy. "All the people here are already dead," he said. I wrote for his memorial:

> Leslie Barklamb's death has left a big hole in the centre of my life. He was a father, a mentor, and a friend, and the principal cause of my having made my life in music.
>
> I met him when I was ten, and began my studies with him shortly thereafter. A year later my father died and it seemed those studies would end. Instead, he taught me without charge until I started at the university. Through my high school years I would go to the Conservatorium after school for my lessons - to his corner room where his patience and encouragement kept me going. I remember those treasured moments when he actually seemed emotionally moved beyond his normal positive response. I remember the thrill of playing duets with him - what a sound! And I remember the smell of the music drawer. This was the moment of greatest excitement, when he decided I needed a new piece. The drawer would be opened and he would go through its wonders as the aroma drifted up, until he made a selection and the lesson would continue.
>
> He had so much more confidence in me than I had in myself, and pushed me headfirst into performing and teaching experiences I couldn't possibly have deserved, but at which I then had to succeed so as not to let him down. He was always there for me when I had a problem, and his serious consideration usually produced a solution.
>
> As I got to know him better, awe changed to respect and finally love, as my experiences started to include a cricket match at music camp, a whisky in his living room, a footy game at the MCG, a dinner at his favourite restaurant with a special red from his cellar. His reminiscences covered Australia's musical history, and every now and then his eyes would moisten as he relived a magical musical moment.
>
> I was blessed in having Les Barklamb share his great generosity, enthusiasm, wisdom and humanity with me. He was always giving, and always seemed to have more to give. He gave flutes, and he gave music, he even gave me a Melbourne Football Club tie, but mostly one remembers that he gave himself. I once thought

that when I grew up I would repay him for his generosity, but he never wanted that, and I came to realise that the only way to repay him is to try and follow in some small way his example. Then I know he will go on smiling, and his eyes will twinkle, and he'll say, "Good on ya, John!"

Leslie Barklamb, 1985.

We planned another California trip for my Thanksgiving break. We would visit the Daniels at their new Santa Barbara house, then continue up the coast to Big Sur, then San Francisco for Thanksgiving at Vicky's sister's, and then up to Mendocino. Vicky was returning from another trip, so we would meet at the airport. A strike had been called at American Airlines, raising some question as to whether our flight would happen. As a result we had back-up reservations on United. As I approached the American terminal ramp, the traffic barrier was down, so I told the driver to continue on to United where I expected to find Vicky. Not seeing her and thinking she must have checked in and gone to the bathroom, I proceeded to check in and get my boarding pass. Unable to get through to anyone at American, I waited as long as I could, and finally just boarded, thinking the next five hours would be the longest of my life. But once airborne, seeing a phone, I called home and found a message from Vicky. She didn't know where I was, but *she* was at American and flying to Los Angeles. On my arrival, I went to the American terminal to find that her flight had just landed. I headed towards the baggage area and there, way down on the escalator, I saw her. "Vicky," I shouted. "John," she shouted, not seeing me. We met at the bottom and hugged each other with teary eyes. We had a great vacation after that.

At the end of this year I agreed to sub at *Phantom of the Opera* and went to "watch the book" at the matinee before my scheduled evening debut. I was quite overwhelmed, not by the actual notes but by the "roadmap." Jump from here to here, then back to here. Cut this, then turn to here, etc. If I had not been scheduled to play that evening, I would have cancelled. Instead, I took the part home and studied it as I cooked and ate dinner, until I had to leave for the theater. I survived, and in fact went on to sub whenever the regular sub was unavailable. I found it strange going backstage at the Majestic for *Phantom*, as I had spent so much time here when I had played *Camelot* thirty years earlier. Very little was the same, as the entire area under the stage, where we had our lockers and gathered, was now taken over by the machinery that provided the effects in *Phantom*. After a break of more than a year, I was called again, but with the warning that much more amplification had been added in the pit, and that the experience was quite unpleasant. I declined, and so ended my Broadway subbing.

By year's end, I had finished volume five of my opera series, and now seemed to be able to produce a book in six months.

1994

Before school started Vicky and I took a Caribbean trip – Bequia, again, to visit the Carolis, then Grenada and St. Lucia, both for the first time. The hotel in St. Lucia was spectacularly sited on a steep hill, up from the water which provided magnificent snorkeling.

The year at the opera was particularly depressing. The administration finally admitted that the summer season was not working (I never felt that they promoted it properly with tourists) and reverted to the fall/spring seasons. To achieve this, they gave no performances from the end of the previous season in November 1993 until the fall of 1994. I was, again, the only person not seriously affected by this; indeed it made my life easier. But hereafter my life would be harder, as both season openings would coincide with the start of the school semester. I had difficulty working my teaching around the rehearsal schedule, and this would eventually lead to my decision to retire from NYCO. The first spring season would, however, not present a problem, as I had been granted a sabbatical for the first semester of 1995.

The latest of the Pavarotti specials took place in January. He shared the stage with sopranos Elizabeth Holleque, Aprile Millo and Deborah Voigt and the wonderful baritone, Dwayne Croft.

I had decided to create two more CDs from my early Molique/Romberg LPs. By a stroke of sheer luck I had the master tapes of these recordings. I had noticed a final sale of my quintet LP in the Musical Heritage catalog some years before and phoned to order some copies. I learned that they did not plan to reissue the LP on CD, and that all such tapes in their catalog were about to be thrown away. They were quite happy to send mine to me instead, now that I expressed an interest, but would not otherwise have contacted me. In similar fashion I acquired the tape of my concerto LP. As I had done with the French LP, I applied to my university for grants to make the transfers and to record an extra piece to add to each, as was possible in the new format. Each CD would be devoted to the one composer.

In March, for the Molique CD, I recorded his *Duo* for flute and violin. He wrote this charming but virtuosic piece early in his career to play on his tours with Theobald Böhm. I was fortunate to have Mitchell Stern, then on the Hartt faculty, as my associate. Mitch died not long after at the age of forty-five. He was a wonderful violinist and supportive colleague.

The session went well. I still had the occasional moment when I didn't meet the technical demands, but the Alexander work had helped a lot. The performance was less exciting and enthusiastic than it might have been when I was younger, but I felt it had some nice lyricism and musicality.

Working around the spring semester, Vicky and I made short trips to St. Barts and New Orleans, where we first became acquainted with the cooking of chef Emeril Lagasse before his TV fame.

In June, we made a trip to London, Paris (where we caught up with Australian friends, Russell Meares and Stephen McIntyre), and Burgundy. This latter was built around a barge trip on one of the canals and had been arranged by Carla Hunt, travel writer and former neighbor at 180.

Also participating were our mutual friends Bonnie and Bill Daniels, originally from 180, and Carla's husband, Tom Marcosson. We all met for dinner at Au Pied du Cochon, our favorite brasserie near the former Les Halles market, and agreed to meet under the clock at the railway station the next morning for our trip to Dijon. Carla had all the tickets.

We arrived on time but saw no sign of the others. We had not traveled with them before and decided perhaps they were just not punctual. Train time approached, however, and they hadn't arrived. Finally, a desperate Vicky ran up an escalator to the platforms and saw Carla waving frantically. We raced up with our bags and scrambled on board as the train pulled out. The others were all relaxed in their assigned seats. We had arrived by subway and had not realized that we were one level below the street entrance to the station, which, of course, also had a clock.

On the barge in Burgundy, 1994 (Photograph by Carla Hunt).

Carla was an experienced traveler and great organizer, so everything from there on went smoothly. The only problem occurred on the barge trip itself. Bill had become quite a celebrity from his St. Elsewhere program, and the others on the barge wanted to rub shoulders a bit too much. He is a private person and didn't take too well to this. Things were a bit tense by the end and eased up only when the six of us headed off again on our own for Lyon.

In July, Vicky and I took off again, this time to Austria for the first time. Having enjoyed our earlier train trip around Switzerland, we decided to try it again and found it most relaxing. We began in Vienna, where of all the magnificent sights we saw, I felt most moved to be walking along the path by the brook where Beethoven strolled from his summer workplace for his meals. Heiligenstadt, where he wrote his famous testament relating to his encroaching deafness, was now at the end of the subway line. The path had been surfaced, but it was still quiet and shady, and one could easily imagine him walking there, hearing the birds and rippling water that he incorporated into his *Pastoral Symphony*.

From Vienna we visited Linz, Salzburg, and Innsbruck, before crossing the Alps into Italy to visit Bolzano, Cortina, and Merano. We had planned Vicenza as our last stop, but we found everything closed, and on a whim took the train to Venice.

At the NFA Convention, my flute and piano edition of the Romberg *Concerto* was performed at the Newly Published Music concert. This concert is presented each year, bringing together the winners of two separate competitions – one for the publications themselves, and one for professional performers who compete for the opportunity to play those pieces. When I had been president of the NFA, I proposed that these winning publications be used as required material in all the following year's performing competitions, such as the Young Artist, Masterclass, and High School competitions, feeling that this would stimulate sales and encourage new publications. Now that I was in a place to benefit, I learned that the practice had been discontinued. Such lack of continuity of policy was an ongoing problem with changing administrations and committee chairs.

With the Daniels and Vicky in Burgundy, 1994 (Photograph by Tom Marcosson).

In the fall season at the opera, the only productions of interest were Delibes's *Lakmé* and Bernstein's *On the Town*. Adolph Green was involved in the revival of this show from his youth, and one had a sense of history seeing him in the theater.

I was already planning my spring sabbatical, and prepared a recital program that would serve me in planned trips to Mexico and Australia. I included two pieces I wanted to learn – sonatas of Liebermann and Humble – along with standard Bach and Reinecke. I also wanted to play another Hartt recital, and had planned it for early that year. Irma Vallecillo, who had recently joined the piano faculty, agreed to play with me, but an eye problem she developed forced a postponement. We had to squeeze it in before school ended in December. To fill out the program, Mitch Stern played the Molique Duo with me.

Vicky and I took a quick trip to London after school, just to see plays. We had the neat idea of staying on New York time, and it served us well. We got up around noon, saw a matinee or went to a museum in the afternoon, and saw a play at night followed by dinner and a long read or TV movie. I couldn't have had a nicer way to start my sabbatical.

1995

Vicky and I spent New Year's Eve in Mexico City with Michael and Elena Emmerson, and the following week I taught at Elena's flute class and played a recital. The Emmersons were perfect hosts, showing us around the city and spoiling us with their kindness. My recital with Zoe Smith took place at the beautiful Anfiteatro Simón Bolívar with its Diego Rivera frescoes. I played my Hartt program, substituting the Perilhou *Ballade* for the Molique.

I had been dealing with the question of my US legal status for some time on three fronts. The green card I had received after entering the US in 1958 was now coming apart, and I had been told to have it replaced before it was taken from me. The New York office of the INS was so overrun that one had to write just to get an appointment. I was given an appointment with only a few days notice, by which time I already had a work obligation and had to request a new date.

I had been reluctant to take US citizenship because Australian law at the time was such that I would then have lost my Australian citizenship. A bill to change this was before Parliament, and I was monitoring its progress.

In the meantime, Vicky suggested I write to the State Department – perhaps the law under which I had lost my original US citizenship had been revised. The grounds stated for loss of citizenship were that I had voted in a foreign election, as I was required to by Australian law at the age of twenty-one. I was only Australian before that as a minor whose parents had naturalized him. Less than a year after reaching twenty-one, I had returned to the US, where I had now spent my adult life for thirty-five years.

I wrote, explaining all the details, and included the documentation. A form reply came back after a while stating that I had not included the appropriate fee. I responded to the effect that I was happy to pay any fee, but that I thought my request had been misunderstood. Another reply returned my material and informed me that I had directed my request to the wrong office. I thought it strange that my request could not be redirected, but I dutifully sent it off again and eventually forgot about it.

After many months, I was surprised to receive an official letter stating that my case had been reviewed and my US citizenship restored. I used this letter to obtain my first US passport. I was eligible to vote, and didn't have to use the non-US line coming through immigration. And, as I had not had to swear allegiance to the USA, I would keep my Australian citizenship.

My former student and current colleague at NYCO, Janet Arms, covered my sabbatical at Hartt. Now she was the one juggling two jobs, along with a new baby. I helped by offering my Hartford apartment. She was also able to touch base with me each week at the opera. I knew my students were in good hands. Indeed, as a result of her work she received an invitation to join the adjunct faculty at Hartt.

Of interest during this leisurely spring season at NYCO was a new opera by Stewart Wallace, *Harvey Milk*, based on the life and death of the gay San Francisco supervisor.

With Stephen McIntyre, 1995.

At the end of the season we headed off to Australia again. We had arranged a house exchange for a terrace house in East Melbourne, close to the city center, which proved to be a great base. I taught for a week at the Victorian College for the Arts and played two recitals, both with my good friend Stephen McIntyre. The first was part of a fortieth reunion for my class at Trinity College. We played a warmly received concert in the school chapel. At the reception afterwards I caught up with many classmates I had not seen since 1958.

The public recital was organized by the University of Melbourne and the Victorian Flute Guild, and took place in Melba Hall at the conservatorium where I had been a student. I chose the same program as I had played in Mexico, and I was looking forward to working on Keith Humble's sonata with him beforehand.

Keith and Jill took us out for dinner a few days before the concert and we had a wonderful evening of reminiscences. The next day he had a stroke and fell into a coma. Jill phoned and said he had gone for a walk, returned, and sat down to rest in his armchair. It was quick, as he had forecast. I was saddened that he would not hear my performance of his piece, but the major concern was that he would not recover. In fact he did not regain consciousness and died in the hospital in Geelong on May 23. I lost a mentor and true friend.

Keith Humble, 1927–1995.

While he was in a coma we had, at Jill's insistence, continued with our prearranged travel plans, and visited the northeast Australian coast around the resort town of Port Douglas for a few days before flying home from Sydney.

In June I joined Vicky, who was working in Prague. Her first staging, years earlier, had introduced Balanchine to the company, long isolated by Russian control. That trip had started out as a bit of a nightmare for her, being dumped in a semi-private room in the suburbs and having to find her way to work on foot because of a transit strike. With each successive visit, however, she found more people speaking English, more restoration and revitalization, more restaurants, and more joy. Prague had become a place she loved to return to. I now saw why – the city was truly charming. We stayed in a former monastery in the center of town, where the ballet studios were located. Some of the rooms had been turned into modern apartments for the convenience of guests. While Vicky worked, I explored the old town and walked into the dreary Soviet-era suburbs. I got a ticket for *Russalka* at one of the opera houses, and the two of us saw *Nabucco* at another. A third house, The Estates Theater, which had been refurbished by director Miloš Forman for the movie *Amadeus*, was presenting *Don Giovanni*. The performance was sold out, but the company provided us with two chairs at the end of a row. I was moved to see this masterpiece in the tiny, elegant theater where it had premiered just over two centuries before.

Vicky's busy summer proceeded with her annual visit to Banff to stage a Balanchine ballet. She scheduled a week off and I flew out to join her for a trip to Glacier National Park in Montana. We drove the Sunrise Highway west and returned north to Canada.

After the NFA Convention in Orlando, my fall season at NYCO began. Our big production was Paul Hindemith's *Mathis der Mahler*, with Christopher Keene conducting. He was seriously ill and needed a microphone to talk during our rehearsals in the acoustically live promenade of the theater. He had to turn over the final performance to his assistant and died a year later. Christopher was brilliant and articulate, if not a particularly expressive musician. He seemed to dislike rehearsing and worked quickly to cover the material. He had developed a clean stick technique and easily negotiated the most difficult score, at which point he seemed to lose interest in delving any deeper. Apart from our moment of difficulty, I had a good relationship with him and enjoyed his wit and erudition. His attitude was straightforward, and he seemed to make difficult decisions easily.

I was by now an active participant in the Internet FLUTE list run by Canadian Larry Krantz. I enjoyed answering students' questions, and Larry began collecting my posts, with which he created a "John Wion Corner" on his website. Later on I lost interest in responding to the same questions over and over. Other younger professionals took over with skill and enthusiasm.

I had nominated Steve Gryc for an NFA commission to write a piece for the semifinals of its Young Artist Competition, and he entered my performance of *The Moon's Mirror* as an example of his flute writing. To our delight he won the competition and created the beautiful *Shadowdance*, which I would publish. Plowing ahead with my opera volumes, I completed volume seven before the end of the year.

1996

In the fall of 1995, a hurricane struck St. Barts, and we were apprehensive about what we might find. The hurricane hit right on St. Jean beach, creating wide devastation. Our house, our secluded retreat for the previous few years, had lost its fence and all vegetation; the sand now swept right up to our porch. With the sand came tourists and noise and distraction during the day, and an eerie isolation at night. The restaurant next door was destroyed, and the other houses nearby were empty. We were alone and unprotected, and for the first time felt vulnerable in our former paradise. In fact we *were* vulnerable and came home from dinner one night to find we had been robbed. Fortunately my flute and our passports were untouched, but we were distraught and felt incapable of spending the night there. Unable to reach the emergency number of our agents, we went to the nearest hotel and took a room. The next day, as our anger and fright eased, we were shown other possible accommodations, but we were afraid to be isolated in any house. We finally settled on an apartment hotel at the other end of St. Jean beach. Les Ilets de la Plage consisted of separate bungalows running up the steep slope from the beach, and one of these "islands" became our new paradise.

My brother David, 1934–1996.

In February, my oldest brother Frank called to tell me that our brother David had had a stroke and had fallen into a coma. A couple of days later he died. I was devastated. David was only sixty-two, the same age as my father, with the same cause of death. Estranged for some years from his wife, Dave had bought a property in Victoria's Grampian Mountains, where he ran an environmental retreat for schoolchildren. The Wions were never very successful at business, and Dave was no exception. Kids loved their visits, but the retreat was never solidly booked. Vicky and I had visited and thoroughly enjoyed the open bush and wildlife. David had sold the property the previous year and was establishing a new life. He apparently had had some chest pain, but when visiting his doctor had not mentioned it, accepting the doctor's opinion that he seemed to be in good health. Time would not permit my reaching Australia before the scheduled cremation and service, but I felt good that a piece from my French recording was played for the large gathering of his friends. David had an easygoing personality and was loved by all who knew him.

One expects to lose one's parents, but losing a sibling was a disturbing reminder of the imminence of one's own death. To compound things, my younger brother, Dick, unexpectedly had sextuple bypass surgery. I was teaching at Hartt when David died. Somewhat panicked, I went to the nearest drugstore and used its machine to check my blood pressure. The reading was wild and I phoned my doctor for an appointment. He reassured me that I had normal pressure and that the machine was poorly calibrated. Nevertheless, he scheduled me for a thalium stress test later in the spring, which showed no sign of a heart problem.

During this time, I developed a project to arrange several arias for flute and piano, with support and advice from Helen Spielman of the Internet FLUTE list and Ross Prestia from my NFA years. Realizing how much my flute playing had changed as a result of my years of listening to singers, I had begun to formulate some new teaching ideas. Additionally, I had been singing to my students in lieu of playing during my worst hand years. Not surprisingly, I proposed Sing! as the title of the book. It would become my most popular publication and would win the NFA's Newly Published Music Competition in 1998.

The spring opera season included an always exciting revival of Rosenkavalier, and introduced Gottfried von Einem's The Visit of the Old Lady with George Manahan conducting. Also this semester, I recorded an excellent piece, Shape Notes, for flute and two percussionists by Hartt composer David Macbride.

Following the opera, the orchestra played yet another Pavarotti extravaganza, after which Vicky and I headed off to England for London theater and then to the Cotswolds. We arranged to meet up with our New York friends, Bob and Mary Sue Hauck. Bob, the opera's principal trombonist and a colleague from my Royal Ballet tour of 1960, had met Mary Sue at Camelot, where she was a member of the cast, having moved over from My Fair Lady. The Haucks had become our close friends, visiting us in St. Barts, and eventually becoming annual vacationers there. We also coordinated with our California friends, Bill and Bonnie Daniels. With the latter we visited the wonderful Quat'Saisons for dinner and overnight, and met again at a B&B. All six of us saw the pretty dreadful production of Macbeth at Stratford. From London we flew with the Daniels to Greece.

Our dinner in Athens, 1996 (Photograph by Carla Hunt).

Bill Daniels had decided to hire a yacht to sail the Aegean and had invited us to join the party, which would include their son Michael and his girlfriend, Carla and Tom Marcosson from the Burgundy canal trip, and George and AllynAnn Gaynes. I knew George casually from Dynamite Tonight, the Bill Bolcomb show in the early sixties. He had since moved to California, where he had a particular success with the movie Police Academy. We had not met his wife, AllynAnn McLeary, who had had a successful career on Broadway, including being the original Amy of "Once in Love with Amy" in the Frank Loesser show Where's Charley. Just before the projected trip, Bill was advised that the company had double-booked the yacht and we were being upgraded. After a night in Athens, we all headed for Pireus and the start of our adventure.

The *Ariadne* was splendid and had been the temporary home of many a shah, prince, and movie star. Our compatible group wended its way down the

The Ariadne.

With George Gaynes (left), and Bill and Michael Daniels on the Ariadne, 1996.

channel between the Greek coast and offshore islands, always anchoring for the night. We had visions of simple fish dinners at quayside tavernas, but the lunch served on board each day was so enormous that we had difficulty contemplating additional meals. Vicky led exercise class for the ladies each morning. Bill and George fished. We made excursions by foot, donkey, or taxi to see ancient sites. We did much reading and napping. Altogether it was a memorable trip.

In July, we took a second trip to Europe – this time to Italy. We flew into Milan and began our vacation in the Cinque Terra area of the northwest. We walked the cliff paths between the little villages and took the train back to our base in Levanto. From there we visited Lucca, where Vicky's dance friend Olga Evreinov had a summer cottage which she lent to us. From Lucca we drove back to our Malfiano retreat in the Tuscan hills, where we met up again with our Scottish friends, Richard and Joyce Milner, and were visited by our Australian friends, Tony and Janneke Casson. Livio and Betty Caroli were also in the area and joined us for an incredible feast outdoors at Malfiano, arranged in our honor by the Lucarelli family. From there we headed north again to visit Stresa on Lake Maggiore.

Back in New York, the NYCO presented Virgil Thompson's *Four Saints in Three Acts* as a part of the Lincoln Center Festival.

In August, the NFA convention returned to New York. The program chair, Eric Hoover, had the previous year picked my brain as he developed his program, and he eventually asked if I would play a concerto by New York composer Glen Cortese. The work had been written originally with string accompaniment, but Cortese had composed a revised version with added winds. This would prove to be my last appearance at a convention, and I was delighted it would be in New York where my family could come to the concert. The first rehearsal took place in a basement ballroom in New Jersey (the orchestra was the New Jersey Symphony). I thought I sounded awful and completely covered by the orchestra. I went home discouraged and fearful. However the run-through on the concert stage at the convention hotel went much better, and in the end I enjoyed the performance. Now that I no longer had any need for publicity, I found my photo attached to the *Times's* review of the concert.

THE NEW YORK TIMES, TUESDAY, AUGUST 20, 1996

MUSIC REVIEW

4 Premieres by Flutists, Performing for Flutists

By ANTHONY TOMMASINI

For a flutist, performing before an audience of some 2,500 other flutists has got to be intimidating. Still, a festive atmosphere prevailed during a concert on Sunday night in the Broadway Ballroom of the Marriott Marquis Hotel, the final event of the four-day annual convention of the National Flute Association.

One reason for the excitement, no doubt, was the program: world premieres of four works for flute and orchestra (one actually a concerto for piccolo, which almost all flutists also play). Flutists can disagree vehemently about embouchure, fluttertonguing technique and a range of other insider issues, but they bemoan with unanimity the dearth of works for flute and orchestra. Needless to say, there was eager anticipation over the prospect of some new ones.

Presenting these particular works on the same program was not an ideal way to showcase their individual qualities, for all four shared a rather post-modern style. The program began with Variations for Flute and Orchestra, by Glen Cortese, also the evening's conductor.

The music is steeped in the language of Barber and Copland. There are attractive stacked-up harmonies, wistfully soft melodic lines for solo flute, a modal melancholic hymn, restless passages of flute recitative. It is nicely wrought but familiar-sounding. John Wion played the solo part with plaintive tone and elegance. Mr. Cortese drew sonorous playing from members of the New Jersey Symphony Orchestra.

A new work for two flutists and orchestra by the prolific William Thomas McKinley is playfully titled "Goldberg Variations II" — a joint homage to one of the soloists, the esteemed Bernard Goldberg, and to Bach's masterpiece of the same title, which is quoted toward the end. Both Mr. Goldberg and his co-soloist, Grzegorz Olkiewicz, must alternate among flute, alto flute and piccolo, and the inventive, coloristic writing for all three instruments in various combinations is the work's most striking achievement.

Though Mr. McKinley has a tendency to stretch thin his elemental musical materials, the music is accessible and mostly effective, especially a slinky waltzlike section with crunchy clashes of notes between the flutes in duet, and a jittery march with piping piccolos that recalls the patriotic music of the American Federalist era.

Augusta Read Thomas's "Eclipse Musings" for solo flute (Bonita Boyd), solo guitar (Nicholas G-

John Wion, soloist, in one of four world premieres at a convention of the National Flute Association.

The convention served me well in other ways too. The judges had chosen my edition of Keith Humble's *Sonata* as a winner in the Newly Published Music competition, and it was performed as part of the program honoring the winners. The six semifinalists in the Young Artists Competition played Steve Gryc's newly commisioned *Shadowdance*, and I appeared on a panel discussing performance injuries. Two of my colleagues, James Galway and Michel Debost, have big upper bodies, which has served them well as flutists. The large audience, obviously looking for help with problems, was not impressed with their suggestion that if you held the flute correctly and stood correctly you wouldn't have a problem. Having gone through my own challenges, I could be a bit more helpful. Vicky and I also hosted a dinner at our apartment on one of the convention nights. We invited the Emmersons, the Carolis (with Livio's brother Enzo who played on one program), Paul Dunkel (who would conduct the closing concert), my new internet friend, Helen Spielman, and Patty Adams. Multi-talented Patty had provided me with a beautiful memento of the 1986 convention when she had drawn a picture of a flute with the title "The Flute that John built." In tiny letters inside the flute were the names of everyone who had performed.

In the fall, the NY Yankees made it to the World Series in what would be the start of a remarkable post-season run. Our son Russell, with his Major League connections, got us tickets to what turned out to be the thrilling final game. Afterwards, an exultant Wade Boggs rode around on the back of a police horse.

At Hartt I took on the administration of the chamber music program, which was in disarray. I instituted midterm juries so that groups would be encouraged to begin work sooner, and turned both these and the final juries into concerts attended by all the participants, each of whom had to offer written comments. I also set aside a weekly time when everyone would be free, so that coaching and rehearsals could more easily be arranged. I encouraged people to form their own groups, and tried to get things started at the end of the previous semester whenever possible. Some time was needed for a new sense of direction and purpose to take hold. But today, long after I have given up the reins, I am gratified to attend the juries and find a high standard of preparation and music-making presented in a professional manner.

Of interest that fall at NYCO was *Falstaff*. I also played my last recital for the Long Island Flute Club, performing the Bach E♭ *Sonata*, the Milhaud *Sonatine*, the Taffanel *Andante Pastorale et Scherzettino*, Anne Boyd's *Goldfish Through Summer Rain*, Debussy's *Syrinx*, Varèse's *Density 21.5*, and Steve Gryc's *fish in shallow water*.

Thus ended another decade in my life. The next decade would see me cutting back my performances even more and dealing with my retirement from the opera. I would find more time to relax and travel and read, while at the same time having more energy and enthusiasm for my teaching.

My Sixties

1997

My sixties covered a major transition in my life as I moved to close my performing career. I imagine that many people, perhaps most, look forward to retirement, after many years spent at something that is basically earning an income. Performing, at least in my case, is rather more complicated, representing an activity begun in childhood and one which is deep in my identity and psyche. Would I still be myself if this element were removed?

Without doubt, my situation at NYCO was not good. The two separate seasons ran concurrently with the two school semesters. I was committed to three or four days at school, so I had to manipulate my participation in NYCO activities to fit around my teaching schedule. To participate in a new production, I had to play all rehearsals and performances. The new administration developed a standard routine for new productions, either a Friday afternoon dress rehearsal with a Tuesday opening, or a Tuesday afternoon dress rehearsal with a Friday opening. Either way, I could only participate if I broke up my teaching week and made two round trips to Hartford. I did in fact do this for a couple of new operas that I really wanted to play, but it made for a tiring week, and the students suffered by having their lessons rescheduled. Although many members of the faculty operated this way on a fairly regular basis, I believed my students, particularly the undergrads, developed better discipline and advanced more quickly when they had a set lesson time. I discovered that if they had ten days between lessons, they took it easy for a day or two and produced only a week of work. When lessons were less than a week apart, they were unable to produce a full week's work.

By juggling things around I was able to participate in some worthwhile productions in the first part of this decade. In addition to *The Visit of the Old Lady*, based on the Friedrich Dürrenmatt play which I had seen during my first year in New York, Kurt Weill's *Seven Deadly Sins*, which I first saw at NYCB after my arrival, with Lotte Lenya singing and Allegra Kent dancing, also brought back memories. Verdi's *Macbeth* was an exciting new find, and we added Donizetti's *Don Pasquale* to the repertoire. We also did Gluck's *Orfeo ed Euridice*, but in the version without the ballet and its famous flute solo. Strauss's *Intermezzo* was perhaps the most difficult score I ever had to learn – or was I just getting older? A lot of fun was Rossini's *Il Viaggio a Reims*, something he had put together for a particular occasion, and which had only recently been reassembled. One scene has an extensive flute obbligato. I read that an English production had the flutist in costume on stage, but that was not the case at NYCO. I did some lovely playing, I thought, but a particular repetitive arpeggiated passage sent my hand into spasm, and lessened my enjoyment in this otherwise satisfying way to be ending my career. Finally, the opera undertook *Porgy and Bess*, which for all its great songs contained some passages that were awkward to the point of impossibility, at least at the speed we had to tackle them.

As my schedule forced me to delegate more and more of the new productions to Janet Arms, my own participation sank into a routine of playing standard repertoire, Friday through Sunday. I understand that to many musicians the opportunity to play a diet of *Bohème*, *Butterfly*, *Traviata*, and

Magic Flute may sound pretty good, but I had been playing each of these operas five or ten times a year for over thirty years.

When I came in to play over the weekend, however, I also felt considerable stress. Stress had always been a part of my experience, as part of the collective stress of opening nights for example. Now I was feeling that my routine Saturday matinee *Carmen* was like an opening and that my colleagues were comparing me to Janet, who was covering the repertoire early in the week. Silly? Maybe.

Throughout my career I had seen colleagues play into decline. Nobody ever told you that you weren't playing as well as you once did, and even if you were to ask, you could not accept an encouraging response at face value.

I heard of a couple where the wife was told that her husband should seriously think of retiring. She replied that she thought he was sounding better than ever, and he truly wasn't. I was determined to leave sooner rather than later; I hope that I did.

I began collecting my opera pension in my early sixties by a since-rescinded quirk of the American Federation of Musicians' fund. The pension was not much, having started some years into my tenure and with minimal contributions for many years after, but it enabled me to cover the loss of salary when my teaching prevented me from playing the required weekly performances. At sixty-five I would add my social security pension, making my combined pension earnings about the same as my opera income, so money was not a factor in my deciding to retire.

Much as I was not enjoying playing at the opera, I still loved the idea of playing in an orchestra, which has been my thrill since I was a teenager. Indeed what I liked about playing a concerto was that I had a really good part to play. Realistically, I had to accept that I would no longer have an opportunity to participate in this activity. I had long since cut my ties to freelancing, and union rules now provided tenure to those holding positions in established freelance orchestras.

Moving towards making the decision to retire, I took advantage of my second sabbatical in the spring of 2002. My seniority at NYCO gave me the right to take off a full year without pay, but I decided to take a leave for only the fall 2001 season to experience just teaching. Not missing the opera, I then took a second leave for the spring 2002 season, so that with my Hartt sabbatical I would have a sense of complete retirement. Confident that I was making the right decision, I handed in my resignation to NYCO thirty-seven years after I had begun in the fall of 1965. I have not regretted the decision. If anything, I am sorry I didn't give up some income and retire sooner. In an ideal world I would love to play a *Figaro* – maybe even a *Bohème* – once a year. But as my dear friend Lew Waldeck said when I asked for advice: "How long have you been at NYCO?" ... "That's a lot of opera."

In the meantime, I had a lot else going on in my life. Early in the year I received an inquiry from Indiana University where a faculty position had opened up. I had a wonderful phone conversation with one of the members of the committee and I was seriously interested. A few days later, in a conference call with the entire committee, I got an entirely different sense, a lack of enthusiasm. After some thought, I wrote and had my name removed from consideration. Much later, I ran into my conductor friend Imre Pallo who had been there for some years. "Why didn't you come?," he enthused. "It would have been so great!"

Another call came from Nyuki Miura, formerly a bass player at NYCO and now a presenter of concerts of Japanese music. He was organizing a tribute to Toru Takemitsu, the composer who had died the year before. This included two concerts with a considerable flute representation. Would I play? In so far as I didn't know any of the pieces and didn't have much time to prepare, it represented a huge commitment. I asked to think about it. Over the next couple of days it developed that for various reasons other flutists needed to be involved, and, with considerable relief, I finally played a single piece – alto flute in a trio with lute and vibraphone.

In April I was invited to join the judging panel for the annual *Flute Talk* Competition in Chicago. As part of our duties, we were asked to give a talk on some subject. I used the theme of the Schubert *Variations* to talk about phrasing, and the way this theme is played by the typical flutist who had not heard anyone sing the song. I was trying to follow up on my book *Sing!* by choosing a song that the audience knew, but I don't know if I made an impression. I expanded this theme later in the year, when the NFA asked me to contribute an article to its proposed volume on aspects of flute playing. I reworked my introduction to *Sing!*, with prodding and valuable help from editor Martha Rearick, and made a good contribution.

I wrote several articles for the magazine *Flute Talk* over the years with some frustration at their editorial policies. They consciously tried to make all the articles sound the same, making them, in my opinion, boring. One article I wrote was prompted by a part I played from during a Bolshoi Ballet season. This particular part had started out as a poor manuscript, to which a sequence of flutists had added various pencil markings. These were now a permanent part of the copy. Careless Xeroxing meant that missing notes at the end of a line had to be written in by hand. I wrote a light article pointing out all these little things, intending it to be funny and an object lesson in what one had to deal with in the profession. What was published was totally humorless and sounded as if I were being snooty.

The lowest point with *Flute Talk*, however, came when someone at the magazine actually wrote an article and signed my name to it. The intention was good (to promote my first volume of opera excerpts) but the article contained misinformation. The magazine printed a retraction in the following issue. I finally reached an understanding with the person I dealt with that, regardless of editorial changes, I would have the final word.

In May, Vicky and I participated in another adventure organized by Carla Hunt, who had arranged our Burgundy barge trip and been a part of the Greek trip. Our destination was the Galápagos Islands. Along with Carla and her husband, Tom, were the Daniels and Gaynes from the previous trip, the actress Barbara Barrie and her husband, Jay Harnick, and four more friends of Carla's. Our boat, *Isabela II*, was a pleasure. With twenty cabins it could carry forty passengers, but we had it to ourselves thanks to Carla's credentials and clout.

A four-hour flight from Miami took us to Quito, the capital of Ecuador. The city is high, nestled between even higher mountains, originally sited to be above mosquito level. I am embarrassed to admit that I knew nothing about Ecuador and found it to be a thriving democracy of seemingly happy people. While we were there, they had a national referendum on changes to their constitution. Every literate adult has to vote and voting is on Sunday, so people are both free and able to get to their place of registration. Additionally, no liquor can be sold (even with meals) from Friday until Monday morning during the election weekend. Ecuador has fine painters and skilled artisans. We were able to attend a charming evening of folkloric dancing accompanied by five musicians – rhythm, guitars and, of course, native flutes of all sizes, both recorder type and pan flute type. I brought home an artistic collage of all the Andes flutes – miniatures made of wood, named and mounted on a board. We made a trip outside of Quito to the north to visit a market in the town of Otavalo, where the Indians bring in their handicrafts every Saturday morning. This whole area is a shopper's paradise – all things woven, jewelry, leather goods, and primitive artwork. A beautiful woolen sweater was $30 for example; an elegant suede jacket $75. We crossed the equator, where we had the obligatory photo taken.

Our group on the equatorial line, 1997.

After a half-hour flight to Guyaquil near the Pacific Coast, an hour-and-a-half more took us to Baltra in the Galápagos Islands, five hundred miles out in the Pacific.

These volcanic islands, largely uninhabited, were discovered by sailors some three hundred years ago and used by whalers and buccaneers as a place for water and food. The water came from the craters, the food from the teeming wildlife, tame birds, and huge tortoises from which the islands got their name. The islands were made famous by the visit of Charles Darwin in 1835. His observations on how birds and plants had adapted to the circumstances of each individual island in order to survive inspired some of his most famous work. Access to the islands is strictly controlled to preserve them – no more than ninety people a day are permitted on any island, and those people are guided and restricted to paths that keep them out of nesting areas and other sensitive locations.

We didn't get to relax much. Activities often started at 6:30 AM and went on until near 6 PM. These daylight hours included snorkeling trips, and breakfasts and lunches featuring Ecuadorian fruits and juices. (Everything on the boat came with us from the mainland except water, which was desalinated on board.) Briefing on the next day's activities was at 7 PM, dinner at 7:30, and bed at 9 if you could keep your eyes on a book till then.

Our guide, a young Ecuadorian, was personable, witty, extremely erudite, and fluent in English. He was equally at home on land and under the water. One of the absolute highlights of an extraordinary week was to see him lead a group of playful sea lions down twenty feet and watch them rise to the surface surrounding him. Or to see one of them balance a shell on its nose and push it through the water. These animals are not trained and they are everywhere – on the shores, in the water, on the paths.

We sailed most nights, often all night, to get to the next approved island, and had a couple of visits from dolphins that "bodysurfed" in the boat's bow wave – six or so coasting along, wheeling away, leaping into the air.

Each island is different in size, age, flora and fauna. We saw a barren "moonscape" and a tropical rain forest, lava flows, lava tunnels, and giant sink holes where these tunnels have collapsed.

Our only disappointment was that the giant turtles were currently in an area that was unreachable due to a delayed rainy season. We did see some at the center that is trying to increase their numbers and repopulate their colonies. The center has regained several of the adults that had been taken to the mainland as house pets. Several dozen babies that are hatched each year at the center are kept until they can survive on their own.

The bird life was incredible and mostly endemic to the islands: boobies (blue footed, red footed, and masked), gulls, frigates (the wooing male puffs up an enormous scarlet gullet), albatrosses, pelicans, and the Darwin finches. We saw courting rituals and nesting sites and learned some of their habits. Birds with five-foot wingspans nest near the cliffs so they can take off unhindered. The finches were numerous because their islands were green from unusual rainfall. When a shortage of food arises, many will die; so the females mate only with males that have longer beaks, making them better able to forage for seeds. I could go on forever – this was a trip of a lifetime.

A quite different trip was the one Vicky and I alone took the following month. We had found a house on a Bordeaux canal that was for rent. After a few days in Paris, we took the train to the city of Bordeaux, rented a car, and found our place. The old farmhouse was lovely and the lawn led right down to the canal. But it rained. And rained. We spent most of the week in front of the enormous kitchen fireplace. We did make some little trips – to Bordeaux, to Toulouse to visit friends, to some vineyards – but it was really pretty dreary and not something we would repeat.

In July I had a rare trip without Vicky when the Bronx Arts Ensemble was invited to play a concert in Santa Fe. I had not been there before and I loved walking its downtown streets and driving about the surrounding area. We played in the atmospheric Santuario de Guadalupe; the wonderful Rachel Rosales was the soloist in Hector Campos Parsi's moving *Sonetos Sagrados*.

At the end of August we left once more for Australia, where Vicky was working. Our first stop was in Sydney, where Russell and Sue Meares had moved into their spectacular new harbor home designed by Australia's leading architect, Harry Seidler. The structure was definitely unique, with its curved roof, two-story living room overlooking the patio, overlooking the harbor. The master bedroom suite also had a window that overlooked the living room that overlooked the patio that overlooked the harbor. As a home, it was not very private or livable, and they didn't stay long. In the meantime, we found it most glamorous, and the four of us had a great reunion.

In Melbourne, we were housed in a new central hotel with an impressive atrium. While Vicky worked I caught up with friends and family, and together we joined a gathering of old Trinity friends at Jim and Robin Grimwade's home. I made a dashing overnight trip a thousand miles north to Brisbane to advise the committee of local flutists on its planned convention. I also taught a class while I was there.

Trinity friends and wives at the home of Dr. James (*seated right*) and Mrs. Robin (*standing left*) Grimade, 1997.

Jet-lagged, I arrived in Chicago for the twenty-fifth NFA convention, where I made an improvised and ineffective presentation on *Sing!*. The wonderful Sam Baron had died earlier in the year and a moving memorial for him had been scheduled. Oboist Ronnie Roseman, Sam's longtime colleague in the New York Woodwind Quintet and Bach Aria Group, had come to participate. We had not seen each other since I had been fired from

Musica Sacra, and we had a warm reunion. The program chair, Patti Adams, had put together an evening memorial to all the members of the NFA who had died over its twenty-five years. Accompanied by new age music performed by Jim Walker, slides were projected with the names of the deceased. To be confronted like that with all those people who had been such a part of my life was a numbing experience. I was sitting next to Kathy Borst Jones, the current president, who had recently lost her husband, whose name was on the list. I squeezed her hand harder and harder as we both sat stunned. I never went to another convention.

That of course was not the only reason. I had been feeling for some time that the association was headed in a direction and making policy decisions with which I didn't agree. I was never much of a joiner, and it is remarkable in retrospect that I became so involved in the first place. As I saw myself marginalized as a performer, presenter, and advisor, I became more aware of how stressful I actually found these conventions. I was bothered by even the silliest things like not recognizing someone who came to speak with me, and being too embarrassed to look down at the name tag.

In the fall our younger son, Anthony, began courses at Yale toward his MBA, and we were again paying tuition bills – although this time as a loan.

1998

My first interesting assignment of 1998 was to perform John Corigliano's lovely *Voyage* with a string orchestra at Hartt. More significantly, I completed my opera series. I discovered some time before that each volume sold fewer copies than the previous one, but I still believed in the value of the project and determined to finish it. My compromise was to condense the final three projected volumes into two. I now received volume nine back from the printer. My first step was to send a signed copy as a thankyou to the group of people who had supported the project from the beginning. Some years later, with almost a thousand copies of volume nine still unsold, I sent another hundred or so to all the professional flutists in the country. I received a number of warm thanks in return, but did not notice an increase in sales as a result. I eventually revised volume one and two to correct errors and improve the layout. I couldn't justify the expense of a print run by the time I got to volume two. Instead, I spent much time figuring out how to print individual copies as needed. I had to find a printer that would handle the unusual music size of 9"x12" folded and covers even bigger so the borders could be trimmed, I had to find paper in these sizes, and I had to find a program that would turn my inkjet printer into a postscript printer that would print the music accurately. I also had to find a stapler big enough to reach the center of a 12"x18" sheet, and some kind of guillotine to trim the covers. I had to revise the book and set it up so that the 64 pages would print in the correct order. Each sheet took five minutes to print, so each book took almost three hours to produce. That was not a satisfactory solution, but it took years to find a better one.

I published a few more pieces on an "on demand" basis, but I could do those in a more conventional format with much less time and trauma.

In May, Vicky and I made a trip to North Carolina, South Carolina, and Georgia. Near Asheville, we stayed with Bobby and Virginia Barnett, Vicky's longtime friends from her early NYCB days. Ginny and her sister had used an inheritance to buy a mountain in the Smoky Mountains where they each built their dream home. The Barnetts' was quite spectacular and appropriately theatric. The entrance hall staircase was from the set of an Atlanta Ballet *Romeo and Juliet*, and the house was filled with a lifetime's collection from travels all over the world, finally in an appropriate setting. In their living room, a beautiful oriental screen rose to the ceiling at the press of a button, to reveal an entertainment center. And the kitchen had everything – new to me was a faucet producing boiling water. All of this was in beautiful taste and not ostentatious.

We had a couple of nights in Charleston, where Vicky showed me many sights discovered on her working trips there. Then we moved to Savannah to stay with another ballet friend, Una Kai. Una, after her own dancing and teaching careers, was now a guide in this historic city, which had reached heightened fame with the publication of *Midnight in the Garden of Good and Evil*. So we had our own private guide for the whole city, including of course all the sites from the novel.

After Hartt's year ended in May, we set off again, this time to London for some theater, then on to a highly recommended manor in Devon. We had a lovely few days of good English pampering there and walked on the moors in the mist and rain, thinking of the *Hound of the Baskervilles*.

In July, as a part of the Lincoln Center Festival, our orchestra played for two visiting German companies. The programs were *Romeo and Juliet*, *Eugene Onegin*, a Bernstein evening, and a Mahler *Fifth* brilliantly conducted by Klaus-Peter Seibel.

Rehearsing with Enzo Caroli at Belluno, 1998.

At the end of the month, Vicky and I went to Venice for a few days, en route to Belluno in the Dolomites, where Livio Caroli's flute-playing brother Enzo had invited me to teach and play a duo concert with him. I was not paid a salary, but the director and his wife, and Enzo of course, were such perfect hosts and fed us so well that I hoped it might become an ongoing part of my life. (That didn't work out. I think that when they totaled up all they had spent on us, it just wasn't feasible to repeat the offer.)

One thing I learned there was the art of the siesta. I worked hard teaching in the morning, but then took a long break for lunch and rest before continuing later in the afternoon. I found this so helpful that I incorporated it into my Hartt schedule – three hours in the morning, two-hour lunch break in my apartment, three hours in the afternoon.

In August our younger son, Anthony, was married to Amy Rogers at a lovely ceremony in Connecticut.

Anthony and Amy's wedding, August 1998.

1999

I spent the early part of this year developing my web site, which would contain my expanding memoirs and the results of my genealogical research, in addition to material relating to my teaching.

I created a page on my site relating to the history of orchestral principal flutists, having become aware of how easily this information is lost. Although some large orchestras have archivists, most do not. Records of employment are destroyed in wars (as were La Scala's) or floods (such as Houston's), or are thrown away (as in the case of my own orchestra). Sometimes the only remaining records are programs, and they did not always identify the principals or even list the members of the orchestra at all. In my own orchestra members were not listed for the company's first twenty-five years. I contacted as many older players as possible to have them search their memories before it was too late. In the end, my file contained the principal flutists of more than a hundred orchestras worldwide, many of them going back to their origins. In the case of the Leipzig Gewandhaus that was 1743.

I developed a file of errata in printed flute music, and another on vibrato. In addition to my thoughts on vibrato, I included clips of flutists playing a few bars, and clips of those same bars slowed down so the vibrato could be studied. Finally, I used the site to sell my recordings and publications, and to make available some of my live performances. The site gets about a thousand visitors a month. Most visit the principals' page. Every now and then I get an order for a CD or music.

I played some interesting performances during the year. The first was organized by NYCO clarinetist Laura Flax at the Cooper Union Hall (where Abraham Lincoln had once given a speech). My contribution was Amilcare Ponchielli's wonderful spoof of an operatic quartet scored for four high winds, originally with orchestral accompaniment. Laura played B♭ clarinet, and our NYCO colleagues Steve Hartman and Randy Wolfgang played E♭ clarinet and oboe, respectively. I also participated in a faculty trio recital at school with pianist Margreet Francis and cellist David Wells. The three of us played the Weber Trio, and Maggie and I played Steve Gryc's new *Shadowdance*, which we were preparing to record in May. For the Bronx Arts Ensemble I played Janácek's *Mladi* in one concert and the Debussy *Sonata* and Jolivet's *Pastorales de Noel* in another. At year's end I performed Bernstein's moving *Halil* with the school orchestra.

Vicky and I spent much of the summer in Europe. Apart from vacations in Paris and at Malfiano in Tuscany, where we caught up with our Scots friends Richard and Joyce Milner and hosted the Carolis who were in the area, I taught and played a recital at two festivals. The first was in Stratford-upon-Avon where Elena Duran and her husband, Michael Emmerson, had started a two-week International Flute Festival. The second arose from the previous year's Belluno week. The

With Livio Caroli and Richard Milner at Malfiano, 1999.

pianist there ran his own festival in another town in the Veneto (Conegliano) and invited me to participate. I had an interesting time, but I was unable to attract a class due to students attending the NFA convention, and I was not invited back. My program at both festivals consisted of the Mozart K13 and Reinecke sonatas, Milhaud's *Sonatine*, Gryc's *Shadowdance*, and Anne Boyd's *Goldfish through Summer Rain*.

Our year ended with Vicky's sixtieth birthday on New Year's Eve. Our children offered to cook some of the dishes and made the wine suggestions. We shared this imposing feast with them, their wives, and close friends.

A New Year's Eve Dinner
Celebrating Vicky's 60th Birthday
December 31, 1999

Caviar
Peconika Long Island Hamptons Vodka

Oysters
Greco di Tufo

Shrimp Remoulade
Pierre Sparr Gewurtztraminer 1996

Trout Mousse with Madeira Truffle Sauce - Fernand Point
Chateau d'Epire Savennieres 1997

Ravioli filled with Eggplant
Maculan Breganza 1988

Foie Gras with Haricots Verts
Chateau Suduiraut Sauternes 1995

Mini Beef Wellingtons with asparagus
Castillo Ygay Gran Riserva Especial Rioja 1989

Roasted Quail with mushrooms
Chateau Talbot 1990

Truffle Cheese with grapes
Castello Di Fagnano Chianti Classico 1996

Stilton with dried apricots
Cockburn's 20 Year Old Tawny Porto

Persimmon Sorbet
Tarte au Citron with blueberries
Bittersweet Chocolate Cake with creme fraiche, strawberries
Yalumba Museum Muscat

Espresso / Liqueurs

Midnight Champagne Toast
Veuve Cliquot

Vicky's sixtieth birthday party and menu.

2000

Bronx Arts concerts this spring included the Stravinsky *Octet*, the Beethoven *Serenade*, and a new *Quintet* by Robert Baksa whose *Octet* and *Nonet* we had recorded so successfully. The recording of the *Quintet* was altogether different. The session was scheduled for a Friday evening at New York's Town Hall. The engineer had an arrangement with the management to record at a reduced price when the hall was free. That evening we were to follow a rehearsal for *The Prairie Home Companion*. Unfortunately, some members of that cast were arriving by air and thunderstorms delayed arrivals. They were waiting for them, then they weren't; we were waiting for the rehearsal to finish, then we weren't. When could we re-schedule? – not for months. Just when we were on the verge of going home, we were told that they were about to finish. The situation was strange; as we were not officially there, we could hardly complain. To add to our problems, our violinist, the wonderful Gerald Tarack, was recovering from an accident and was on heavy pain medication. We managed our way through the piece under the low-keyed observation of the composer. The ensemble had some co-ordination problems in the finale, and the engineer finally suggested we take a nice easy tempo. With no complaint from the composer, we laid out a successful, if leisurely version. I was invited to comment on the final edit some months later and picked up on a missing beat and a missing bass note. Then I was surprised to hear that the composer felt the finale was too slow. Modern technology took over, and a satisfactory speed was attained. A CD was issued, adding the Quintet to a re-release of the Octet and Nonet from the original LP.

Our big adventure this year was a visit to China. After considerable research we finally decided to join a tour, and in retrospect we made the right choice. Much of the time we were the only people on our tour, so we had our own car and guide. While we expected great contrasts between the old and the new, what really staggered us was what had happened in the last twenty years, indeed in the last five years. We swept across Shanghai, for example, on a highly elevated expressway, with an endless vista on either side of high-rise buildings. Yet behind these were the yet to be cleared hovels of the old China, the dirty streets, and the hordes of poor immigrants from the countryside. At the tourist sites we were besieged by the poorest of all, trying to sell some trinket or postcard.

The ten years of the Cultural Revolution made a visible hole in the society, and we could see a marked difference in personality and attitude between the younger and older people. Just as the food and hotels varied from ordinary to excellent, so did our guides. The younger ones were full of vitality and enthusiasm for their jobs, the older ones perfunctory. One explained that as an English major she had been assigned to her job. Now that change was possible owing to the reforms of Deng Xiaoping, she was, at thirty-five, too old for a new career. (Most women are retired by fifty-five.) She had her one child and lived on the top floor of a walk-up apartment building. All the guides were surprisingly candid about the mistakes made by the government, and the older ones had all suffered hardships. Our Beijing guide's father, a tenor, had been sent away for rehabilitation, and the son had been sent to live with relatives in Mongolia. Chosen to represent his school at Mao's funeral at Tiananmen Square, he had later been there when the army moved in to crush the student revolt.

We saw little sign of militarism or control on our trip, though we do know that CNN was not offered on cable except in classy hotels (and even there censored if deemed necessary). The missing four-page leaf from one Herald Tribune was explained as having been removed by the government. On a later trip there for work, Vicky was amazed that the death of the pope was not even reported.

A considerable part of our goal was to visit China's famous historical and scenic sites, and we were never disappointed, unless it was from an overdose of Buddhas. In Beijing we walked through the Forbidden City and onto the Great Wall, took a rickshaw around the old area and visited the immaculate if small home of a retired army engineer. Because the city was so huge, we spent a lot of time admiring the way our driver avoided the chaotic traffic everywhere. What used to be mostly bicycles now included an equal number of cars. VW was the first Western auto maker into China, and it seemed to have a good hold on the market with its locally made Santana.

We loved the vitality of Shanghai, enhanced throughout by our guide, the charming young Seven. She explained that her social life with her co-workers was limited because they were all so much older. During the Cultural Revolution no English was taught, hence a gap in ages of English-speaking guides. We walked around the downtown area and appreciated the flow of life, whereas the museum with its excellent acousti-guide and an evening acrobatic performance were each fascinating in entirely different ways.

Beijing, 2000.

We had wanted to visit Suzhou, "The Venice of the East," famed for its gardens. En route we stopped at Zhouzhuang, another canal village recently opened to tourism, which we found charming if not quite "ready for business." Suzhou itself was a bit of a disappointment though the new Sheraton is spectacular. We did not see as many of the walled gardens as we had hoped, and the canals could not be visited due to summer odor. An example of how tourism is still getting organized was an evening concert of traditional arts in one of the old garden villas in Suzhou. The performers were excellent and the setting ideal, but the presentation was somewhat amateurish. An atmospheric flute solo, played on a terrace and viewed from across the garden pond, was abruptly curtailed when the performer got a cell phone call. What *was* spectacular was a visit to the embroidery institute. The skill and delicacy of the artisans was remarkable, as they "painted" their unique works of art using silk thread in an infinite range of colors. The fur of a white cat was so real you felt you could lift the ends.

A central part of our trip was a cruise through the Yangtze River gorges, which would largely disappear when the new dam was filled a few years later. For this relaxing cruise we joined a group of nine on a similar tour, along with their dynamic young Beijing guide, Alena. They all proved to be enjoyable touring companions and some became good friends.

This dam and its implications were astonishing. The site, cleared by channeling the river off to one side, was maybe a half mile across, and looked like something out of a James Bond movie, with cranes everywhere and endless movements of trucks and people – over 25,000 in three eight-hour shifts, seven days a week, all living in barracks on site. A five-level lock would bring ocean ships through the dam and open up sea trade to central China. An elevator would lift smaller traffic. The housing for the first six turbines was near completion, with that for the next eight taking shape. After these turbines were installed the river would be diverted back, the dam would start to fill, and the final series of turbines would be installed on the far side. When completed, the water level above the dam would be some 200 yards higher. About a million people would be relocated. When we learned that the frequent flooding of the river could take 100,000 lives the perspective of disruption changed. The government believed that the $28 billion cost would be recouped in five years by the sale of electricity generated, and the dry northeast of the country would be revitalized by irrigation. The gorges were indeed spectacular, and we were sorry they would be lost; but it was hard not to be swayed by the desperately needed advantages of the dam. As we moved upriver towards Chongqing and took side trips to view tributaries and towns, we saw the periodic markers reminding residents where the new water line would be, and we saw the new towns, villages, roads, and bridges being created above that level.

Staying with the same group, we next visited a site of ancient Buddhist stone carvings at Dazu, dropped in on a local farm village (they may lead simple lives but they have their color TVs), then flew northeast to Xi'an. The internal airlines used Boeings, left on time, arrived on time, and one even offered a Royal Ballet *Swan Lake* as the in-flight entertainment.

The Yangtze River gorge, 2000.

Far from being the small town we expected, Xi'an was another six-million-plus sprawl around the impressively reconstructed wall of the old city. This former capital is the site of the terra-cotta army of the first emperor's tomb. The tomb itself, believed to be a city, still lies untouched beneath its man-made hill covering. The protective army – life-sized infantry, archers, charioteers, and officers in the thousands, each individually created and painted – was drawn up in formation before the tomb. Then the whole was covered and disappeared from history, until a farmer digging a well struck a corner of the site. In the new China, that farmer now sits and autographs the tourists' photo books at a dollar a pop. (Off-site you can get the same books at half price by bargaining, but you don't get that signature.) A wonderful surround-movie re-enacts the creation of the army and brings the whole astonishing site to life.

With the sinking of the roof over the centuries most of the figures were shattered, and the paint has long disappeared, but huge areas of the trenches have now been opened up, with hundreds of figures reassembled and placed back in formation – an awe-inspiring sight. A highlight of a professionally-presented evening based on traditional Xi'an song and dance was a virtuoso pan-piper, Mr. Guo. His presentation included astonishingly realistic imitations of birdcalls.

We then flew south to Guilin, famed for its limestone mountains rising precipitously on all sides. These are the misty vistas seen in so many Chinese paintings, and magical they were. The town was charming with its riverfront promenade and dragon boat rehearsals, though it lacked the excitement of the big cities.

That changed with our arrival via hydrofoil from Guangzhou into Hong Kong. What a vibrant and magical place it is. Although Vicky had been there a decade ago, I had not seen it since 1963. At that time the harbor was filled with residential junks and sampans, and the

Guilin, 2000.

hillsides were covered with tin-roofed shanties. Now the boats had gone, and the shoreline of the island was a pincushion of glass and metal skyscrapers, shimmering by day, glittering by night. We saw wealth everywhere here, and no signs of the grinding poverty always hiding behind the facade on the mainland. We did the conventional touring – Victoria Peak, Stanley Market, and Aberdeen (no longer a fishing village but a marina for glamorous yachts), and wandered around downtown and across the harbor in Kowloon. But perhaps most fascinating was watching the downtown Sunday gathering of all the Filipino maids. On their one day off, they meet by the thousands, and their high-pitched chatter sounds like geese cackling.

In a trip of such contrasts, the sheer number of people in China was the overwhelming constant. With such numbers labor is cheap, and everywhere we saw signs of this as crews of men repaired and built at all hours of the day, and all days of the week. As old and new mixed, we saw, for example, a modern turnstile at a superb new museum, but one person sold the magnetic admission cards, another placed them into the turnstile for us, and a third retrieved and returned our cards after we entered. After almost three weeks, this continuous press of people had lost its novelty, and we were ready for the comparatively large personal spaces of New York.

2001

The spring season was to be my last at the opera. Although I would not officially retire from orchestral performance, I did not pursue any engagements, so one chapter in my career did close. I continued to play some chamber music concerts with the Bronx Arts Ensemble, whenever rehearsals for the Sunday concerts could be scheduled toward the end of the week. I particularly enjoyed the *Wind Quintet* of John Harbison, finding it well worth the considerable time I had to spend preparing my part. The Poulenc and Thuille sextets with piano on the other hand were old friends and always a pleasure. I also had another crack at Honegger's *Concerto da Camera* with Marsha Heller playing the English horn part. Apart from being a wonderful musician, Marsha is a gifted painter. Vicky and I bought a painting each, and two more for the kids. This art has given us all much pleasure.

We have acquired a few paintings over the years from talented friends. The first two were abstract oils by Gregory Reeve, the brother of my oboist friend Basil. "Jake," as he was called, was gifted in so many areas, including music and photography. We also have a large geometric acrylic by my high school friend Jeremy Barrett. A particular favorite is Sandra Leveson's 1991 acrylic, *Glissando*.

Sandra, Russell Meares's second wife, reached a peak of recognition around that time, with paintings in most Australian galleries, and a certain international success. Over the years, we followed her development from delicate pointillist abstracts to the striking landscape-type abstracts of the nineties. Sandra's studio in Sydney was a converted factory, which included a darkroom and a swimming pool. She had hung the walls with her favorite paintings, ones she had chosen not to sell. Her method of working was to take a large number of photographs of a subject – a field of poppies or the rusting side of a freighter – and develop a book of small pastel sketches from those photos. The next step would be a larger-sized series of silk screens or something similar. Then would come the full-sized acrylics, four feet by four feet or larger. The whole project might occupy her for a year. I was always trying to buy something, but Sandra always deflected me. Finally, Vicky approached her, asking her to paint something as a surprise for me. They had an interesting discussion about price, by the square foot. I worried that she might paint something I didn't care for. We were also concerned about getting a painting from Sydney to New York. Suddenly, Sandra proposed that we look at slides of some unsold paintings sitting in Texas following an exhibition there. We quickly made our choice. I used it later on the cover of my publication of the Humble *Sonata*.

Glissando, 1989 by Sandra Leveson.

I made yet another trip to Australia, when I took advantage of Vicky's working in Melbourne. We stayed in an old brick cottage on the grounds of the Victorian College for the Arts. We found it convenient and pleasant, once we moved the bed into a back room away from the screeching of the trams. I taught a single master class at the college and gave some private lessons. My playing career did indeed seem to be coming to an end.

September 11 of that year, with its attacks on the World Trade Center, brought, among other things, the realization that from then on we would always feel a sense of vulnerability in Manhattan. Everyone has his own story of that day. I was teaching in Hartford that morning. Vicky was flying to Atlanta. On the airport train to the terminal there, she overheard people talking on cell phones. When she heard more definitely what had happened, she phoned my studio to tell me she was safe. In a common area at school a TV was set up, and staff, faculty, and students watched, horrified, as the towers slid to the ground. Work got us through the next days, and then Vicky had to face flying home.

I felt I had to go to the site. Otherwise it would remain an unreal thing, reduced to the size of a television screen. Together, Vicky and I went and stared at the horrific sight. Just as overwhelming, and never to be forgotten, was the smell.

Life after the Opera

For the remainder of my sixties I continued moving away from performing and focused my professional activities on teaching. As these things happen, it was not a straight line. To start with, in the spring of 2002 I was granted my second sabbatical and practiced being completely retired. As before, I chose the second semester of school as being the less disruptive to my students. I could get everyone started, particularly the incoming students. Elena Duran proved to be an excellent choice to replace me. Her enormous enthusiasm and focus on areas such as memorization gave the class a different perspective and a real lift.

In May, I was invited to participate in the Seventeenth International Flute Festival in Lima, Peru. The experience was unique but not very productive for me. Nor did I think my presence added much. Confusion and local politics surrounded the activities, and the only international aspect to the festival was the six visiting performers. But the high quality of these guests was significant. My main contribution was to play the Gryc *Shadowdance* and the Copland *Duo* on one of the concerts. Beyond that I joined in some ensembles and helped entertain a variety of audiences. I was the only guest not invited to participate in the concerto concert. That hurt, but what really got to me was that I never did teach. Only when I raised the issue was a class assigned to me on the last day, and then the car didn't show up to take me there.

A concert in Lima, 2002 – Ilari Lehtinen at left, Robert Dick at right.

Vicky joined me in Lima at the end of the festival and we visited the Incan sites in the Andes. Macchu Picchu was an amazing experience, though an impending train strike meant we couldn't stay overnight as planned.

As a result of the festival, I was invited to Finland in the fall of the following year by a fellow guest, Ilari Lehtinen. The event in Tampere was the twentieth anniversary of the Finnish Flute Association, and Ilari had put together the weekend's activities. The focus was "The Singing Flute." At his request, I played *Shadowdance* and taught a class. I had a wonderful time and thought the Finns had a society to be envied. Their values were so different from those in the United States, with a strong focus on music performance and social security. My former student, Kathy Weidenfeller, who had done postgraduate work in Helsinki and settled there, was my constant guide from the moment I landed. After the festival she arranged a moving visit to Sibelius's home. I loved everything about Finland and couldn't wait to go back.

Class in Tampere, 2003.

My return would be two years later, when Vicky and I planned a northern European trip. I had been hosted in Tampere by local flutist Päivi Järkäs, who with her husband welcomed us into their spectacular home overlooking a lake. Vicky had to imagine the combination of yellow birch leaves and green firs that had framed the view in the fall, but summer had its pleasures too, a swim in the lake and dinner on the patio.

The whole northern trip was a pleasure. The impetus had been a desire to see St. Petersburg, so that is where we started. We flew there with great anxiety, worried about safety, our lack of language, and the reported difficulty with officials. Things were indeed difficult, but we survived and had great adventures. Vicky remembered enough Cyrillic alphabet from 1962 that we could negotiate streets and restaurant names, and we never felt threatened.

The city is beautiful, but with such a level of construction and renovation that one imagined an even better treat awaited next time. I mostly wanted to see the painting collection at the Hermitage, which was indeed remarkable, but I had not expected to be so overwhelmed by the rooms of the palace themselves – such grandeur, such elegance.

We saw a performance of *Bayadère* at the Mariinsky, and a somewhat "summer pops" concert by the symphony in its acoustically marvelous hall. Our culinary highlight was dinner in the grand restaurant of the Europa Hotel. With violin, piano, and wonderful alto on the stage, we tasted the local caviar served Russian style and had a splendid meal while looking at the wood paneling and stained glass roof of the imposing room. Peterhof, a summer palace, despite its delightful fountains, showed us the kind of extravagance and arrogance that could surely lead to a revolution.

We went then by train to Helsinki, one of the few places that I had been to that Vicky had not. We enjoyed the waterfront market and had a lovely dinner with my former student, Kathy Weidenfeller, on an island just offshore. On the 11:30 PM ferry home it was still light. Our final stop in Finland after the Tampere visit was at the port city of Turku, where another flutist, Hannu Lehtinen, kindly showed us around. We then took the overnight ferry to Stockholm.

As we walked all around the harbor and the old city we both agreed that this was the prettiest of the Scandinavian capitals. The highlight was definitely the museum housing the sixteenth-century galleon *Vasa*, which sank on its maiden voyage. Astonishingly preserved in the mud of the harbor, it had been resurrected in the 1960s and lovingly restored to its original splendor.

Half way across Sweden, at Örebro, we were met by our Australian friend, Michael Long. Mick had followed two of his children to Löa where he had now bought a house. Through his generosity and warmth he had made himself a part of the community, and as his friends, we were in turn welcomed and invited into homes for dinners and an evening of folksongs. Between times, we walked in the countryside and relaxed, a perfect four days.

With Mick Long at Löa, 2005.

A long bus ride took us to Oslo, where our run of great weather finally ran out. But the train trip across Norway to Bergen was spectacular, and the sun was shining when the train stopped en route, so we could all get out and look at the glacier field. Bergen is a very pretty port, with a bustling marketplace where we bought fresh sandwiches piled with tiny shrimp or smoked salmon, and local berries. We spent our second day at "Norway in a Nutshell," an all-day trip via train, cog railway, boat, and bus. The weather was dreary, but even so the sights were grand. The cog railway wound its way from the mountain heights to the Sonnenfjord's edge, where a boat took us through the fjord for a couple of hours. Then a bus took us up to the heights again to meet the return train to Bergen.

We have tried to make traveling to a new place a part of our yearly plans and visited Ireland, Wales, and Cornwall during these years. The latter two were built around a second, non-performing participation at the Stratford festival in 2003. More confident about handling Russia, we would like to make an extended trip there. I would like to visit Ephesus in Turkey, and Morocco, and Singapore and ... maybe make another trip around the world. We have an arctic trip planned for 2007 and we have a list of favorite places to return to. Traveling will certainly be a big part of our future as long as our health permits.

Australia will be a part of our lives too. Vicky is always in demand there to stage a Balanchine ballet or to teach, so I join her when possible and do some teaching too. In January 2004 I was able to take part in a summer school in Melbourne, for example. And the following year I became a performer again.

My longtime friend Leonard Spira retired to Noosa in Australia's northeast – its Florida. He became involved in the local music scene and wrote to ask if I would play a recital in 2005. After much deliberation, I agreed, and spent a year getting back into some kind of performance shape. He asked for an unchallenging program for the audience, so I chose Bach E♭, Schubert *Arpeggione*, Reinecke, and Poulenc. Stephen McIntyre agreed to join me. Thus committed, I arranged to play the same program for the Sydney flute people and also have it serve as a part of a fiftieth reunion at Trinity in Melbourne.

Sydney was planned as a dress rehearsal, with Stephen arriving the day before from Europe. He was jet-lagged and I was nervous. I convinced myself that I was playing for a group of amateurs, but the first face I saw was a beaming Imre Pallo, longtime conducting friend, who was working in Sydney and saw my concert listed. He wanted to say hello but couldn't stay; my pulse dropped back to normal anxiety. Then as I walked on stage, I saw the face of a professional I knew and all my composure flew out the window. I had breathing problems and tone control issues, but Vicky said it went well, and people were gracious in their comments afterwards.

I taught a class and gave some private lessons, and had a great time catching up with our hosts, Russell and Sue Meares, in their latest harbor-view apartment. Then we flew to Noosa in the sunny north. The Spiras made us feel so welcome in their beautiful home and fed us such a healthful diet that I started to feel quite relaxed; indeed I felt better about the concert this time. Gail Spira even asked me to offer an encore, and "Send in the Clowns" made a great ending.

In Melbourne, Vicky had arranged to teach for two weeks, and we did a lot of socializing in the evenings. The Trinity concert was in the dining room where so many formal and informal meals had been taken fifty years before. Finally I was playing for friends. After it was over, and a few tears shed over Sondheim, I thought, *I could really make a habit of this*. I would just have to stay in shape

At the Spiras in Noosa, 2005 (Photograph by Gail Spira).

and actively pursue concerts. But neither seemed to be a priority. I had spent so much of my life making concerts happen, and I just didn't have the enthusiasm and drive to do it any more. And without a deadline, it became harder and harder to maintain a serious practice routine. I found it hard enough to keep enough muscle tone to not embarrass myself playing duets with my students.

Rehearsing with Stephen McIntyre in Noosa, 2005.

I thought I had played my last concert, but then the Boston Flute Club asked me to play at its annual weekend. I played *Shadowdance*, but more important, two of my former students and one current one were on the same program. Afterwards, an elderly gentleman who is a leading teacher introduced himself and told me he always plays my French recording for his students to emulate.

My students have been a joy. I get great pleasure from watching them develop at school, and then following their lives. Some of the more talented ones have chosen to pursue careers in performing and have had gratifying success. Others, not necessarily less gifted, chose different paths – becoming librarians and teachers and chemists and engineers, and one a midwife. Another, while still doing graduate work at New England Conservatory, honored me by interviewing me and having the results appear in *The Flutist Quarterly*. In 2003 a competition with a $10,000 grand prize was begun at Hartt for undergraduate instrumentalists. In its first year my students took first and third places. Two years later my student again won the grand prize. My students have enjoyed other competition successes in and out of school, and have won opportunities to play concertos and recitals.

In my early years at Hartt I wrestled with the morality of directing students towards a career in which opportunities were both limited and dwindling. But I decided that as long as I was honest and helped them understand the realities of their choice, they were spending these years in a positive manner. In addition to the joy of performing and the satisfaction of developing their talent, they learned valuable skills such as discipline, coordination, organization of time, and how to manage interpersonal relationships. My belief has been strengthened by letters from students whose careers have moved away from performing. None seem to regret their Hartt experience.

I don't know how long I will continue to teach. I find much routine in what I do and dealing with emotional students is draining. I know I will have to leave *some* students in midstream *sometime*. I plan to see my most gifted student through her four years, but then I start seeing a younger talent blossom and wonder if I will stay to see her through.

In January 2004, my dear friend Lew Waldeck died after some years of slow decline. He figures here and there in this story, but he led many lives himself, and affected countless other

lives with his intellect and totally unreserved love. He was a tuba player, master chef in a variety of cuisines, poet, philosopher, photographer, movie maker, stalwart leftist, union organizer, and one of the first computer geeks, writing programs before most of us knew what a computer was. He was always at the other end of the phone when I needed help or advice, and I miss his wisdom and his love.

In April of the same year my half sister Jocelyn died in Napa at the age of 89. She figures less in this story as I only met Jo a couple of times, as I did her sister Kathryn.

Lew Waldeck.

We are blessed to have close friends still with us, though one only after a near-death struggle with cancer. We assemble in different combinations and numbers as our busy lives permit and immediately continue where we left off. We can usually count on most for Labor Day at our country house.

Labor Day weekend, 2005 with 6 close friends

We take great pride in our two children, who have developed in ways totally different from their parents, but who, like their parents, have made happy marriages and careers, love to cook, and enjoy each other's company.

Finally, we have had great joy in the births of our two grandchildren, Charlie in 2003 and Annie in 2005. We hope to have long lives if for no other reason than to see them develop. They are very special.

Afterword

Life goes on, and not always quite as expected, or as written in an autobiography. In the spring of 2007, I decided that after thirty years the right time had come to retire from teaching at Hartt. I was principally motivated by my decreasing enthusiasm for the commute to Hartford and my wanting to spend more time at home. I hope to continue teaching in New York, however, and coaching young flutists to prepare for college.

The previous fall I received a totally unexpected phone call informing me that the National Flute Association wished to honor me with its Lifetime Achievement Award. I was humbled to be thought worthy of inclusion in a list that includes Jean-Pierre Rampal and Julius Baker, and will attend the annual convention in Albuquerque, New Mexico in August to receive the award. I have also agreed to perform.

I have written in these memoirs about my final convention performance and the unlikelihood of my attending another convention. At that time an offer of such magnitude was beyond my imagination.

When I programmed the 1986 NFA convention I asked Geoffrey Gilbert if he would consider performing. I had in mind the rarely heard *Romanza Siciliana* for flute and orchestra by Carl Maria von Weber. He graciously declined, saying his days of public performance were over. I hope I have not been unwise to propose this piece now for my own contribution, rather than follow his lead.

More important than both of these honors was the NFA's proposal for a tribute concert, to be played by former students. I was moved that all those I asked to perform accepted, and that many agreed to play music that I have published. Only the time allotment kept me from including more worthies. I find that satisfying.

I also agreed to give a recital this May in a church in Flinders, near Melbourne, Australia, where Vicky will be working. One recital became three when I offered to repeat the program for both my high school and my college.

Vicky and I sold our summer cottage too, and with the proceeds plan to travel extensively to places both familiar and new. Next autumn will be my first opportunity to fully enjoy the splendor of that season. I would like to follow the changing foliage in the Northeast by driving south from Canada. Or I might help bring in the grapes at our beloved Malfiano in Tuscany. In the spring we could observe the awakening blossoms by driving northwards from Georgia.

Thus refreshed and rejuvenated, I look forward to catching up on my reading and listening, and enjoying further, as yet unknown, stimulating challenges.

New York, May 2007